THE TROUBLE WITH

The Trouble with Psychotherapy

Counselling and Common Sense

Campbell Purton

 macmillan education palgrave

© Campbell Purton 2014

All rights reserved. No reproduction, copy or transmission of this publication may be made without written permission.

No portion of this publication may be reproduced, copied or transmitted save with written permission or in accordance with the provisions of the Copyright, Designs and Patents Act 1988, or under the terms of any licence permitting limited copying issued by the Copyright Licensing Agency, Saffron House, 6–10 Kirby Street, London EC1N 8TS.

Any person who does any unauthorized act in relation to this publication may be liable to criminal prosecution and civil claims for damages.

The author has asserted his right to be identified as the author of this work in accordance with the Copyright, Designs and Patents Act 1988.

First published 2014 by
PALGRAVE

Palgrave in the UK is an imprint of Macmillan Publishers Limited, registered in England, company number 785998, of 4 Crinan Street, London N1 9XW.

Palgrave Macmillan in the US is a division of St Martin's Press LLC, 175 Fifth Avenue, New York, NY 10010.

Palgrave is a global imprint of the above companies and is represented throughout the world.

Palgrave® and Macmillan® are registered trademarks in the United States, the United Kingdom, Europe and other countries.

ISBN 978–0–230–24190–9

This book is printed on paper suitable for recycling and made from fully managed and sustained forest sources. Logging, pulping and manufacturing processes are expected to conform to the environmental regulations of the country of origin.

A catalogue record for this book is available from the British Library.

A catalog record for this book is available from the Library of Congress.

Printed and bound in the UK by The Lavenham Press Ltd, Suffolk

For Dinah and Tom

Science is rooted in what I have just called the whole apparatus of common sense thought. That is the datum from which it starts, and to which it must recur [...] you may polish up common sense, you may contradict it in detail, you may surprise it. But ultimately your whole task is to satisfy it.

Alfred North Whitehead

A philosopher is a man who has to cure many intellectual diseases in himself before he can arrive at the notions of common sense.

Ludwig Wittgenstein

Before I studied Zen for thirty years, I saw mountains as mountains and rivers as rivers. When I arrived at a more intimate knowledge, I came to the point where I saw that mountains are not mountains and rivers are not rivers. But now that I have got its very substance I am at rest. For it's just that I see mountains once again as mountains and rivers as rivers.

Ch'ing Yuan (8th century)

Contents

Acknowledgements	x
Introduction	1
The origins of the book	5

PART I
THE TROUBLE   11

1 The Effectiveness of Psychotherapy   13
    The place of theory in psychotherapy   17
    A postmodern alternative   21
    The identity and commitment issue   26
    Summary   27

2 Theories and Common Sense   30
    Theories, regularities and explanatory pictures   30
    Reasons for rejecting a theory   33
    Incoherent theories and misleading pictures   35
    Common sense and everyday language   41
    Summary   45

3 Historical Prologue: Behaviourism and Behaviour Therapy   46
    Introduction   46
    The common-sense core of behavioural therapy   47
    The theory and its confusions   50
    The theory and its dangers   57
    Summary   58

4 Person-Centred Therapy   59
    The common-sense core   59
    Variants of the person-centred approach   63
    The 'core conditions' and common sense   64
    Self-deception   65
    The theory and its confusions   67
    The theory and its dangers   77
    Summary   80

5	**Psychodynamic Therapy**	**81**
	The common-sense core	81
	The theory and its confusions	85
	The theory and its dangers	93
	Summary	98
6	**Cognitive-Behavioural Therapy**	**99**
	The cognitive procedures of CBT	99
	The common-sense core	101
	Cognitive theory and its confusions	103
	The theory and its dangers	114
	Summary	117
7	**Process-Experiential/Emotion-Focused Therapy**	**118**
	The common-sense core: 'treatment tasks' in PET	120
	The theory and its confusions	123
	Dialectical constructivism	126
	Summary	129
8	**Existential Therapy**	**131**
	Three principles of existential therapy	132
	The practice of existential therapy	135
	The existential approach and its dangers	136
	Summary	139
9	**Neuroscience**	**140**
	Relating the person to their brain	142
	Summary	148

PART II

STARTING AGAIN   149

10	**The Troubled Client**	**151**
	Psychiatric classification: The *DSM*	153
	A common-sense classification	156
	Type A troubles	158
	Type B troubles	158
	Type C troubles	159
	Therapy, psychiatry and medication	162
	Summary	164
11	**Psychotherapy Integration**	**166**
	A common-sense account of what therapists do	166
	Three therapeutic accounts	171
	Integrating the accounts	172

	Attachment patterns	176
	'Balancing' and the 'zigzags'	177
	A traditional background for the common-sense rationale	180
	Summary	183
12	**Implications for Practice and Training**	**187**
	Summary of the suggested principles of therapy	187
	Implications for practice	188
	Implications for training	193
	Summary and conclusion	198

References 200

Index 210

Acknowledgements

This book draws on my work in both therapy and philosophy. I would like to thank all those friends and colleagues who have discussed its themes with me, and especially those who took the time to read and comment on drafts of the book – Rose Battye, David and Maureen Cockburn, Christiane Geiser, Martin Langsdon, Judy Moore, Eamonn O'Mahony, Clive Perraton Mountford and Dinah Robertshaw.

The University of East Anglia Counselling Service (alas, like many others, now deeply affected by the trends that I discuss at the end of Chapter 6) provided me with a wonderful counselling workplace for 28 years, and I would like to thank especially Brian Thorne, Judy Moore and Jane Ramsbottom for all that they did to create an atmosphere in which counsellors and clients could work together in a very human and common-sense way with the personal problems of both students and staff of the institution.

David Cockburn and Hans Julius Schneider were especially helpful in connection with the philosophical context of the book, and saved me from some (I'm sure not all!) misunderstandings of Wittgenstein's thought. I owe a special debt of thanks to Gene Gendlin, philosopher and psychotherapist, whose writings first drew me into detailed work on the philosophy of therapy. I have come to disagree to some extent with his approach, but Gendlin's thought has been an enormous inspiration for me. I also owe much to the earlier influence of Heinz Post in the philosophy of science, David Hamlyn in the philosophy of mind and Frank Ebersole who helped me see the transformative effect of looking at philosophical problems in a Wittgensteinian way.

Thanks are due to Pete Sanders of PCCS Books for permission to reprint an extract from my book *The Focusing-Oriented Counselling Primer* (2007) in Chapter 7, and to Taylor and Francis for permission to use material in Chapter 4 that is taken from my paper 'Incongruence and "inner experience"' which first appeared in *Person-Centered and Experiential Psychotherapies* (2013) 12 (3), 187–199 (www.tandfonline.com/; http://www.tandfonline.com/doi/full/10.1080/14779757.2013.840670). The Wittgenstein epigraph is an excerpt from Ludwig Wittgenstein *Culture and Value* (1980), p. 44e (copyright © in the English translation Basil Blackwell 1980), reprinted by permission of John Wiley. The Whitehead epigraph, from his address to the British Association in 1916, is included by permission of the MacTutor History of Mathematics Archive at the University of St Andrews.

I would like to thank Catherine Gray at Palgrave, who patiently stayed with this book through the very different forms it has taken over the last few

Acknowledgements

years. She suggested the book's title. Also to her successor Peter Hooper was most helpful in the final stages, and suggested the subtitle. Three anonymous Palgrave reviewers also made helpful suggestions that greatly improved the structure of the book.

Finally, as always, my thanks to my wife Val for 'being there' throughout.

Introduction

This book is addressed to psychotherapists, counsellors, clinical and counselling psychologists and therapy trainees who are puzzled or troubled about the present status of the psychotherapy profession. I hope it may also be a source of stimulation for those who have not given the matter much thought, since I think that the issues at stake are fundamental for anyone who is engaged in psychotherapy. These issues can be briefly summarized in the following way.

People who come to therapy are troubled and often vulnerable. A responsible therapist needs to have reasonable confidence that what they do (or how they are) in their sessions with a client will be helpful to the client, or at the very least not harmful. In short, the therapist needs to 'know what they are doing'. Such 'reasonable confidence' in what they are doing has traditionally been grounded in the theory of human nature and of psychological disturbance to which the therapist subscribes, as well as in their clinical experience of the kind of procedures that seem to work.

Until recently, the empirical evidence for the effectiveness of psychotherapy was slight. The psychologist Hans Eysenck famously maintained that although clients in psychoanalysis (and other 'talking therapies') *do* significantly improve over a period of years, this improvement is no greater than that which occurs through 'spontaneous remission' of symptoms. If that were so, of course, it would be very hard to justify the effort and expense of psychotherapy at all. The results of psychotherapy outcome research in the last 30 years have dissolved *that* potential crisis for the psychotherapy profession, but they have also precipitated a different kind of crisis. For, while psychotherapy has been shown to be very effective, no significant evidence has been found for one school of therapy being more effective than any other. Yet the schools are in many ways very different, being grounded in different theories of human nature, as well as sometimes having distinctive values.

This finding is disturbing because it makes it difficult for a therapist, or trainee, to make a reasoned decision on which school of therapy to be associated with. A therapist, if they are to 'know what they are doing', needs to have some theoretical grounding. It might possibly be said that all that is required is a list of therapeutic techniques that have been shown to be effective; one could then simply use these techniques without knowing *why* they work. Such an eclectic and purely pragmatic approach might be a last resort for psychotherapy, but it seems very unsatisfactory. There are *many* therapeutic procedures that seem to be effective, and a therapist with no understanding of *why* they work can make only a random selection. Further, if a procedure wasn't helpful in a particular case, the therapist would have no background understanding of *why* it was unhelpful in that case, or how it might reasonably be modified, or what might be a better approach with that client. A therapist with a battery of available techniques but no *understanding* of them cannot be said to 'know what they are doing'. They cannot be seen as a *professional* in the field of psychotherapy.

The traditional theories of psychotherapy, psychodynamic, cognitive-behavioural, person-centred and so on, have up to now been seen as providing the kind of understanding that allows psychotherapy to be more than just a set of pragmatic techniques. They provide the therapist with a firm *grounding* for their practice, something that is enormously important in a field where clients' happiness, and even on occasion their lives, depend on the therapist's knowledge of what they are doing. Therapists need to have confidence in what they are doing, but to base one's practice in one's own personal confidence, without having any reasoned basis for it, seems unprofessional and even unethical. For example, in assessing therapists for professional registration, the British Association for Counselling and Psychotherapy (BACP) has always insisted that the applicant must show how their practice *derives from* their theoretical position. Someone who cannot do this will not be professionally accredited. What the BACP has never been able to do, however, is to require that the theoretical position of the applicant should itself be a sound position. *That* would require professional consensus over what psychotherapy involves and why it is effective. Such a consensus would involve an agreed rationale or generally accepted theoretical background for psychotherapy, in terms of which it could be assessed whether a particular *approach* should be accredited. Current attempts to establish 'empirically supported treatments' (ESTs) (Wampold 2001, pp. 18–19) for particular client difficulties do not go far in this direction. They simply assess particular procedures by comparing their effectiveness with 'control groups'. Leaving aside the empirical and conceptual difficulties involved in setting up appropriate controls, this approach to the validation of psychotherapy would mean that the hundreds of currently available psychotherapy procedures would each need to be investigated, whether or not they have any real plausibility. Without a broadly accepted theoretical background for the profession, it is not possible to make effective judgements of plausibility; from a purely empirical standpoint, almost anything is possible.

Regarding the justification of therapeutic practice, the situation of accrediting bodies such as the BACP is little different from that of therapists, trainees and indeed clients. The results of psychotherapy outcome research give none of these groups any reason to trust in one therapy approach rather than in any other. Yet therapists, trainees and clients *need* to have trust in the approach they select. This, if not obvious anyway, is confirmed by research that shows that therapy carried out by people who don't actually believe in the principles of what they are doing is much less effective than that carried out by 'believers'. (This situation can arise, for example, where one kind of approach is being compared with another, using the same therapist in both cases.) It is also well established that *clients* need to be able to trust in the therapy that is offered to them, if it is to be effective.

A further consequence of the current situation relates to the statutory regulation of psychotherapy. Given that there is considerable public demand for therapy, that those seeking therapy are in some ways vulnerable and that few of them have any knowledge of what exactly therapy involves, it is understandable that governments should feel a responsibility to provide at least some guidance on what counts as genuine psychotherapy. It seems reasonable to suggest that not just anyone should be able to advertise psychotherapeutic services but that the term 'psychotherapist' should be reserved for properly qualified practitioners. But who is to decide what counts as a 'properly qualified practitioner'? Established governmental bodies have little understanding of what is involved in psychotherapy; so it is reasonable for governments to turn to the professional bodies. What do *they* consider to be an appropriate training for psychotherapists? What body of theory does a trainee psychotherapist need to master? But here governments run into the problem that the professional bodies find it difficult to agree on what constitutes an appropriate training. What seems appropriate to the psychoanalysts seems quite inappropriate to cognitive-behavioural therapy (CBT) practitioners, and vice versa. In Britain, the disagreements between the different groups of therapists led the government of the time to place the issue in the hands of the Health Professions Council, in spite of its lack of knowledge of psychotherapy. Then, as it happened, there was an election, and the new government elected in 2010 dropped the plans for statutory regulation. In some other European countries (but not all), statutory regulation has been enforced, but in a seemingly arbitrary way. Austrian legislation recognizes 16 different methods of individual psychotherapy, Germany four (behaviour therapy, psychoanalysis, 'methods based on depth psychology' and client-centred therapy), Sweden three (analytic therapy, behaviour therapy and cognitive therapy) and Finland two (psychoanalytically oriented therapy and cognitive therapy) (Austrian Health Institute 2003).[1]

There is then something of a crisis in the contemporary psychotherapy profession. At the heart of the difficulty is the fact that belief and trust in the principles of a therapeutic approach are psychologically, ethically and professionally necessary for therapists. On the other hand, given that all the approaches are equally effective, there are no convincing grounds for selecting one approach over any other. The choice, it seems, can only be a personal one. But that places therapists and trainees in an uncomfortable position. One can select an approach simply because it feels congenial, but once one is committed to that approach, one will find that it orients one's thinking in ways that are fundamentally incompatible with other approaches. Becoming a psychodynamic therapist commits one to thinking in terms of the unconscious, so that a CBT approach, for example, will seem superficial. Given the research evidence, one must reluctantly concede that CBT can be effective, but this will seem an anomaly which one would like to forget about. From a psychodynamic point of view, CBT is grounded in an account of human nature and of psychological difficulties that is just *wrong*. Insofar as CBT can't just be ignored, the question of why it gets the results it does will at best be something that needs to be investigated. (It might, for example, be argued that CBT can have a superficial impact on the *symptoms* of disturbance, but that it doesn't engage with the underlying unconscious conflicts.) The more solidly and professionally grounded one is in the psychodynamic approach, the less accepting one can be of approaches whose theories conflict with one's own deeply held views. On the other hand, if one opens oneself to the possibility that another view might after all be true, then to that extent one undermines the principles which sustain one's own work.

For any pair of approaches the same situation arises. If you are a person-centred therapist, you *believe in* the basic principles of person-centred therapy. You also know from the research findings that person-centred therapy is effective. So what is the problem? It is that down the street from your office works a fully accredited behavioural therapist. From your perspective what they are doing is theoretically all wrong, although somehow it seems to be effective. What should your attitude be to someone who 'does it all wrong'? Should they even *be* an accredited therapist? And then further down the street is a bio-energetics practitioner who also gets good results. They are 'accredited' by some bio-energetics institute, but does that really *count* as accreditation? And then at the end of the street is a popular and charismatic astrological counsellor who also uses crystal healing. People report to you how effective this therapist is. What do you say? That they really shouldn't be mixing crystal healing with astrological work?

This book will be concerned initially with two possible responses to the current situation. One is to argue that the effectiveness of each of the therapies rests neither on their particular theories nor on their practices. Rather, it is something like a placebo effect: what therapy really depends on is a good relationship with the therapist, the client's belief that the procedure will be effective and perhaps also the client's *belief* that the procedure does have a well-grounded rationale (for what is being done in therapy must *make sense* to the client). However, *what* the procedure is, and whether it *really* has any rationale, simply doesn't matter. According to this sort of view, the theories of therapy, or the rationales for the procedures, at best function as 'healing fictions'. They are, none of them, *true*. The opposite kind of approach is to say that far from *none* of the theories being true, they are *all* true. This move requires some sympathy with postmodern thought, according to which there is no single reality, but multiple, 'socially constructed' realities. From such a perspective, a psychological problem could be *at the same time* the result of incongruence of self-concept with organismic experiencing, a manifestation of unconscious conflict, the result of unfortunate conditioning contingencies and the effect of negative automatic thoughts.

I will argue that neither of these responses is satisfactory, and the rest of the book is then devoted to finding another way through. A reader of an early version of the book asked whether it is a book about theory or about practice. The answer is that it is in the end about practice, but more specifically about how

Introduction

practice can reasonably be justified. I will argue that the current theories don't provide adequate justification for their practices and I develop a way of thinking about therapy that is not dependent on the theories. In doing so, I develop an understanding of therapy that might itself be called a 'theory', although it does not move very far from 'common-sense' ways of thinking about psychological difficulties. This new way of thinking about therapy allows much of the current *practice* of therapy to remain as it is, though it also leads to some suggestions for change. This is consistent with the fact that much current practice is remarkably effective – 'If ain't broke, don't fix it!' The difference, which I believe to be an important one, is that this new way of thinking provides us with a crucial background understanding of what therapy is and why it works. Without that, as I have suggested above, therapists cannot have reasonable trust in what they do, and that is a necessary requirement for good *practice*.

The origins of the book

It may be helpful to say briefly how I came to write this book. My own training was initially in person-centred therapy, a school of therapy that today incorporates several different 'tribes' or sub-schools (Sanders 2012). I specialized in the tribe known as 'focusing-oriented therapy', deriving from the work of Rogers' younger colleague Eugene Gendlin, and over many years I have been closely involved in this approach. I taught on a postgraduate counselling training course at the University of East Anglia, UK, and gradually introduced focusing-specific elements into that course. Later I set up specifically focusing-oriented training courses in England and in China and wrote two books (Purton 2004, 2007) on that kind of therapy. I still think that it is a form of therapy that is rather neglected, and it has sometimes seemed to me to contain at least the seeds of a solution to the problem of how the schools of therapy can be integrated.

So far as procedures are concerned, the focusing-oriented view is that pretty much any procedure can be used so long as clients themselves experience that procedure as being helpful; the important thing is for the therapist always to check back with the client's experience of the procedure. Regarding the different theories, Gendlin's view is in a way similar to that found in postmodern philosophy, that is, there can be multiple theories and multiple truths, none of which is *the* truth. In practice the therapist can use whichever theory works best in illuminating the difficulties of a particular client.

However, Gendlin, who is himself a philosopher as well as a therapist, holds that there has to be *something* to which the theories are answerable; it is not that any old theory will do, so long as it appeals to both the therapist and the client. This 'something' is what he calls the client's *experiencing*. A client's 'experiencing' is their immediate awareness, especially of their situation or problem. They may express or articulate their experiencing in a variety of ways, such as 'I feel flat', or 'It is a sort of heavy feeling'. The therapist may then bring a range of theoretical notions into relationship with the client's experiencing, for example through considering that the client may be burdened by conditions of worth, or trapped in automatic thoughts, or be working through their Oedipus complex. In Gendlin's terms, these are all ways of *symbolizing* the client's experiencing; they all provide linguistic, conceptual forms for the experiencing, but the experiencing in its fullness goes beyond concepts and language, even though, as Gendlin puts it, experiencing responds differently to different ways of articulating it.

The notion of a form of experiencing that lies beyond concepts is central to Gendlin's approach, and this notion can seem to provide a basis for understanding how there can be many theories, yet also something *beyond* the theories, to which they are answerable. After I encountered focusing-oriented therapy, I became intrigued by the philosophy which lies behind it. I was myself trained as a philosopher before moving into the field of therapy, and I set about reading all that Gendlin had written on the philosophy behind focusing-oriented therapy. I also incorporated some of this philosophical framework into my own writings on therapy. However, after ten or 12 years of this involvement, I began to have doubts about whether Gendlin's notion of 'experiencing' can really do the job it is designed to do.

Some fairly extensive discussions with Gendlin, by email and phone, helped me to clarify my thinking, but perhaps because of the differences in our philosophical backgrounds (his in phenomenology, and mine in 'ordinary-language philosophy'), we encountered fundamental disagreements. These were disagreements about how one should *conceptualize* the practice of focusing-oriented psychotherapy, not about the practice itself. I suspect, in fact, that many of Gendlin's insights into psychotherapeutic practice can in fact be reformulated in a way that does not use his notion of 'experiencing'.

In Gendlin's view, it is important to turn one's attention to one's 'experiencing' in a way that is not very different from the practice of the earliest school of modern psychology – that of the introspectionists. Yet introspectionism never worked out as a viable approach to psychology, being superseded by behaviourism and subsequently by cognitive psychology. I reflected on the fact that the theories of these later schools, together with the less academic tradition of psychoanalysis, have *all* been severely criticized (often of course by adherents of other schools), and that none of them has established itself as *the* theory of psychology, any more than any of the theories of therapy has established itself as *the* theory. I also reflected on how different this is from the situation in sciences such as physics (my first degree was in that subject) and biology, where in spite of significant differences of opinion at the growing points of the science, there is an extensive and well-established body of knowledge (such as relativity theory, or the theory of evolution) that is not controversial.

In the case of the existing theories of therapy, I have come to think that there is little prospect of any of them becoming established as *the* theory, a view shared I think by many therapists. The current trend seems to be in the direction of an eclecticism of techniques and a pluralism of theories, but that brings us back to the question of whether there are then alternative realities, or whether there is just one reality – but a reality beyond language and concepts. Both these suggestions are intriguing philosophical ideas, but they seem far from the everyday concerns of clients and service providers, who understandably want to engage in a form of therapy that is well grounded in some established body of knowledge. That seems crucial to the question of whether there can be a genuine *profession* of psychotherapy at all.

The theme of this book is that of how therapeutic practice can be grounded. It may be suggested that a grounding will one day be found in some philosophical system, such as Gendlin's system, or existentialism, or postmodernism, but I am sceptical about this, if only because such philosophical positions are at least as controversial as the theories of therapy themselves. What I have come to think is that we may be able to find a grounding, not in any philosophical system, but in something that is so close to us that it tends to elude our notice, and that is our everyday understanding of human nature and personal troubles. I will suggest that it is *this*, and not 'experiencing', to which our theories are answerable.

My thinking about this has its own philosophical roots in the philosophy of Wittgenstein and, to a lesser extent, the writings of 'ordinary language philosophers' such as John Austin and Alan White. I have been particularly influenced by Wittgenstein, but in this book I am not concerned with the details of Wittgenstein's philosophy. Wittgenstein himself denied that he had any philosophical thesis to advance, so it is doubtful whether he even counts as a philosopher in the traditional sense. He might instead be called an 'anti-philosopher'. Rather than proposing a new philosophical system, he recommended a particular sort of *practice*: that of reflecting on *how words are actually used*. The philosopher Rupert Read (2012, p. 200) puts it like this: 'Ordinary language offers only [...] a call to us to return to ourselves, to be honest, to ask ourselves whether we are really on balance willing and wanting to use such and such a word in such and such a way.' One consequence is that this book, which is strongly influenced by Wittgenstein, does not require the reader to be familiar with Wittgenstein's philosophy, or indeed with any philosophy. It is not a study of Wittgenstein's thought but an application of it.

I think, with Wittgenstein, that many of the problems surrounding the nature of psychology and psychotherapy are rooted in conceptual confusion – in thinking that our language works in one way when in fact it works quite differently. As we will see in the course of the book, the *actual* use of words, and hence their *ordinary* meanings, is often different from the ways that psychologists and traditional philosophers try to use them. This can result in a lot of confusion, and the task of the Wittgensteinian 'philosopher' is not to propose new theories but patiently to work on how a particular kind of confusion has arisen. The outcome may then be that the problem is not so much solved as *dissolved*; it no longer arises. Such a way of looking at things is hardly possible to justify in general terms; it can only be demonstrated in practice through seeing what the confusions are, how they arise and how they can be sorted out. This means that the confusions within the different theories need to be sorted out in a case-by-case way; so the first part of the book is largely devoted to criticisms of some of the major schools of psychotherapy. I have limited the discussion to consideration of *individual* therapy; family and couple therapy raise issues that are beyond the scope of this book. There are, of course, many schools of individual therapy apart from those that are discussed here; indeed, it is said that today there are something like 400 schools of therapy. For reasons of space I cannot consider here more than six or seven approaches, and must apologize to the reader who finds that their preferred school is not included. On the other hand, I hope that anyone who comes to appreciate the *kind* of thing that is awry in the schools I do consider will be able themselves to apply the principles of criticism that I have described to any other school of therapy.

The book need not necessarily be read in the existing order of chapters. In Part I, after the first three chapters, which provide a general orientation, the reader may like to look next at criticisms that are made of one or two approaches that are of especial interest. Some sections of later chapters do rely on material in earlier ones, but at least the earlier sections of Chapters 4–8 can stand on their own.

Part I is concerned with criticism of the various theories, and this criticism typically takes the form of (a) consideration of whether the *practice* of the particular theory can be understood in a common-sense way that does not require any reference to the theory in which the practice is supposed to be grounded; (b) discussion of ways in which the theory is confused or incoherent; and (c) discussion of ways in which commitment to the theory (not the practice) can be positively harmful. The discussions of the ways in which the theories are conceptually tangled up can at times be rather complicated, but this is unavoidable, because the confusions themselves are complex. Wittgenstein (1967, §452) once wrote, 'Philosophy unties knots in our thinking; hence its results must be simple, but philosophizing has to be as complicated as the knots it unties.'

Part II presents my suggested way through the difficulties that have emerged. Readers whose primary interest is in practice rather than theory may prefer to begin with this part. The main aim of Part I is to eliminate the theories, but readers who were never much impressed by the theories will not necessarily want to know *what* exactly is wrong with them. In Part II, I bring together the 'common-sense cores' of the various approaches, in a way that provides an integrative understanding of psychotherapy practice. This could itself be seen as a 'theory', but it is one that does not stray far from our ordinary ways of thinking about personal troubles.

Note

1. There is the added complication that in some countries a distinction is made between 'psychotherapy' and 'counselling'. In Britain, during the debate over statutory regulation, all attempts to reach agreement on what is involved in this distinction failed. It is easily agreed that there is a difference between 'psychotherapists' and other professionals (or volunteers) who employ 'counselling skills' either as workplace counsellors or in the context of other professional activities (McLeod 2009, pp. 9–11). But professionals who prefer not to be called 'psychotherapists'

can distinguish between 'counselling' and 'counselling skills' in much the same way as the others distinguish between 'psychotherapy' and 'counselling'. In some countries the term 'psychotherapist' is associated with a training in clinical psychology, but that seems to be just a surreptitious way of restricting the term 'psychotherapy' to the kinds of approach, especially cognitive-behavioural approaches, that predominate in a clinical psychology training. (It may be worth noting that the term 'counselling' was initially introduced by Carl Rogers simply because the medical profession of the time was not prepared to have the term 'psychotherapist' used by practitioners who were not medically trained. Its use did not imply any difference from 'psychotherapy' but was a purely political move.)

PART I
THE TROUBLE

CHAPTER 1

The Effectiveness of Psychotherapy

The world of psychotherapy has changed dramatically in the last 40 years. In the early 1970s it was characterized by a fairly limited range of therapies, such as psychoanalytic, behavioural, humanistic and early forms of cognitive therapy. These schools of therapy saw themselves as in many ways opposed to one another, both in terms of their underlying beliefs about the nature of psychological problems and their preferred ways of responding to such problems. At that time there was no consensus about whether *any* of the approaches were effective; Hans Eysenck, in the 1950s and 1960s, had argued that the rate of success of psychotherapy was no greater than the rate of 'spontaneous remission'. This suggestion led to many studies of the effectiveness of psychotherapy, but the results were initially conflicting; some studies concluded that psychotherapy was effective, but others concluded that it was not. The situation began to change in the late 1970s, with the publication of the first meta-analysis of psychotherapy outcomes by Mary Smith and Gene Glass (Smith & Glass 1977). Meta-analysis, a technique now widely used in many fields, is a statistical method that re-assesses the conflicting findings of previous studies and leads to an overall judgement of which findings are reliable. The meta-analysis of Smith and Glass found that psychotherapy was remarkably effective, and although some criticisms were made of this analysis, and of other early meta-analyses of effectiveness, there is by now almost universal acceptance among psychotherapy researchers that therapy is indeed effective (Wampold 2001; Cooper 2008).

During the same time period psychotherapy research has also established that the *relative* effectiveness of different kinds of therapy is about equal. Here and there studies have suggested that one form of therapy is more effective than another, but these apparent differences have usually disappeared when the factor of 'therapist allegiance' is taken into account, that is, when the analysis takes into account whether the investigators themselves had allegiance to one of the approaches being compared (Wampold 2001). The established equivalence of therapeutic approaches has come to be known as the 'Dodo-bird' finding, after the story in Alice in Wonderland in which, following a race, the

Dodo announces: 'Everyone has won, and all must have prizes.' This idea itself dates back at least to 1936, when Rosenzweig first referred to Lewis Carol's story of the Dodo in a paper on psychotherapy outcome; however, it is only with the development of meta-analytic statistical techniques that Rosenzweig's suggestion has been confirmed by systematic research.

One consequence of the findings has been the development of both 'eclectic' and 'integrative' forms of therapy. The more eclectic forms are not very concerned with theoretical explanations for the effectiveness of various procedures; they simply draw on procedures that have been demonstrated to be effective, whatever the original theoretical grounding of the procedures was. The more integrative forms try to find ways of bringing together at least some of the theoretical schemes underlying the major schools of therapy, though this has proved a very difficult undertaking, since the schemes are embedded in very different conceptions of psychological disturbance and indeed of human nature generally.

The impact of the research developments has thus been mixed. On the one hand, they have removed the earlier pervasive doubts about whether therapy is effective at all. They have also reduced the earlier ideological tensions over which approach to therapy is preferable. Forty years ago this tension led to acrimonious disputes 'with mutual antipathy and exchanges of puerile insults between adherents of rival orientations' (Norcross 2005, p. 3). Such 'schoolism', as Cooper and McLeod have called it, is likely to be detrimental to the professional practice of psychotherapy.

On the other hand, the research findings have made it more difficult for therapists to give their allegiance to any particular form of therapy. This is important clinically as well as theoretically. It is not just that researcher allegiance to an approach biases the research findings, but that whether the therapist has allegiance to a particular approach makes, as one would expect, a significant difference to whether the approach is effective (Wampold 2001, pp. 162–168). The dilemma here, which I will discuss below, is that while there is strong evidence that it is important that the therapist should 'believe in' their approach, there is also strong evidence that no approach is better than any other. One of the aims of this book is to find a way through this dilemma.

It may be worth emphasizing at the start just how effective psychotherapy is. In technical terms, the 'effect size' of psychotherapy (a measure of how strongly therapy is correlated with beneficial changes in the client) tends to be around 0.8, which entails that the 'success rate' in those having therapy would be about 69% compared to about 31% for those not having therapy (Wampold 2001, p. 53).[1] This effect size is substantially larger than those of many medical and surgical procedures, where effect sizes average 0.5 (Cooper 2008, p. 22). A psychotherapy effect size of 0.5 would mean that the success rate in those having therapy would be about 62%, compared with about 38% for the others. Another useful comparison is that effect sizes for antidepressant medication (compared with placebo) are quoted as around 0.3 or 0.4 (Vöhringer & Ghaemi 2011), although there is controversy over whether these estimates are too high (Kirsch 2009). Effect sizes higher than 0.8 have sometimes been reported for some procedures; an effect size of, say, 3.0 would mean that practically *all* members of the therapy group did better than those in the control group, but very few effect sizes of this magnitude are found in the biological and social sciences, and it would be quite unreasonable to expect them in connection with psychotherapy. In sum, it can be said that psychotherapy is about as effective as any approach to psychological disturbance could reasonably be expected to be.

Turning to the *relative* effectiveness of the different forms of therapy, the 'Dodo-bird finding' is by now well established. It is a surprising finding because there are very significant differences between the major schools of therapy: differences in background philosophy, in theory and in practice. One response to the finding has been to suggest that in spite of the differences that exist between the schools of therapy, there are also many common factors, and that it is these factors that are the real motor of effective therapy. Research has already indicated what some of these common factors are (Orlinsky et al. 1994; Bohart & Tallman 1999; Hubble et al. 1999; Wampold 2001; Cooper 2008). They include (a) factors pertaining to the client, such as whether the client expects the therapy to be effective, and whether the client is open to change, (b) factors pertaining to the therapist, such as whether the therapist is empathic and non-judgemental, but also whether the therapist believes in the therapy that he or she practices and (c) factors pertaining to the interaction between therapist and client, such as whether they agree on what the goals and tasks of therapy should be.

Given these findings, one view of what is involved in psychotherapy is that its effectiveness comes not from any specific techniques but from the general context that is common to almost all forms of therapy. This general context is constituted by the factors that I have mentioned, such as the establishment of a good working relationship between therapist and client, and client expectations concerning the effectiveness of therapy. A detailed account of this sort of view was developed by Jerome Frank, whose book *Persuasion and Healing* was first published in 1961, long before the Dodo-bird research was carried out. Frank sees psychotherapy as a contemporary version of much older traditions of healing in which the client's relationship with the healer and trust in the effectiveness of the healing procedure are central. According to Frank, the essential components of effective psychotherapy are (1) a confidential and emotionally charged relationship with the therapist, (2) a healing setting (such as, today, a therapist's consulting room) in which the client believes that the therapist can provide help, (3) a therapeutic rationale that provides an explanation for the client's difficulties and (4) a procedure based on the rationale, which requires the active participation of both therapist and client (Frank & Frank 1991, pp. 40–44). The rationale need not be grounded in scientific evidence, but in addition to it's being accepted by the therapist, it needs to be consistent with the attitudes, assumptions and general worldview of the client, or at least the client must become persuaded of its 'truth'. Frank argues that these conditions for psychological healing are met not only by psychotherapeutic practice but also by various forms of religio-magical healing, both historical and contemporary. In Frank's view, what distinguishes psychotherapy from other forms of psychological healing is that the rationale in psychotherapy takes the form of a psychological theory. It is of no consequence *which* theory is involved, so long as it provides a rationale for what the therapist and client are doing. Whether the theory is true, whether the entities and processes it postulates (such as the unconscious, cognitive schemas, stimulus-response connections) actually exist, is beside the point. Frank understands psychotherapy theory in terms of myth, and psychotherapy practice in terms of ritual:

> [T]he adherence of therapist and patient to the same therapeutic myth creates a powerful bond between them... By inspiring expectations of help, myths and rituals keep the patient coming for treatment and are powerful morale builders and symptom relievers in themselves. (Frank & Frank 1991, p. 44)

The mathematician and psychotherapy researcher Bruce Wampold (2001) has called this kind of view 'the contextual model of therapy', since it attributes the effectiveness of therapy to general contextual factors rather than to specific procedures. He contrasts it with 'the medical model of therapy', according to which psychotherapy should be seen as treating identifiable disorders with specific remedies, based on an understanding of what the underlying nature of the disorder is. Many schools of psychotherapy adopt this latter way of thinking. For example, cognitive behavioural therapists see the client's disorder in terms of maladaptive thoughts and use techniques such as reframing to help the client see things in a more adaptive way. Psychoanalysts see the underlying nature of psychological disorder in terms of unconscious conflicts and use techniques of free association and interpretation to make the unconscious conscious. According to the medical model of therapy, one needs to have a good theoretical understanding of what is wrong with the client, so that the therapeutic technique can be applied in an appropriate way to the specifics of the client's complaint.

Wampold has investigated in detail whether the psychotherapeutic research literature confirms one or other of these models of psychotherapy. His conclusion is that almost all the statistical evidence supports the contextual model rather than the medical model. It is an impressive conclusion, since while Frank presents an appealing view of how psychotherapy is best seen as a variation on more traditional forms of healing, Wampold relies entirely on the kind of quantitative research that is typical of the medical model, in order to show why such a model must be rejected. Wampold's version of Frank's account is that effective therapy involves first a good 'therapeutic relationship' or 'working alliance' with the therapist, which covers

> (a) the client's affective relationship with the therapist, (b) the client's motivation and ability to accomplish work collaboratively with the therapist, (c) the therapist's empathic responding to and involvement with the client, and (d) client and therapist agreement about the goals and tasks of therapy. (Wampold 2001, p. 150)

The 'therapeutic relationship' is the most frequently mentioned common factor in the psychotherapy literature (Grencavage & Norcross 1990; Wampold 2001, p. 149) and seems to correspond roughly with Frank's first and fourth conditions (affective relationship and active collaboration). A second common factor is the 'expectancy' effect, that is, the element in improvement that is due to the client's belief that they are being treated in a way that is likely to help them. This seems to cover Frank's second condition (a healing setting in which the client believes that the therapist can be of help). A third common factor is 'therapist allegiance', that is, the extent to which the therapist believes in the effectiveness of what they do (Wampold 2001, pp. 165–168). This seems to connect significantly with Frank's third condition (the existence of a therapeutic rationale, accepted by the therapist as well as the client).

Wampold's conclusion, then, is that psychotherapy research has established that much of the effectiveness of therapy arises from the common factors of 'therapeutic relationship', 'client expectancy' and 'therapist allegiance'. That doesn't mean that there will be no theory or 'rationale' involved in the therapy, but the crucial point, in relation to the Dodo-bird finding, is that the *details* of the rationale don't matter. There needs to *be* a rationale since, without one, client expectancy and therapeutic allegiance would have no focus, and there could be no working alliance in connection with the aims of therapy.

One way of putting this position would be to say that psychotherapy works essentially in the way that a placebo works in medicine. The effectiveness of the placebo (such as a capsule containing cornflour) seems to depend on the human relationship that the doctor establishes with their patient, the client's belief or faith in the placebo and the doctor's trust that the placebo will work. Just what the placebo capsule contains is irrelevant. The analogy in psychotherapy is the view that pretty much any theory (and its associated practices) will work so long as the therapist relates well to the client, and the client believes that they will be helped. Compared with traditional accounts, this is of course a radically different view of the place of theory in psychotherapy.

The place of theory in psychotherapy

Wampold (2001, p. 231) writes:

> Psychotherapy is indeed effective, but not in the manner one would expect from a medical model conceptualization.... Perhaps, as Jerome Frank has intimated, psychotherapy is indeed a myth, created by Freud and maintained by people's belief in the endeavour. In any event, it is a valuable myth and one that should be revered, cherished, and nourished – and not folded into the field of medicine, where it will be suffocated.

Such a view of psychotherapy raises important questions. As discussed above, there is strong evidence that the therapist must give allegiance to, or believe in, the form of therapy that he or she practices. Yet, according to the Dodo-bird finding, there is no reason to prefer one theory to any other. Wampold's

(2001, p. 219) response to this dilemma is that the contextual model therapist (the therapist who believes that therapeutic effectiveness depends on the general context of therapy, not on specific ingredients)

> should promote belief in treatments, albeit at a different level. The contextual model therapist understands that it is the healing context and the meaning that the client gives to the experience that are important. A humanist therapist could administer systematic desensitization and believe in its efficacy because the therapist understands that it is the client's belief that is paramount – this therapist would administer the systematic desensitization with enthusiasm, faith and allegiance. Under the contextual model, the following equation holds: **client belief + healing context = therapist belief.**

This is ingenious, but it seems to lead to the conclusion that therapists can employ *any* form of treatment that is consistent with client beliefs. For example, irrespective of whether there is any truth in approaches such as Neuro-linguistic Programming (NLP) or Eye Movement Desensitization and Reprocessing (EMDR), Wampold's equation would seem to authorize their use. But how far can this be taken? If a client finds astrology a helpful framework for thinking about their problems, should the therapist endorse their view of things and engage enthusiastically in astrological counselling? There are of course any number of other non-standard forms of therapy, each of which has its own devotees (Singer & Lalich 1996). Many of these therapies may be effective; indeed, given the evidence for the contextual model of therapy, we can be fairly sure that they *will* be effective, and even satisfy the criteria for 'empirically supported treatments' (ESTs). Wampold (p. 224) mentions a form of bio-energetic couple therapy that was reportedly effective, but rather ironically comments: 'Fortunately, no-one subjected bioenergetic analysis to clinical tests that might have validated it through the criteria for an EST.'

Wampold (p. 224) seems to approve of a religious version of cognitive therapy that 'gave Christian religious rationales for the procedures, and used religious arguments to counter irrational thoughts, and used religious imagery procedures'. He remarks that 'religious imagery does not have a basis in psychology...nevertheless at a higher level the therapist realizes that compatibility with the attitudes and values of the client is important, and thus embedding cognitive techniques in a religious cloak may be therapeutic'. On the other hand, he insists that

> the contextual model does not imply that psychologists can use any treatment...Psychologists should only find treatments that are well-grounded in psychological principles to be congenial and convincing. That is, theoretical approaches and the concomitant techniques must be consistent with knowledge in psychology.... EMDR has met many of the criteria for an EST but nevertheless involves rapid eye movement, which has a dubious basis in neurophysiology.... Interventions administered by clergy, indigenous healers, occult practitioners, motivational speakers may be effective and even as

effective as psychological treatments. Nevertheless, such treatments are not allowed within the set of psychological treatments.

It seems that Wampold's position is that (a) any form of therapy is likely to be effective so long as the client believes in it, but (b) only treatments consistent with, or based on, accepted psychological knowledge can count as *psychological* treatments. However, the qualification in (b) seems to be a merely verbal caveat. From the client's point of view, what does it matter whether the treatment is called 'psychological'?

Another way of approaching the difficulty that Wampold faces is the following. According to the research evidence, it is important that the therapist gives full allegiance to their own approach. For the contextual model therapist, this involves giving allegiance to the principle stated in Wampold's 'equation' above. That is, the therapist must give allegiance to the principle of following the client's belief. However, the research findings also point to the importance of the therapeutic alliance, and agreement between therapist and client on the goals and methods of therapy. Yet in the kind of case that concerns us (say astrology), the therapist and client *don't* agree. The client believes in astrology; the therapist believes in going along with the client's beliefs whatever they happen to be. An honest discussion between the two would quickly reveal how much they differ, as would such a discussion between the humanist therapist and the client who believes in the value of systematic desensitization. The kind of commitment that is involved in Wampold's 'equation' is not a commitment that can be upheld in therapeutic practice. One might genuinely believe that any kind of therapy will work if the client believes in it, but one could only put the belief into practice with a client who shared *that* belief, rather than having, say, a belief in astrology. I think then that there is a fundamental incoherence in Wampold's position, which shows up in his vacillation between tentatively endorsing some kinds of non-standard therapy, yet refusing to accept that, according to his 'equation', therapists can use any kind of treatment that appeals to a client.

What is called the 'placebo effect' seems to include at least three interconnected elements: (1) the patient's belief in the effectiveness of the treatment, (2) a trusting relationship between doctor and patient and (3) the doctor's belief in the effectiveness of the placebo. There is some contradiction between these elements, as we have just seen, since what the patient believes is different from what the doctor believes. This contradiction can perhaps be 'fudged' in the case of medicine (although contemporary ethical standards concerning informed consent (Shapiro & Shapiro 1997) make this increasingly difficult), but it is hard to see how it can be fudged in psychotherapy, where the evidence is that agreement on the aims and methods of therapy plays a significant part in therapeutic effectiveness.

A second objection to the Frank–Wampold view on the effectiveness of therapy is that some effective forms of therapy do not involve an interpersonal 'healing context' of the sort proposed. There is good evidence (Hubble et al. Ch 4; Prochaska et al. 1994; Norcross & Aboysoun 1994; Bohart &

Tallman 1999, p. 160) that *self*-therapy can often be effective. For example, there is the use of self-help books and computer therapy programs, self-help CBT techniques, as well as 'common-sense' practices such as journaling, or simply 'sitting with', or meditating on, one's difficulty. Gendlin's 'focusing' procedure is a good example of a self-therapy procedure, although it was originally formulated in the context of client-centred therapy and has a central place in focusing-oriented therapy. Considerations such as these suggest that any plausible account of the effectiveness of psychotherapy needs to allow for the existence and effectiveness of various forms of self-therapy. It is not *just* the interpersonal 'healing context', together with client faith in that context, that matters but also certain kinds of client and therapist *activities*.

This takes us to a third difficulty for Frank and Wampold, for there are cases where one can, as it were, *see how* the therapeutic procedure is working. For example, when a therapist uses an exposure technique in connection with a traumatic phobia, and the client's anxiety gradually reduces, it is hard to believe that what is going on is just a placebo effect. It seems undeniable that through gradually 'getting used to' an initially alarming situation, one will indeed become accustomed to it, and no longer respond in such an anxious way. This seems very different from, say, experiencing anxiety reduction following EMDR. EMDR may work, but if it does that is something of a surprise. The effect could be connected with integration of the functioning of left and right brain hemispheres, although there is evidence that the eye movements are not in fact essential (Cooper 2008, p. 173). We might also speculate that it is a placebo effect. But we don't *speculate* about why people feel easier about situations to which they have gradually accustomed themselves. That this sort of thing happens seems too basic to human living to require any *explanation* of why it is so, although we might of course investigate what goes on in the nervous system when it happens. I will discuss this further in Chapter 3; my purpose in drawing attention to it here is just as an example of a therapy procedure whose effectiveness cannot reasonably be attributed to 'people's belief in it' or simply to 'the therapeutic relationship'.

Similarly, I think, it would be very implausible to suggest that a placebo effect is the explanation for how therapy works when a client reflects on what they are feeling, considers their actual situation and how they are responding in it, and then, after trying out various ways of putting things, finally admits that the fact is that they are *jealous*. Following this, they then proceed to make significant changes in their life. This sort of procedure, which could be understood theoretically in terms of 'making the unconscious conscious' (Freud) or of 'becoming more congruent' (Rogers) clearly involves the sort of reflection and self-examination that people do outside of therapy, and while some account of it can no doubt be given of it in terms of overcoming self-deception, it seems absurd to propose that the beneficial consequences within therapy are a placebo effect. I will discuss this further in Chapters 4 and 5; here it is again just a matter of making it clear that there *are* effective therapy procedures that go beyond the effects of client hope and expectation, and also cannot be reduced to the effect of the other main common factors, that is, 'the therapeutic relationship' and 'therapist allegiance to the rationale of the therapy'.

A postmodern alternative

Put briefly, Wampold's view, like that of Frank, is that theories of psychotherapy should be seen as healing myths. They provide clients with helpful pictures within which to frame their difficulties, but these pictures are not to be taken as scientific truths, and they can only work effectively in a context where the therapist gives allegiance to the same general mythological framework as the client. In short, the theories give meaning to the client's difficulties, but they are, none of them, *true* in the way that we think that scientific theories are true, such as the theory that the earth is a planet, or the theory that matter is composed of atoms, or the theory of evolution. We would not say that *these* theories are just appealing myths.

An interesting alternative to the mythological view is found in the writings of some recent therapists who are sympathetic to the postmodern notion that there is not just one reality but many different realities. They refer to their approach as 'pluralist therapy'. Such a perspective opens up the possibility not that all the theories are, strictly speaking, false but that they are *all true*. The difference between the two positions may not be as great as it seems at first, since a follower of Frank might want to say that while none of the theories is literally true, they can all be mythologically or poetically true. However, I think that the postmodern therapists want to say, rather, that all the theories really *are* true; it is just that truth is not unitary.

Cooper and McLeod (2011, p. 3), following Hollanders, have recently criticized what they call 'schoolism', that is the tendency of therapists belonging to a particular school 'to defend passionately the truth of their own school and attack with vigour the "error" of rival schools'. They think within a postmodern philosophical framework in which there is no single 'truth' about the nature of psychological disturbance, or about the best way to help clients who come for therapeutic help (Cooper & McLeod 2011, pp. 14–20). Instead of making any particular theory of therapy central, they suggest that what should be central is clients' goals. Their own approach to therapy is to begin by discussing with the client what the client wants from therapy and also the general way in which the client prefers the therapist to work (e.g. in a directive or non-directive way). Then the therapist draws on whatever ideas and procedures they think will be helpful to the client (which may be taken from any school of therapy), while every so often checking with the client whether the client is happy with what is being done.

I think there is something to be said for this approach, which has a strong common-sense tone to it. Indeed, I think that the general principles that Cooper and McLeod are advocating are not restricted to the practice of therapy; in any project where we are engaged in helping a person, we will need to clarify what the person wants (allowing for the possibility that what they want may change as we proceed), and it will be important to find a style of working that the person feels comfortable with. For example, if someone wants to learn to play the guitar, the guitar teacher will do well to discuss at the beginning whether the student is interested in learning classical guitar, flamenco guitar, whether they mainly want to learn chord sequences for vocal accompaniment, or whether they don't really know about all that, but simply want some broad general instruction – perhaps they just like the idea of being able to play the guitar. Then again, it will almost certainly help if the teacher can pick up early on whether the student prefers very structured teaching, learning of scales, learning of musical notation, periodic preparation for music exams, or whether they prefer starting with some tunes they like, gradually learning some chords, making use of the simplified guitar 'tablature' rather than learning the full musical notation, and generally following their own feeling for what they like.

Thus it seems to be very much a matter of common sense that in helping someone with any activity we need to clarify what the person wants, and also what style of helping appeals to them. If someone were to doubt these basic principles, it would be hard to know how to respond to them; indeed, I think we would be rather at a loss to know what someone could possibly *mean* if they suggested that in trying to help someone it would be better not to be very clear about the person's goals, and also better not to adapt one's helping style to what the person preferred. When I refer to 'common sense' in the course of this book that is the sort of thing that I have in mind: principles, or ideas, or ways of thinking that just about everyone would accept. Such principles are not 'absolute truths' – there can always be special contexts in which we would be forced to admit that the principle does not apply, or in which what seems to make no sense does make sense after all. It is just that *without some special background story* it makes no sense to doubt the principle. Another way of putting it would be to say that *normally* the principle holds: its holding is the norm, so that cases where it doesn't hold need some special accounting for. The principles which Cooper and McLeod are invoking seem to me to be of this 'common-sense' nature.

What is involved in pluralism is clear enough in connection with therapeutic practices, procedures and interventions. Within the different schools of therapy can be found all sorts of procedures, and the pluralist approach suggests that any of these procedures can be used if they are helpful to the client, which seems an admirably commonsensical view. It is not so straightforward in connection with the theories that are associated with the different schools. These theories, as both Hollanders (1999, pp. 487–488) and Cooper and McLeod (2011, p. 157) acknowledge, involve widely different philosophical and psychological assumptions. Psychodynamic therapists think in terms of 'the unconscious mind', and an important part of psychodynamic therapy involves, as Freud said, 'making what is unconscious conscious'. However, behavioural, cognitive and person-centred therapists don't 'believe in' the unconscious mind. Similarly, cognitive therapists hold that psychological disturbances arise from dysfunctional thinking, but behaviourally oriented psychologists and person-centred and psychodynamic therapists don't believe this.

From a common-sense point of view these are disagreements about what is or isn't true, and the different theories can't *all* be true. However, in this connection, Hollanders (1997, p. 487) refers to the position of the historian of science Thomas Kuhn (1970), who argued that scientific theories do not arise directly from observation and experiment but are constructed partly under the influence of personal, social and economic influences. This has led some writers to suggest that since theories are human constructions, there is no reason to object to the idea that alternative constructions are possible, and that there is no single truth to be discovered. As Hollanders and Cooper and McLeod both note, this kind of view is also to be found in the philosophical tradition of social constructionism and postmodernism, which 'challenges the idea that there are any single definitive truths (e.g. Derrida 1974)... [F]or postmodern thinkers such as Derrida, the fact that all knowledge rests, ultimately, on language, means that we can never penetrate down to the 'true' essence of how things are'.

Nevertheless, there is a difficulty in using social constructionism or postmodern philosophy as a foundation for an account of psychotherapy integration. These traditions of thought are themselves highly controversial as philosophies (e.g. Hacking 1999), as is Kuhn's account of the development of scientific theories (Sharrock & Read 2002). Adopting postmodern philosophy might solve the problem of how different psychotherapy theories can 'all be true', but it lands us with a similar dilemma at the meta-level of what kind of philosophical approach we should take to the theories. One can't both be a postmodernist *and* a follower of Popper (1959), who held that science moves in the direction of a single truth, *and* a follower of, say, David Cooper (2002) or Eugene Gendlin (1997) (if I understand him correctly), who hold that there is a single truth, though it can't be expressed in conceptual terms. Should we then consider moving to a meta-meta-level at which all these incompatible philosophies become acceptable?

I am not concerned here to discuss postmodernism, or the nature of 'truth' in a philosophical or metaphysical sense. Such a discussion would take us much too far from the concerns of this book. Nevertheless, something needs to be said about the idea that Cooper and McLeod seem to be recommending, that is, that there can be 'many truths', and that, for example, we can accept the truth of psychoanalysis, *as well as* the truth of cognitive theory, and behaviourist theory, and person-centred theory. Cooper and McLeod (2011, p. 157) acknowledge that one cannot accept all of these theories as 'fixed exclusive truths', but suggest that they can all be accepted at the same time if they are 'held lightly'. This is reminiscent of Carl Rogers' (1959, p. 191) view that a theory is 'a fallible, changing attempt to construct a network of gossamer threads which will contain the solid facts'.

I think there are serious difficulties with this 'gossamer threads' view of theories. It certainly doesn't fit well with how 'theory' is understood in most branches of science. For example, modern biology accepts the Darwinian theory of evolution, and biologists hold that this is a true account of the origin of species. Similarly, modern physics accepts Einstein's theory of relativity and holds this to be an important part of the truth about the physical world. These theories are not held as 'absolute truths' that could *never* be revised; the history of science is littered with theories that were once confidently held but were later abandoned. Yet contemporary scientists do believe in these theories and accept them as true. The theories are not at all like 'gossamer threads'; rather, they are an established backdrop to most work in the relevant fields. This may seem paradoxical, but it is not so if we understand 'truth' in a common-sense way. When a biologist says that the theory of evolution is true, they mean that it provides an overall framework for biological thought that accounts for a multitude of biological facts; that they can take it for granted because it works so well; that there are no serious alternatives to it. In short, it is a theory that has proved its worth, so that they can trust it. 'Truth' in its common-sense use is indeed linked with 'trust' (with which it is also linked etymologically): a true friend is a friend one can trust; a carpenter's rule is true if the carpenter can trust it; if we tell someone that something is true, we are saying that they can trust what we say. This is the opposite of 'gossamer threads' that will bear little weight; to say that something is true is to say that you can rely on it, that it will bear a great deal of weight.

Much the same applies, I think, in the case of theories in psychotherapy. A psychoanalyst *believes in* Freud's theory of the unconscious mind. That means that they think in terms of it; they find the theory highly plausible; they see it as explaining a multitude of psychological phenomena that other theories cannot account for nearly so well; they see it as providing insights into human life more generally – such as insights into art, literature and religion. They see their clinical practice in terms of the theory, and where they encounter something hard to explain, they are either sceptical about whether it really happened, or they consider ways in which the theory might be amended or extended in order to account for the new observation. The truth of the theory as a whole is not something they question, but that does not mean they might *never* question it. It is the same as in evolutionary biology or modern physics. Recently, some physicists reported the results of experiments that, in contradiction to relativity theory, suggested that some sub-atomic particles can travel faster than light. The community of physicists reacted to this neither by saying 'Well, relativity theory is just gossamer threads, so we can let it go' nor by saying 'Relativity theory is the final truth, so these experimental results must be flawed, and we can ignore them.' The reaction was more like 'I just don't believe this, but since the experiments were carefully conducted, we need to check them out.'

The point I want to make is that we have a common-sense notion of truth, such that it makes sense for a therapist to say that they think that Freud's theory that psychological disturbance is caused by unconscious conflicts is true (and similarly for the cognitive therapist's theory that it is caused by dysfunctional thoughts, or Roger's theory that it is due to incongruence, or the behaviourists' theory that it is due to faulty conditioning). One can hold that such theories are true while not being committed to saying that one would *never* abandon them. To say that they are true is not to say that one *has to* hold to them, but just that one *does* hold to them. One trusts them, relies on them, centres one's thinking around them. One comes to believe in a theory through first hearing about it, finding it initially plausible, discussing it with other people, realizing that some objections to it are groundless, taking part in training courses that presuppose its truth, attending meetings and conferences where the finer details of the theory may be questioned, but the broad truth of it is accepted by everyone there. Coming to believe in a theory of therapy is a kind of initiation process (Purton 1991) in which one is drawn into membership of a professional community that sees things in a particular way. What distinguishes membership of such professional communities from membership of a *cult* is, of course, that a professional community is in the end open to well-argued fundamental criticism, both from inside and from outside its ranks. Most physicists were highly sceptical about the 'faster-than-light' results, but they did not just dismiss them.

I think that our common-sense notion of truth is the one we need to stick with if we are to get anywhere with the question of whether all the theories of therapy can be true. My sense is that Cooper and McLeod move uneasily between two different ways of understanding 'all of them are true'. One way is the 'gossamer threads' way: we can say that they are all true if by this we mean that we 'hold lightly' to all of them and can use ideas drawn from any of them 'as offerings that may or may not be of use to a client' (Cooper & McLeod 2011, p. 157). The other way of understanding 'all of them are true' is grounded in the philosophy of postmodernism, according to which there are multiple realities that are socially constructed. This philosophical position is controversial, and arguably not as novel as it may seem, since throughout the history of philosophy there have been 'relativistic' views of truth; for example, Protagoras, the 5th-century BCE Greek sophist, held that 'man is the measure of all things'. Whatever the long-term fate of 'postmodernism' and 'social constructionism', the notion of 'truth' around which such discussions centre is not the common-sense notion. Discussions of postmodernism are related to the question of whether particular worldviews are 'True' in some metaphysical sense and are irrelevant to the concerns of therapists.

What therapists are concerned with is the question of whether they can in practice accept the truth of, say, Freud's account of psychological difficulties as arising from repressed mental contents *and* Rogers' theory of such difficulties as arising from incongruence between self-concept and organismic experiencing, *and* the cognitive account of the difficulties as arising from dysfunctional thinking, *and* the behaviourist account of the difficulties as arising from unfortunate conditioning contingencies. It seems to me that if we understand the notion of 'truth' in an everyday way, along the lines I sketched above, then the answer must be 'No'; you can't accept (trust, give allegiance to, take for granted, think mainly in terms of, habitually relate your clinical experience to) more than one of these theories at a time. But couldn't one be a psychoanalyst on Mondays and a behavioural therapist on Tuesdays? I don't really think so – any more than one can be an Arsenal supporter one day and a Chelsea supporter the next. Someone who claims to be like that doesn't really count as a football supporter at all; they just don't take football seriously. So, taking 'true' in its common-sense meaning, a therapist can't hold that psychoanalytic theory and behavioural conditioning theory are both true. If someone did say that, I think it would simply be unclear what they meant.

The identity and commitment issue

The difficulty with the notion of 'plural theories' is not just that it seems to make little sense to say that all the theories could be true. There are also more practical implications, which are related to the issue of 'therapist allegiance' which, as discussed earlier, is a very significant factor in therapeutic effectiveness. Dave Mearns and Brian Thorne write (2007, pp. 213–214):

> We are alarmed when we read in an entry in the Directory of the British Association for Counselling and Psychotherapy that a practitioner is describing herself as psychodynamic, person-centred, gestalt and rational emotive behavioural – or some other unlikely combination. We cannot even begin to conceptualise what such a self description might indicate. Does it mean that the counsellor combines all these approaches in some amazingly integrative or eclectic fashion, or does it suggest that on a certain day, at a certain hour, she dons one mantle and the next another – psychodynamic for this client but person-centred for the next... [T]he depth and coherence of the counsellor is critical. The counsellor will be placed under varied and at times dramatic demands, and the depth of their grounding will give a coherence as well as a stability to their working.

The issue here is important in practice because it bears on a therapist's sense of identity and commitment. As Szasz (1974, p. 41) put it, 'the therapist who tries to be all things to all people may be nothing to himself; he is not "at one" with any particular method of psychotherapy'. Hollanders (1999, p. 489) tries to avoid the difficulty by suggesting that 'identity and commitment need not be seen as the province of the single schools alone'. In a pluralist approach, 'the committed practitioner is one who does not hold tenaciously to a single approach, but instead accepts with humility the validity of different systems. Commitment is not to a school but to the whole project of therapy.' Hollanders then quotes Prochaska's (1984, p. 367) view that the committed practitioner is centrally concerned with 'what is the best way to be in therapy; what is the most valuable model we can provide for our clients, our colleagues, and our students; and how can we help our clients attain a better life?' Yet surely the 'best way to be in therapy' (and so on) is closely related to what we take to be the truth about human nature and the nature of client troubles. Practitioners of different kinds of therapy disagree very profoundly on what is the best way to be with clients (e.g. whether to be directive or non-directive, emotionally close or emotionally distant), and these differences are rooted in the theoretical differences that divide them.

I don't doubt that there is something right about the idea that therapists (like scientists) should hold to their theories with humility, if this means acknowledging that their theory could turn out to be wrong. Similarly, it is important to acknowledge that rival theories could be right. But such humility is not incompatible with having trust in a particular theory, and a corresponding mistrust of others. To say 'this theory is true' is not to say that one couldn't possibly be mistaken, but just that one *isn't* mistaken. It is an assertion of one's trust in something, and one can trust in something while being aware that any kind of trust *could* turn out to be misplaced. Cooper and McLeod's (2011) way of dealing with the 'commitment issue' is to suggest that what therapists should commit themselves to is pluralism, but they tend to slide between pluralism of theory and pluralism of practice. They write that 'trainees can be encouraged to feel confident and proud about the work they do while also seeing the value in alternative practices' (p. 139), which is unexceptional, but how could anything similar be said in connection with incompatible theories? For example, I think it would be true to say that most person-centred therapists and cognitive-behavioural therapists honestly think that psychoanalysis is fundamentally mistaken, and probably in some ways harmful.

Cooper and McLeod see their own commitment to pluralism as paradoxical (ibid., p. 158): their commitment is to the prizing of diversity and difference but *that* commitment is 'to a large extent, not considered negotiable'. I take it that they say 'to a large extent' in order to cover the possibility that they might at some time have to revise their values, even though they can't imagine revising them at present. But if that is right, I can't see how their position is fundamentally different from that of someone who is committed to, say, psychoanalysis. In either case there is a commitment to something that just *might* turn out to be wrong. But there is nothing paradoxical in that; it is how it is with any commitment.

Summary

One way of putting my conclusion would be to say that there *may* be a postmodern philosophical sense of 'truth' in which 'all the theories are true', but whether any sense can be made of this idea is philosophically controversial, and is likely to remain so. There is also the idea that all the theories can be true in the *different* sense that one can draw useful ideas and insights from any of them. That seems undeniable, but it also seems to be very different from saying that all the theories are true. As I have tried to show, there is much more to saying that a theory is true than just finding that one can get some useful ideas from it; to say it is true is to give allegiance to it. So either way, I suggest, it is implausible to say that all the theories are true.

That seems to leave us with the conclusion that after all there can only be one true theory. It might be one of those currently under consideration, or it could be a theory that has yet to be developed. It seems pointless to speculate about theories that have not yet been developed, so it seems we are left with the traditional idea that just one of the current theories is the true one, or at least that just one of these theories is on the right track, and needs only to be worked on until it becomes fully satisfactory. I take it that committed psychodynamic theorists would say that psychodynamic theory is *the* theory, and similarly for the other school-based theorists. Eclectic therapists and some pluralist therapists of course don't have an overall theory, and other pluralist therapists would seem to be committed to postmodernism as *the* theory (although it is a theory on a different level from the others).

I don't think the possibility of there being just one theory that is *the* theory can be entirely ruled out; psychotherapy theory might develop in a quite unexpected direction. But given our present position I do share Cooper and McLeod's (and many other people's) scepticism about accepting any one of the current theories as *the* theory. So we reach the conclusion that none of the current theories are likely to be the one true theory, but also that there is little to be said for the idea that *all* the theories are true. This returns us to the position of Frank and Walpole that, except in a mythological sense, *all the theories are false*.

There is a sense in which most therapists already agree with this conclusion. Suppose – the exact figures don't matter – that roughly one-fifth of therapists are integrative or pluralist, one-fifth are psychodynamic, one-fifth are person-centred or 'humanistic', one-fifth are cognitively oriented and one-fifth are behaviourally oriented. The integrative and pluralist therapists don't 'believe in' psychodynamic theory or in any of the other theories. They don't think that *any* of the theories are true in the common-sense meaning of 'true'. The psychodynamic therapists don't believe in cognitive, or person-centred or behavioural theory, and similarly the other kinds of therapist don't believe in the theories of the other three. Thus a large majority of therapists don't believe in Freud's theory; but an equally large number don't believe in the theories of Rogers, or Beck or Skinner. All the theories are rejected by a majority of therapists, a partially different majority in each case, but a majority nonetheless.

In this book I will argue that the majority of therapists is right, and that all the theories should be rejected. However, my reasons for rejecting them will be rather different from the reasons given by therapists committed to any particular school. A psychoanalyst will reject other theories largely on the grounds that they are incompatible with psychoanalytic theory, which is *the* theory. And similarly for all the other approaches. In this book I will not be grounding my discussion in the truth of any particular theory; my view is not that *all but one* of the theories is false but that they *all* are false. That then raises the question of whether there remains any possibility of understanding psychological disturbance and ways of alleviating it. My answer will be that there is the possibility of such understanding, but that it does not require any of the current theories. The resources of common sense and of our common ways of thinking and understanding can take us a long way towards the understanding we need. Common sense may need some extension or correction in the light of clinical experience and the findings of other disciplines such as sociology or neuroscience, but the basic framework of therapy need not take us far beyond common sense. We may extend our everyday way of thinking about people, and in that sense begin to develop new ways of thinking about therapy, but we need not *replace* it with views that are grounded in theoretical concepts such as those of 'the unconscious mind', or 'organismic experiencing', or 'conditioning contingences' or 'dysfunctional cognitions'. I will argue that *these* theoretical concepts are fundamentally flawed because the theories in which they are embedded are themselves incoherent.

In their place I will recommend a view, which perhaps counts as a 'low-level', or 'close to common sense' theory, that organizes and orients some of the common-sense ideas that are already present in the various schools of psychotherapy. I will argue that while the developed theories of the schools have to be rejected, each school contains a core of plausible common-sense understanding that can be retained. These common-sense 'cores of understanding' can then themselves be brought together and integrated into a 'low-level theory'. In order to clarify further what is involved I will need to say something in the next chapter about the nature of theories and of 'common sense', together with an account of the main ways in which theories can be unsatisfactory.

Note

1. 'Effect size' is defined as the number of standard deviation units between the means of the 'experimental group' and of the 'control group'.

CHAPTER 2

Theories and Common Sense

Theories, regularities and explanatory pictures

Theories are distinguished from facts, although the dividing line between the two can be hazy: for example, the theory that the earth revolves around the sun has become an accepted fact. And sometimes a previously accepted fact, such as the fact that the earth is flat, can be demolished by the construction of a new theory. People say things such as 'But that's just a theory' or 'Evolution is not a theory – it is a fact'. Sometimes people use 'theory' in this way to mean much the same as 'hypothesis', but we need to distinguish between hypotheses about what happens in the world and hypotheses about *why* these things happen.

(1) On the one hand, there are hypotheses about regularities or observed patterns – for example, whether it is true that drinking coffee interferes with sleep, or that listening to clients is therapeutic for them. Establishing whether such regularities exist usually requires observation, data collection or experiments. The discovered regularities are straightforward (though often statistical) facts about the world. Things either happen like this, or they don't.

(2) On the other hand, there are theories, which don't simply propose what the regularities or patterns are. They attempt to *explain* why the regularities exist, through putting forward a wider view of the nature of things, into which the regularity can be fitted. For example, once it is established that coffee in some circumstances, and in some people, interferes with sleep, we can investigate what it is about the nature of coffee and the nature of sleep such that the one interferes with the other. The theory is likely to bring in lots of *other* things – caffeine, chemicals in the brain and so on. Once you have the theory you say 'Ah, yes, now I understand why that happens', or at least 'I do see how that *could* explain why it happens'.

A theory of that sort works within familiar concepts and principles – it shows how the regularity fits into those concepts and principles. Working out the explanation is essentially a puzzle-solving activity – the puzzle is how the existence of the regularity follows from our wider knowledge of things. Much scientific research is like this – the historian of science Thomas Kuhn (1970) referred to it as 'normal science'.

However, some scientific developments are not a matter of fitting a regularity into familiar concepts and principles but of developing *new* concepts. This clearly happens in the work of great innovators such as Copernicus, Newton and Darwin, but it probably happens in a less obvious way in many scientific developments. In such cases we do not explain a regularity by fitting it into a pre-existing conceptual scheme, but allow the perceived incompatibility of the regularity with the current concepts to open up the possibility of a change in those concepts.

Theories often draw on pictures, models or analogies (Hesse 1963; Frigg et al. 2012). Consider, for example, the picture of matter as being made up of atomic particles, or Darwin's analogy between the selection of favoured characteristics by animal breeders and an analogous process, *natural* selection, that could take place in nature, without deliberate planning. The picture or analogy invites us to see things in a particular way, so that certain aspects of what we observe are drawn together in a way that depends on our acceptance of the picture or analogy. In highly developed sciences such as physics, the pictures, analogies or models may take us far beyond our ordinary ways of thinking, yet they are in the end still grounded in our common-sense view of things. A high-level theory in physics still needs to connect with down-to-earth observations and experiments in the laboratory whose results can be stated in common-sense terms. What takes the high-level concepts of physics far away from our ordinary view of things is the *length* of the path from the understanding of someone who has not yet studied even elementary physics to that of a leading theorist at CERN; that path normally involves something like two decades of study, but also considerable experience of how *in practice* the pictures and concepts are to be used. There is, as the chemist and philosopher Michael Polanyi (1958, 1966) argued, a significant 'tacit dimension' to the scientific enterprise; not everything that the scientist knows can be spelled out in words. For example, the physicist does not simply learn the abstract theory of electrons but also learns how these particles can be manipulated. Ian Hacking (1983) persuasively argues that it is this practical engagement with sub-atomic particles that inclines most physicists to see them as real entities and not just as 'constructions of the mind'. This is perhaps even more clear in the case of the picture of the earth as a huge ball: the earth-ball is not just a mental construction; we can actually travel round it.

Not all theories in physical science are 'high-level' theories such as the theories involving sub-atomic particles. Others work on a 'lower level' that is not far removed from common sense. Common sense suggests that the earth is a flat disc, but it is not a dramatic departure from common sense to picture the earth as a very *large* sphere, since if it is very large we would not *expect* to be able to tell immediately whether it is flat or not. The theory that the earth is a huge ball involves a certain act of imagination and an invitation to think about our experiences of travel in a particular way, but something of common sense is saved, while at the same time we do now picture the earth in a new way. That is the sort of thing I mean by a 'low-level theory'; it is one that doesn't stray far from common sense, and indeed retains much of what common sense says. Nevertheless, it does re-orient and re-organize common sense to some extent. My suggestion will be that psychotherapy needs a low-level theory of this sort, and while it *could* be that, in the future, higher-level theories will be constructed in the human sciences, whether or not that will happen is a matter of pure speculation. One difficulty is that in the human sciences the construction of theories has an impact on how people see themselves, and hence on how they behave. The theories can *alter* what it is that they are explaining (Hacking 1999). But also it could be that there is, in any case, something about the subtlety and 'mistiness' of human relationships that simply doesn't allow for high-level theory. As in some Chinese paintings, it may be that the mist is an essential part of the picture.

Once a scientific picture becomes established, it may become elaborated indefinitely. The 17th-century picture of the world as made up of material particles governed by Newton's laws of motion originated in astronomy, with the idea that the heavenly bodies are large material particles, but this mechanistic picture quickly led to mechanistic explanations of such things as the behaviour of gases (picturing them as made up of fast-moving particles), and of the transitions between solid, liquid and gaseous states (picturing them as involving different kinds of relationships between the particles). Then later came the development of chemistry and of mechanistic explanations of biological phenomena. Although increasingly challenged in the 20th century, the mechanistic picture of the world led to a huge expansion of scientific knowledge.

In the late 19th century hopes were raised of some parallel development in our knowledge of human personality and behaviour. There were evident difficulties here, since mechanical explanations, since the time of Descartes, were usually seen as applicable only to matter. Late 19th- and early 20th-century psychology investigated the possibility of developing a parallel science of *mind*, though, as we shall see in the next chapter, this was a failure. In reaction to that failure, behaviourist psychology worked with the alternative possibility that a mechanistic approach, in terms of physiological stimulus–response connections, could after all be made to work. This too, by the early 1950s, was seen to be clearly impossible, and from the 1960s there was a return to thinking in terms of 'mental' or 'cognitive' concepts. Currently, there seems to be something of a swing back to the 'physical', with the rapid development of neuroscience, and the picture of *brain processes* as being the foundation for psychological explanation. We will look in a little more detail at this historical sequence of psychological explanations in the next chapter, but for now the point is that such explanations always involve both observed regularities in human behaviour *and* a background picture that provides the framework for explanations of the behaviour.

Theories of psychotherapy, like other theories, have their background pictures against which people's behaviour and difficulties are seen. These background pictures form the major reason for there being very different schools of therapy. In the background of behaviourist theory is the picture of people as stimulus–response organisms; this picture stays close to the mechanistic picture of (pre-quantum-mechanical) physical science. In the background of cognitive theory is the picture of human behaviour as depending essentially on what goes on in our minds, in the sense of what we think and believe. In the background of psychodynamic theory is the picture of the *unconscious* mind, which operates at a 'deeper level' than our conscious thoughts and beliefs. In the background of much humanistic theory is the picture of the person as a living thing (Rogers used the analogy of a potato plant) that, given suitable facilitative conditions, will find its natural way to self-actualization. These very different background pictures set up very different frameworks for the understanding of personal difficulties. They are not pictures that can be *merged*, any more than, say, early earth-centred astronomy can be merged with modern astronomy, or mediaeval alchemy with modern chemistry.

This book is concerned with how the psychotherapy profession can best respond to the situation in which there are several competing candidates for the role of a background picture or framework for psychotherapy. In spite of the obvious difficulties, can a way be found of integrating the pictures? Or, in spite of its current implausibility, should we take seriously the idea that just one of the pictures is essentially correct, while the others are largely mistaken? The idea I will develop is that neither of these options is viable. Instead, I will suggest that while there is something of value in all the current approaches, the *theories* are all flawed, because the pictures that they are bound up with are confused. It is probably true that each of the approaches has done something to illuminate certain aspects of personal difficulties, and some of these more common-sense understandings can be retained. However, as we shall see, the more theoretical developments, which are closely involved with certain pictures of the nature of human beings, need to be rejected.

Reasons for rejecting a theory

There are a number of reasons why theories come to be rejected. The most obvious is that the observed facts or regularities are simply not what one would expect if the theory were correct. The philosopher of science Karl Popper (1959) made *falsification* the key notion in his account of theory change in science. Later writers pointed out that the matter is not quite so simple: if incompatibility with observations was regarded as sufficient to reject a theory, then the laws of physics and chemistry are daily falsified in school science laboratories, where the pupils do not carry out the experiments sufficiently carefully. Further, as Paul Feyerabend (1975) and others pointed out, there is often room for dispute about what counts as a valid *observation*. Galileo observed things through his new telescope that 'falsified' the old Greek astronomical theory, but at the time there was not much reason to trust what one saw through these primitive telescopes (they produced false colours, and other distortions of what was seen). Trust in telescopes developed only along with a theory of optics that explained what could and couldn't be trusted in telescopic observations. Nevertheless, there are limits to how much one can reasonably contest the observations in order to preserve the theory; beyond a certain point it does seem to be reasonable to say that a theory can't be correct if it conflicts with what we observe. *One* reason that most scientists reject astrology as a theory of human personality is that there is little evidence of correlations between personality variables and dates of birth. The alleged regularities just don't exist (although astrologers may contest this matter of fact). Some objections to Freudian theory are along these lines: it is said that what would be predicted by the theory is falsified by empirical evidence.

A different reason for rejecting a theory is that the picture involved in the theory is not sufficiently well developed for it to yield definite conclusions about what we should expect to observe. There is some evidence that homeopathic treatments can be effective, even though in a homeopathic remedy the active ingredient is so diluted that no particle of it is likely to be present in the prescription. The homeopathic theory is that 'like cures like' and that the active ingredient leaves a 'memory trace' in the water even though it is no longer itself present after the successive dilutions. It is this 'trace' that is held to be the effective element in homeopathic remedies. Such a theory is not inherently absurd, and combined with statistical evidence for the effectiveness of homeopathy, it might seem that it should be taken seriously. However, the difficulty is that the theory's picture of 'like curing like' is vague and does not tell us anything about the nature of the 'trace' or of how it is registered in the water, or how the modified water makes an impact on physiological functioning. What we have here is a picture which draws its life from the idea that 'like cures like', but the picture has not been developed in a way that encourages us to take it seriously. There are many theories in psychotherapy that seem to fall into this category. For example, practitioners of EMDR suggest that the therapy works because the eye movements involved restore the balance between excitatory and inhibitory processes in the brain. This *could* be true, but the details of the theory are not sufficiently worked out for it to be investigated as a serious explanation for the effectiveness of EMDR (if indeed it is effective; *that* is the question of whether the alleged regularity actually obtains). NLP, primal scream therapy, crystal healing, neural organization technique (NOT) and many others (Singer & Lalich 1996) also seem to fall in this category.

These two reasons for rejecting a theory (incompatibility with observation and lack of serious theoretical development) do not obviously apply to the major theories of psychotherapy, such as cognitive-behavioural therapy, psychoanalysis, process-experiential therapy and the Rogerian theory of client-centred therapy. The regularities that these theories try to explain are well established: *that* is known from the psychotherapy outcome research. Further, the theories are well developed. That is, they do not simply involve vague pictures, such as the homeopathic picture of a 'memory trace in the water'. Rather, they have more or less elaborate theoretical frameworks that are discussed, developed and sometimes modified in the light of new findings. For a therapist working within the general picture underlying the theory, detailed reasons can be given for preferring one interpretation of a client difficulty to another, or arguments can be presented as to why a particular phenomenon does or does not require a modification of the theory. The literatures of the different approaches are full of detailed and subtle discussions of how exactly the theory in question bears on clinical findings. In this way the psychotherapeutic theories are no different from theories in other areas of knowledge. The point of learning the theory is to acquire a detailed understanding of the nature of psychological disturbance, so that the most appropriate clinical responses can be made. It is this detailed elaboration of the theories, and their relation to practice, that ensures that the various schools of therapy remain largely distinct from one another. Being a psychoanalyst, for example, involves both believing in the effectiveness of psychoanalytic procedure (for which there is good evidence) and thinking about client problems in terms of the elaborate structures of psychoanalytic theory. The analyst uses the theory in the way an experimental physicist uses theory: the theory provides the framework of concepts in terms of which the observations are understood. Yet the distinction between observation and theory is not a sharp one: the analyst *notices* that the client is repressing something (even though 'repression' is a theoretical term), just as the physicist *sees* the behaviour of electrons in a photographic emulsion. The way in which the practitioner *describes* what they see is often influenced by the theory they subscribe to. This is a further reason why the differences between therapists run deep. Therapists from different schools *see* things differently; there is no common 'observation language', or at least the commonalities in description fade out as those observations come increasingly to depend on theory.

Incoherent theories and misleading pictures

Theories may be rejected because the regularities that they entail simply don't obtain, or they may be rejected because their theoretical structure is not sufficiently developed to provide any serious understanding of the regularities. However, there is a third kind of reason for rejecting a theory which is less obvious, and less well known. It is, roughly speaking, that there is a fundamental incoherence in the theory, which arises from a *misleading* picture that lies at the heart of the theory. This idea derives from the thought of Wittgenstein, who held that many philosophical, as well as psychological, systems of thought are rooted in confusions that arise from such misleading pictures. In connection with psychotherapy theory, the most pervasive of the misleading pictures is the Cartesian picture of a human being as a physical system that is conscious; that is, the picture of a person as a composite of 'mind' and 'body'. Central to this picture are the ideas that all that we can know for sure is our own 'subjective experience', that we have no direct knowledge of 'the outside world' and that 'the outside world' (apart from 'other minds') is a physical system devoid of 'consciousness'. If we think within this picture we will suppose that we never perceive people or things as they are, but only subjective images of them. The Cartesian idea is that we perceive only our own experiences.

It is largely through the pervasiveness of this picture that psychotherapy theories tend to assume in one way or another that personal difficulties are rooted either in 'mental disturbances' (unconscious conflicts, defective cognitive schemas, automatic thoughts, etc.) or 'physical disturbances' (faulty conditioning, physiological deficits, brain abnormalities, etc.). Behaviourists reject the Cartesian 'mind', but then they try to understand human psychology in terms of the behaviour (movements) of the Cartesian 'body'. Psychoanalysts reject the idea that 'the mind' always involves 'consciousness', but they still accept the notion of 'the mind', which they divide into 'conscious' and 'unconscious' compartments. Humanist theoreticians often emphasize the idea of 'experiencing' without realizing that this is essentially Descartes' notion of 'mind' reborn. Some neuroscientists try to identify 'mental states' with 'brain states', but this does not begin to get away from the Cartesian picture.

Wittgenstein rejects the Cartesian picture, but it is not my purpose in this book to explain his ideas for their own sake; it is rather to make use of his idea that we can free ourselves from the compulsive power of the picture by attending to how words such as 'awareness', 'experience', 'feeling', 'thought', 'behaviour' are *actually* used, rather than at how we use them when our imagination is captivated by the Cartesian picture. The use made of these words and their cognates by psychologists (and many philosophers) are far from the way they are used in everyday life. Yet it is in the course of everyday life, not psychology, that children come to know how these words are used, and hence what they actually mean. I am not suggesting that we need to hold on to our ordinary use of language, come what may. Language usage changes along with changes in society, new empirical discoveries, changed values and so on. However, our common-sense way of seeing things and the associated ordinary use of words that goes with it are where we must *start*. (I will say more about the notion of 'common sense' in the next section.)

The Cartesian picture of human beings as comprised of 'mind and matter', or 'having a consciousness and a body', is not the only misleading picture that we will encounter, though it is the most important one. Related to it is the picture of language as a *representation* of reality, so that whether a statement is true is pictured in terms of whether the statement 'matches', or 'corresponds with', the facts. This picture pre-dates Descartes and can be traced back at least to Augustine. However, it is a picture that connects closely with the mind-matter picture since the question of whether a *statement* corresponds with reality is very close to the question of whether a *thought* corresponds with reality. In Carl Rogers' theory of therapy, the notion of 'congruence', pictured as the correspondence of self-concept with organismic experiencing, involves precisely this picture. I will discuss this further in Chapter 4.

A third misleading picture that we will touch on derives mainly from Immanuel Kant's response to the problems of Descartes' philosophy. Instead of picturing the world as a material realm that is presented to us in the form of images in consciousness, Kant pictures the world as an essentially *unknowable* realm which does not in itself contain any forms. *On to* this unknowable 'thing in itself' human reason projects its categories of space, time, matter and so on. For Kant, our concepts derive not from the way things are in the world but from the way we need to see things if we are to make any sense of our experience. For Kant, the crucial thing in human knowing is the interaction between our experiencing (which in itself has no content) and our concepts (which provide the content). This picture is influential in the 'schema' notion of cognitive psychology, in process-experiential theory and in Gendlin's theory of focusing. I will discuss the picture further in Chapters 6 and 7. The process-experiential formulation of it (Elliott et al. 2004, p. 36) is '[w]hat one calls a "fact" is actually a joint construction of the "things themselves" and one's knowing process'.

The above three pictures have been extensively elaborated in philosophy, but our concern here is not with the philosophical details. It is rather with how the pictures can lead to misleading ways of thinking and talking about therapy. My suggestion will be that the way that theorists of psychotherapy talk has come adrift from our ordinary ways of talking, and of seeing things. Yet this movement away from everyday language and common sense is not driven by developments in empirical knowledge or changes in society, which would be a wholly natural development. It is driven instead by a fascination with the philosophical pictures I have mentioned, and especially the 17th-century metaphysical picture of people as composites of 'body' and 'mind' that finds its classical exposition in Descartes. This misleading picture feeds, and is fed by, certain theoretical ways of talking that are fundamentally confused or incoherent. I will argue that the only way through this difficulty is to draw attention to how the Cartesian picture has distorted the development of psychotherapy theories. This can only be done by looking at each theory individually, although, as we shall see, there are some confusions and incoherencies that are shared among several of the theories. The following seven chapters are devoted to this task, but first it may be helpful to look a bit more at the *kind* of incoherence that I believe infects the theories.

It is not easy to find *simple* examples of the kind incoherence we will be concerned with. In his own work, Wittgenstein mainly addressed incoherencies in psychology and in mathematics. Much of what he writes about psychology will be helpful in the following chapters; however, his mathematical examples would take us too far from the themes of this book. I will give three examples that may be of some help in understanding what is involved: first, a light-hearted example that may nevertheless help to set the scene; then a slightly more serious example involving the notion of *time* (which, like *mind*, is a fertile breeding ground for confusion); and finally a real-life example from contemporary neuroscience that takes us close to the incoherencies in psychotherapy theories that we will be concerned with.

Example 1: The East Pole

Suppose someone said that since there are four points of the compass, and explorers have already discovered the North and South Poles, isn't it possible that there are still the East and West Poles to be discovered? In one of A.A. Milne's children's stories, Pooh Bear indeed sets out on an expedition to discover the East Pole. If we said to Pooh 'But there is no East Pole!' he might reply 'How do you know – there are many places that have not yet been discovered.' Further, if Owl – the intellectual in the stories – became involved in this discussion, he might suggest that we should at least consider the *possibility* of there being an East Pole. Clearly, the East Pole will be unlike the currently known Poles, since in seeking the East Pole one would be engaged in an endless movement to the east. However, concludes Owl, that just means that we need to extend our understanding of what a Pole can be. The East Pole needs to be understood as an *endlessly deferred Pole*, rather than a place that can be reached. The same clearly applies in the case of the West Pole. However, as Owl as his co-theorists now argue, there is an inherent relation between the East and West Poles: they both, though endlessly deferred, actually cover the same ground, though in opposite directions. They are, in the developing terminology of Polar Theory, *co-extensively deferred*. A member of Owl's group then realizes that in addition to the now accepted four Poles, there must in fact be four others, corresponding to the directions NE, NW, SE, SW. These will all be co-extensively deferred Poles. But then there is a very significant development in the theory. *Between* each of the known Poles there must be an infinite number of other co-extensively deferred Poles so that the various Poles can no longer be conceived as fundamentally separate from each other: they merge into each other. This raises a theoretical problem for Polar Theory, since if polar merger is a general property of Poles, the North and South Poles must in some sense be merged, or even in some deep sense be identical. Perhaps at this stage Owl writes a large, scholarly book on Polar Theory, which he gives to Pooh. Pooh is impressed by the scholarship and intellectual effort that has gone into the book, but he is also baffled by it, and asks Christopher Robin how it relates to his original project of going to find the East Pole. Christopher Robin, having remarked affectionately 'Silly old Bear!', then has to explain what the difficulty is.

The explanation, of course, needs to be that there *really is* no such place as the East Pole. However, it is not that there *happens* to be no East Pole, but that talk of the East Pole makes no sense. The concept of the Poles comes from the idea of the earth as a sphere turning on its axis; the Poles are the end points of that axis – and there can be only two ends to an axis. Pooh has a picture of a pole as a place like a city or a mountain, but it is a misleading picture; if Pooh were taken to the North Pole he might exclaim, 'But there's nothing here – this is not really a *place* at all!' Nevertheless, there is such a place as the North Pole, and there is no such place as the East Pole. Someone who sets out to find the East Pole is engaged in a different sort of project from that of, say, Colonel Fawcett, who in the 1920s set out to find the lost 'city of gold' in the Amazon jungle that he referred to as 'Z'. Fawcett was mistaken about the existence of Z, as could today be demonstrated by satellite photography. By contrast, Pooh is not *mistaken* about the existence of the East Pole; rather the project of seeking the East Pole is a *muddle*, and Pooh is *confused*. We can understand his confusion – after all, we talk about four points to the compass, representing them by the letters N, S, E, W. There are four cardinal directions, and following two of them brings you to a cold place that people call poles. Why shouldn't there be two more poles? Why should we think that E and W are radically different from N and S? All four seem much of a muchness, and of course in the days when the earth was pictured as flat, they *were* much of a muchness. However, with the change of picture from a flat to a spherical earth, the surface similarity in the letters or words becomes misleading. Our current concepts of north and south (how we *use* the words *now*) are very different from our concepts of east and west, a change that comes along with the introduction of the concept of a pole. In terminology that Wittgenstein sometimes uses, there has been a change in the 'grammar' of the term 'pole'. Wittgenstein's sense of 'grammar' is an extended sense, but it is a natural one in that grammar is about the ways in which sentences can and can't be put together. English grammar forbids the sentence 'On cat mat the'; but there is a deeper level of 'grammar' that, barring some special explanatory context, forbids Chomsky's famous sentence 'Colourless green ideas sleep furiously.' Something analogous to grammar in *that* sense forbids us (today) to talk of an East Pole. These words can't retain their current normal meanings *and* be coherently put together in that way. Pooh's picture of poles as just distant, cold places is confused, but once the 'grammar of poles' (the way in which we now use the word 'pole') is clarified, even the 'bear of little brain' will see that the project of looking for the East Pole is incoherent.

Example 2: Time at a place

This derives partly from Wittgenstein (1953/2009, §350) himself: A person remarks that when it is 5 o'clock in New York it is 10 o'clock in London. They then wonder 'When it is 5 o'clock in New York, what time is it *on the sun?*' I have tried out this question in classes and have been struck by how even educated and intelligent people pause and say things such as 'Well, I don't know – perhaps this is a question for the astronomers' or 'I don't know – but clearly it must be *some* time!' or 'Time is such a mysterious thing!' We could imagine a student in the class wanting to go deeper into the question, saying things such as 'There clearly is a time it is on the sun, yet we can't say it is same as the time it is at any particular place on earth; we need some new concepts here that will allow us to talk more effectively about what time it is on the sun.' A particularly bright student might then begin to develop a theory of 'time at a place' (after all, didn't Einstein develop a theory that time is relative to place?). But often, of course, someone spots what the difficulty is, that is, that talk about time at a place is talk about the position of the sun in the sky at that place, so that talk about what time it is on the sun *makes no sense.* We were picturing every place as having its own time, but didn't at first realize that this notion of 'time at a place' only applies *on the earth* (or by extension to the position of the sun in the sky at a particular place on a planet such as Mars). Once one has seen this, one is no longer inclined to *ask* the question about the time it now is on the sun. The problem is not so much solved, but *dissolved,* through being shown to arise through conceptual confusion. At the same time, any theory that had been developed in this context about 'time at a place', however interesting and elaborate it was, would be seen to be incoherent. It would be rejected for *that* reason, and not because it was inconsistent with observation, or insufficiently elaborated.

Those were two simple examples, but they may help at least to indicate the *sort* of thing I mean when later in the book I say that certain theories of therapy are incoherent or confused, or that there is no such thing as 'the unconscious', or 'conditioning', or 'experience' (in Rogers' sense), or 'cognitive processes'. It is not that the theories *might have* been true, but can be shown not to be (like demonstrating to Colonel Fawcett that Z doesn't exist). It is more like explaining that the theories *couldn't* be true, in the sort of way that we might try to explain to Pooh that there *can't* be an East Pole. Unfortunately, showing that a theory is *incoherent* is a much more tricky business than showing that it is *mistaken*.

Example 3: 'Representation' and 'images' in neuroscience

I have already referred to the picture of the world, which we have inherited from Descartes, according to which we do not perceive people or things, but images or pictures of them. The neuroscientist Max Bennett and philosopher Peter Hacker (Bennett & Hacker 2003) have discussed in detail how this picture can be misleading in neuroscience, and I will draw on a small part of their discussion here. The idea that we perceive images rather than people and things is understandable in earlier neuroscientists such as Eccles and Sherrington (quoted in Bennett & Hacker 2003, p. 138), who were avowed Cartesians. Sherrington writes:

> When I turn my gaze skyward I see the flattened dome of the sky and the sun's brilliant disc and a hundred other visible things underneath it... In fact I perceive a picture of the world around me.

However, more surprisingly, we find this idea also in the writings of contemporary neuroscientists such as Damasio (ibid.):

> When you or I look at an object outside ourselves, we form comparable images in our respective brains... But that does not mean that the image we see is the copy of whatever the object outside is like. Whatever it is like, in absolute terms, we do not know. The image we see is based on changes which occurred in our organism.... when the physical structure of the object interacts with the body... The object is real, the interactions are real, and the images are as real as anything can be. And yet, the structure and properties in the image we end up seeing are brain constructions prompted by the object.... There is... a set of correspondences between physical characteristics of the object and modes of interaction of the organism according to which an internally generated image is constructed.

However, as Bennett and Hacker (ibid.) argue, this is confused:

> What one perceives by the use of one's perceptual organs is an object or array of objects, sounds and smells, and the properties and relations of items in one's environment. It is a mistake to suppose that what we perceive is always or even commonly, an image, or that to perceive an object is to *have*

an image of the object perceived. One does not perceive images or representations of objects, unless one perceives paintings or photographs of objects. To see a red apple is not to see an image of a red apple, and to hear a sonata is not to hear the image or representation of a sonata. Nor is it to *have* an image in one's mind or brain, although one can conjure up images in one's mind and sometimes images cross one's mind independently of one's wish or will. But the mental images we thus conjure up are not visible, either to others or to ourselves – they are 'had', but not seen. And the tunes one rehearses in one's imagination are not heard, either by oneself or others.

Bennett and Hacker discuss in detail the difficulties which the Cartesian picture creates in neuroscience, but the same picture, or variants of it, also operates in misleading ways in psychotherapy theory. Two examples that we will encounter are in connection with Rogers' picture of congruence as a matching of 'self-concept' and 'experience', and cognitive psychology's picture of 'inner mental schemas' that are held to represent situations.

Common sense and everyday language

I said above that in developing theories we need to *start* with our common-sense view of things. The theory that we develop may lead to changes in what counts as 'common sense', but at any particular time there will be a set of shared, common-sense views which include the things that need to be explained. For example, the development of astronomy has led to a change in the common-sense view of the earth and its relations to the sun and planets. However, not everything in the old common-sense view has changed. We still see the earth as flat, for most practical purposes, and we still see the sun rise and set. Modern astronomy explains that the earth is a *very large* sphere, so that inevitably it will be flat for most practical purposes. It explains our observations of sunrise and sunset in terms of the rotation of the earth, but that doesn't mean that there is no such thing as the sun rising or setting. It is sunrise and sunset that the theory *explains*. Theories may transform to some extent how we think and speak about our observations, but there have to *be* such observations if the theory is to have anything to explain.

In the case of psychotherapy the 'observations' comprise the things that people do, say and feel when they are, as we say, disturbed, troubled or suffering from some kind of 'psychological disorder'. Now it is an important fact about human affairs that in *describing* them we often also provide some *understanding* of them. To describe someone as listening to a client already explains to some extent why they are sitting there looking at the client. Such explanations do not involve theories; they are a matter of fitting our observations into a familiar pattern. When we explain that someone is crossing the road because they want to avoid a colleague whom they have just seen, we are not invoking any psychological theory, but simply relying on the common-sense principle that people normally do what they take to be necessary for achieving their goals. The explanation works by drawing attention both to the person's wish not to meet their colleague, and to the person's glimpse of the colleague down the street. If it is asked what reason we have for believing in the common-sense principle itself, the answer must be that this principle is bound up with our *understanding* of what human actions, goals and perceptions involve. Someone who doubted whether people normally try to do what they take to be necessary for achieving their goals would show an inadequate grasp of these notions, a failure to understand how these words are used.

Perhaps a little more needs to be said here about the notion of common sense, and its relation to everyday language. The *Shorter Oxford English Dictionary* has two main entries for the phrase 'common sense': '1. An internal sense which was regarded as the common bond or centre of the five senses 1543. 2. Ordinary, normal or average understanding'. The second definition is clearly the current sense of the phrase; the first refers to an earlier usage, which nonetheless has interesting connections with the second definition. In fact 'common sense' is a phrase that has a long and intriguing history (van Holthoon & Olsen 1987). In Aristotelian thought the 'sensus communis' (the Latin translation of Aristotle's *koine aisthesis*) was the faculty by which one sensed what kind of thing something was. The other five senses inform us that an object is red, round, sweet and so on, but there also needs to be a faculty (though it does not have a specific organ) that draws these sensory elements together and informs us that the object is a tomato. The idea was that we not only sense the elements involved in perceiving something but the thing as a whole (van Holthoon 1987, p. 100).

However, the term 'common sense' later came to be used in connection with oratory to refer to the common views and practices of the people that an orator needed to take into account if he were to influence them (Bugter 1987). These common views and practices were seen as those that are natural for people to hold. They are where we all *start*, and the orator, like a good teacher, needs to start 'where people are'.

The two uses of 'sensus communis' seem very different, but they are related. They both draw attention to a knowledge of things that is pre-theoretical. In the Aristotelian view one doesn't start with the perceived redness, roundness and sweetness of the tomato, and then *theorize* that these qualities are the qualities of an 'underlying' material object. Later philosophers such as Locke adopted just that sort of view, but Aristotle stays closer to common sense (in its other sense!): that this is a tomato is not a *theory*; it is a part of common knowledge and everyday language. Children learn the use of the word 'tomato' along with the practice of picking and eating tomatoes, and not through the learning of a theory. However, the use of 'sensus communis' in connection with oratory *also* involves what is pre-theoretical, pre-speculative. The orator needs to take into account what his audience take for granted; their 'ordinary, normal or average understanding'. This is what he or she also, as a member of the same community, takes for granted; it is knowledge of a basic, non-speculative, non-theoretical kind.

It is clear enough that what counts as 'common sense' will depend to some extent on the community involved. In different ages and in different cultures the content of common sense will be rather different, and what is taken to be a matter of common sense may gradually change. For example, when Aristotle argued that the earth is spherical rather than flat, that was a speculative hypothesis, and not at all in accord with the common sense of the time. For almost everyone today the spherical earth is not a hypothesis at all, but a common-sense fact. It is not *impossible* to reject this fact (there are still cultures that have not absorbed the Western worldview, and there is a Flat Earth Society which still has a few hundred members), but for the vast majority of people today the 'round earth' is not a hypothesis; it is a picture of the earth that has become part of common sense.

I am not suggesting that common sense is unitary, even within a particular culture. People sometimes disagree about whether a view is in accordance with common sense, and then there has to be discussion about how the differences can be resolved. That might involve looking at whether such things as prejudice, ignorance, illusion or lack of attention to detail lie at the root of the disagreement. The participants may need to spend some time in finding ground on which they *do* agree, where they do have a *common* sense of what is so. Further, within a single culture a universally held common-sense view may change over time, as in the case of the shape of the earth. However, in spite of all this, there is a large body of common sense that is shared not only within a particular culture but by people from any culture or epoch. For example, in all cultures it is part of common sense that people will normally do things that they believe will benefit them, that sometimes people make mistakes, that they sometimes reflect on what it is best to do, make plans and excuses, have conflicting desires, are not always sure what they want, get used to situations that were at first alarming, and are sometimes self-deceived. And along with these common-sense facts flows the everyday (non-theoretical) language of the culture, the language of beliefs, mistakes, desires, plans, excuses, anxiety, deception and self-deception. There is, in short, a common human form of life involving a common-sense view of how things generally are, although in different cultures this common form of life is elaborated in a kaleidoscopic variety of ways, including all the different *languages*. Common sense, as I will be using the term, is what is not hypothetical or theoretical for us. It is, by contrast, that to which hypotheses and theories are answerable; it is that to which we return when we encounter conflicting hypotheses, or uncertain theories.

Our common-sense view of things is closely linked with our everyday language, as we have already seen from the connection between knowing what tomatoes are and learning how to use the word 'tomato'. At various points in the book I will refer to how we actually use certain words, as I have already done in connection with the word 'truth'. I shall be adopting Wittgenstein's (1953/2009) view that to know what a word means is usually a matter of knowing how it is used. This itself seems to me a common-sense view. For while philosophers may elaborate 'Theories of Meaning', in practice if we don't understand what a word means, we try to find out how it is being used. For example, if we hear that someone is a 'sassenach', we learn the meaning of the word through finding out that it is used to refer to English people in a pejorative way. We learn the meanings of our common words in particular contexts: as I will discuss later, a word such as 'pain' is learned in the context of crying out and tending to the sore place; 'pride' is used in the context of someone being pleased about having done something good. Our word-usage is bound up with the contexts in which the words are used, and we learn the word-usages along with everything else we learn.

Often we learn the use of a word without being able to *explain* how it is used. We may have to think carefully, and try out various scenarios, before we can explain what the difference is between, say, doing something by accident rather than by mistake, or what the difference is between a sarcastic and an ironic remark. However, a little attention to the contexts in which the words are used can make it quite clear what they mean. The 'ordinary language' philosopher John Austin (1970, pp. 184–185) writes:

> 'It was a mistake', 'It was an accident' – how readily these appear indifferent, and even be used together. Yet, a story or two, and everybody will not merely agree that they are completely different, but even discover for himself what the difference is, and what each means.

He gives the following example:

> You have a donkey, so have I, and they graze in the same field. The day comes when I conceive a dislike for mine. I go to shoot it, draw a bead on it, fire: the brute falls in its tracks. I inspect the victim, and find to my horror that it is your donkey. I appear on your doorstep and say – what? 'I say, old sport, I'm awfully sorry, &c., I've shot your donkey by accident? Or by mistake? Then again, I go to shoot my donkey as before, draw a bead on it, fire – but as I do so, the beasts move, and to my horror yours falls. Again the scene on the doorstep – what do I say? 'By mistake'? or 'by accident'?

The important point here is that we have, through our linguistic training, a highly sophisticated knowledge of word-use, and a correspondingly sophisticated ability to make important and often subtle distinctions in the situations that we encounter. Theories of therapy sometimes ignore this ordinary language and everyday knowledge, and that can give rise to much confusion, as I hope to show in the course of the book. Clients frequently have a better sense of what needs to be said than therapists whose talk is contaminated by confused theoretical ideas. For example, as I will discuss in Chapter 6, cognitive therapists sometimes try to persuade clients to say 'I *believe* there is something wrong with me' rather than 'I *feel* there is something wrong with me'. The client rightly senses the difference here, and the therapist's attempt to 'correct' them leads to confusion, and to a mistaken approach to how the client can be helped. A rather different kind of example is that in many schools of therapy there is the idea that the words for emotions are the names of 'inner experiences', as though one could tell whether one was ashamed rather than embarrassed by 'looking inside' at the sensations one has. But as I will discuss in later chapters, this is just a muddle, which originates in the Cartesian picture of 'the inner'. A child doesn't learn the emotion words by attending to their own bodily sensations; the words are learned through learning their use in specific contexts.

Summary

I have argued that there is a level of knowledge and of meaning that is more basic than our theories. It is the level of everyday life and practice that we share with almost everyone else in our community, and to a large extent with people everywhere. We can make sense of many things in a common-sense way, without needing to resort to theories, and I will be suggesting that much of what is done in counselling and psychotherapy can indeed be understood in a common-sense way.

I will not, however, be suggesting that theories in psychotherapy cannot be of value. As I said above, a theory usually involves a picture or analogy that invites us to see things in a particular way, so that certain aspects of what we observe are drawn together in a way that depends on our acceptance of the picture or analogy. A good theory employs a picture or analogy that is effective in organizing a wide range of observations, but also in suggesting new hypotheses that we would not have thought of without that particular way of seeing things. Whether a theory is a good theory or not depends on whether its organizing picture or analogy is a good one. The picture of the earth as a huge sphere is an excellent picture, and Darwin's analogy of living things as undergoing something similar to selective breeding is an excellent analogy. My criticisms of the major theories of psychotherapy will be not so much that they are theories, but that *these* theories employ *misleading* pictures of what is involved in talking about such things as awareness, experience, feelings, thoughts and behaviour. Such misleading pictures prevent us from seeing that at the heart of each theory there is something of a 'common-sense core', which can be set out in a way that doesn't require reference to the theory or its misleading picture. I will discuss the theories and their 'common-sense cores' in the following chapters of this part of the book. Then in the second part of the book, I hope to show how the common-sense cores of the theories can be integrated in a way that is impossible in the case of the theories themselves.

CHAPTER 3

Historical Prologue: Behaviourism and Behaviour Therapy

Introduction

Behaviour therapy today tends to be practiced as one element within the cognitive-behavioural approach (CBT). However, in order to understand CBT it will be helpful first to consider what was involved in behaviour therapy before the cognitive elements were added. To some extent, CBT's behavioural and cognitive elements can be separated, and this can be relevant in assessing the effectiveness of CBT, since there are studies that suggest that in practice the addition of cognitive elements does not add anything to the effectiveness of purely behavioural techniques (Jacobson et al. 1996; McLeod 2009, p. 161).

Historically, behaviour therapy was a distinctive and well-developed approach based on the principles of behaviourist learning theory. Its theoretical background is thus quite different from that of the cognitive therapy developed much later by theorists such as Albert Ellis and Aaron Beck. As we shall see, while behaviourist learning theory has long been abandoned in psychology, some of the behaviourist therapy techniques seem to have proved their worth and have been incorporated into standard CBT practice. CBT has in its background, then, two distinct theories, so that any discussion of 'CBT theory' needs to disentangle these two elements. Since behaviourist learning theory developed first, it will be best to begin with it and to consider later (in Chapter 6) the additions and modifications that come from cognitive theory.

Another reason for beginning with behaviour therapy is that it provides an important example of a form of therapy whose *theory* is now widely rejected. This is in spite of behaviourism having been the dominant school of psychology for something like 40 years, having generated a very large literature, and having been seen as the basis not only for therapy but for many other social practices. The historian of psychology Howard Gardner (1987, p. 110) writes:

The psychology of America between 1920 and 1950 was irremediably behaviourist. Child care, treatment of prisoners, teaching of children, and many other societal activities came to be dominated by behaviourist rhetoric and behaviourist practices. No less an authority than the *New York Times* declared in 1942 that behaviourism marked 'a new epoch in the intellectual history of man'. (Fancher 1979, p. 322)

Gardner then comments that '[b]y the middle 1950s, its program had begun to fall apart; and today the theoretical claims of behaviourism (though not its various applied achievements) are largely of historical interest'. Behaviourism thus provides a clear case of a fundamentally flawed theory in psychology, a theory that is now largely of historical interest. The claim of this book will be that *all* the major theories of psychotherapy should be assigned to that category, but it will be useful to begin with a theory for which the claim is not controversial.

The most important reasons for rejecting behaviourist theory are closely related to the reasons that, I think, should lead us to reject most of the other theories. There is an underlying difficulty in most of the theories which, I will argue, originates in the still influential Cartesian picture of a human being as a composite of 'mind' and 'body'. Some schools of psychology, such as behaviourism, emphasize 'the body' and what is 'outer'; others, such as cognitive psychology and the early introspectionist school discussed below, emphasize 'the mind' and what is 'inner', but all such talk of 'inner' and 'outer' remains squarely within the broad Cartesian tradition. What is needed, I believe, is the sort of break with the Cartesian tradition that is found in the work of Wittgenstein. I will not be discussing Wittgenstein's philosophy explicitly in this book, but the kind of approach that I use is strongly influenced by him. As I mentioned in Chapter 1, Wittgenstein always remains close to ordinary, everyday ways of thinking and talking, so that his thought fits well with my concern to rescue common sense from the psychological theories.

The common-sense core of behavioural therapy

CBT's behavioural procedures are essentially procedures that expose the client to new patterns of reward or 'reinforcement', so that the client's behaviour is gradually modified or 're-shaped'. Although there is in the background the idea of training animals to do what the trainer wishes them to do, behavioural procedures do not have to be directed by the therapist. Once the client has appreciated the basic ideas involved, they may, with the therapist, begin to look at their own patterns of behaviour and consider what they would like to change. Or they may reflect on the circumstances in which they find themselves doing what they don't want to do, the rewards that they get from their behaviour and the fears involved in behaving differently. Then a behavioural modification programme can be drawn up, for example a programme of systematic desensitization of a fear response to the prospect of answering telephones, or in the case of a man who wishes to give up smoking

(McLeod 2009, p. 133), a programme of meeting less frequently with colleagues who smoke, never carrying around more than two cigarettes so that he can't enjoy offering them around, practicing smoking cigarettes continuously until he feels sick or taking up some physical activity that becomes more possible and more enjoyable the less he smokes.

In behavioural desensitization for anxiety states there is the procedure of gradually increasing exposure to situations that provoke anxiety; in other behaviour modification programmes there may be more complex patterns of exposure to the intrinsic 'punishments' of some kinds of behaviour and the intrinsic 'rewards' of other kinds. There is usually an emphasis on proceeding by 'small steps'. The therapist and client will together decide on how big the steps should be; they need to be large enough to arouse the client's fear (or other unwanted response), but not so large that the client finds it impossible to take the step. There is a kind of zigzag between trying out a step, noting its impact on the client's response and then trying another step. The client is moving back and forth between their belief that the next step will be possible, and what they find their actual response to be. Then gradually, step by step, their response comes into line with their belief, or considered view, of what an appropriate response would be.

The behaviourist school of psychology saw such procedures as desensitization in terms of the theoretical framework of 'conditioning'. I will discuss this below, but it is important to see that the procedures of behaviour therapy don't have to be understood in such a mechanistic way. A more human account would be something like the following: The client's current responses are of a rigid, stereotyped nature; for example, the client responds fearfully to phones ringing. The client *believes* that there is nothing frightening about phones, but this belief doesn't inform or make any impact on their response. That, precisely, is the client's problem. However, while the client's belief has no impact on the client's felt inability to pick up the phone, such belief can be brought to bear on whether the client can at least *approach* a ringing phone. The client may think 'It is not dangerous, so I can at least go up to it, can't I?' Informed by that belief, the client may then try approaching the phone. To that extent the client's response comes to be a little more in line with what they believe, but having made the response the client's level of anxiety is reduced, and they may now be able to act on their belief that it would not be dangerous to *touch* the ringing phone. Bit by bit the client's belief that phones are not dangerous is being called upon to enable the client to act as they would like to act. In short, the client's initial rigid response is softened through being brought, step by step, into interaction with what they believe.

Aaron Beck, one of the originators of cognitive therapy, suggests that the behavioural procedures of CBT are largely independent of behaviourist theory. He writes:

> Much of behavior therapy... while ostensibly derived from laboratory experiments and from learning theory, is to a large degree an assortment of

time-honored techniques used by people to deal with their psychological problems. (Beck 1976, p. 21)

I think that is true. For example, in ancient Rome 'aversion therapy' for excessive drinking was practiced by making the 'client' drink a glass of wine in which an eel had been placed (Kazdin 1978, p. 218). The psychologist Padmal da Silva has collected a range of behavioural procedures that can be found in early Buddhist writings, including examples of systematic desensitization, aversion therapy, stimulus control and behavioural management. For instance, the behavioural procedure of 'stimulus control' involves identifying cues that trigger undesired behaviour and finding ways of removing those cues. Da Silva (1984, p. 667) quotes this example:

One monk, Kuddala, found it very difficult to stay committed to monkhood due to his attachment to his main worldly possessions – a pint-pot of seed beans and a spade. He kept leaving monastic life and returning to lay life, which he did seven times. Each time he would till the ground, plant the seed beans, and later, when the beans were ripe, would pull them up, set aside a pint-pot of beans for seed, and consume the rest. He would then return to monkhood. Finally, determined to break this attachment to lay life he threw away what he saw to be the crucial items that lured him; this enabled him to stop returning to a lay life.

Here Kuddala *believes* that it is best for him to be a monk, but finds himself *responding* in the manner of a lay person. He can't simply change this response 'by willpower', but he can draw upon *other* beliefs, such as the belief that if he threw away his spade and pint-pot of beans he would be unable to respond in the lay-person's way. This is a belief that he not only has but one that he can act on, one that can inform his actual responses. *Here* there is no discrepancy between 'view' and 'response', and that is where he has to start.

As an example of the behavioural management of overeating, da Silva quotes the story of King Pasenadi, which can be summarized as follows: Having slept badly, the King consults the Buddha, remarking that he often sleeps badly after overeating, and is also drowsy during the day. The Buddha remarks that overeating is bound to cause problems, and enlists the help of the King's nephew in setting up a training programme for the King. The nephew is asked to memorize a verse containing advice on moderation in eating, and to watch the King whenever he has a meal. The moment the king is about to take the last handful of rice the nephew is to stop him and recite the verse, reminding the King of the Buddha's advice. The King thus distracted would not eat the last handful. Then at the King's next meal the nephew is to bring only the amount of rice that the King had been allowed to eat the previous time. This was repeated, with the King co-operating enthusiastically in his training. In fact, the King contributed an extra element to the programme by giving away a significant amount of money in alms if the nephew had to read the verse as a reminder. This regime made the King lean and energetic again. Da Silva remarks:

> This delightful story could well be re-written as a modern single-case report in the behavioural treatment of obesity and over-eating. There are several familiar elements, in addition to the basic notion of a behavioural training programme:
>
> (a) the acquisition of control over the eating response;
> (b) control of the amount of food served on the plate;
> (c) gradual and systematic reduction of the quantity;
> (d) the use of a pre-arranged verbal cue at a crucial point to interrupt the chain of behaviour;
> (e) the use of a relative or family member to carry out the regime;
> (f) the King's own contribution to the programme.

It seems to me that there is nothing here that can't be explained in everyday terms such as 'wanting', 'realizing', 'reminding' and so on. The King wants to modify his eating behaviour; he realizes he needs help; he can't bring himself suddenly to reduce his eating to an optimum level, so it needs to be done gradually; he needs to be reminded of when to stop, but later becomes able to remind himself. It is hard to see how a theoretical account could add anything useful to our understanding of the procedure, although of course the procedure can be reformulated in the behaviourist terminology of 'eating response' 'stimulus control', 'verbal cues' and so on.

Thus far, my conclusion is that behaviourist conditioning theory is *unnecessary* to an understanding of how behaviour therapy works. I turn now to the questions of whether the theory is itself coherent, and whether a therapist's adherence to it can be potentially damaging for clients.

The theory and its confusions

Behavioural therapy has its roots in behaviourist psychology, which is usually seen to have originated with the publication in 1919 of J.B. Watson's *Psychology from the Standpoint of a Behaviorist,* which in turn drew on Pavlov's account of learning in terms of conditioned responses. Although the behavioural approach is often seen as more 'scientific' than the other approaches (McLeod 2009, p. 30), the behaviourist theory from which it derives was largely driven by philosophical considerations concerning scientific method. The earlier 'introspectionist' school of psychology, which behaviourism replaced, had taken for granted that psychology should study 'the mind', that is, such phenomena as thought, emotion and memory, which were taken to be 'subjective' phenomena, accessible only to the person who experienced them. The introspectionist school, founded by Wilhelm Wundt at Leipzig in 1879, held that

> physics studies the objects of the external world: while this investigation is necessarily mediated by experience, physics is still not the study of

experience itself. Psychology, in contrast, is the study of conscious experience as experience. It must be approached through internal observation, through introspection. (Gardner 1987, p. 102)

This picture of 'external world' versus 'conscious experience' was of course rooted in the philosophy of Descartes, to which I referred above. The Cartesian picture has haunted psychology throughout its history, with periodic changes of emphasis on either 'mind' or 'body'. Introspectionist psychology favoured the mind but was challenged by behaviourist psychology that emphasized bodily behaviour. As we shall see, 'behaviour' in its everyday sense is very different from 'bodily movements', but the Cartesian picture in the background of behaviourism pulls us in the direction of seeing behaviour as movement patterns. Behaviourism was then challenged by cognitive psychology, which re-introduced the notion of the 'inner' in the form of 'internal maps' and 'schemas'. Today, we can perhaps see the beginnings of a swing back to the body, for example in the contemporary interest in neuroscientific accounts of psychological disturbance.

Not all of 20th-century psychology fits this scheme. Psychoanalysis emphasizes 'mind' but not in the sense of 'conscious experiencing', and the 'functional psychology' associated with the names of William James and John Dewey was highly sceptical of centring psychology on introspection and 'inner experiences'. But even before this, researchers in the introspective school had discovered for themselves that there is something awry about the project of understanding psychological phenomena through attending to 'experiences'. For example, in 1901 the psychologist Karl Marbe was investigating how people make judgements about the weights of objects, simply by lifting them. The introspectionist view was that such judgements must be made through noticing what experiences, especially what images, one has when one lifts each object. It was held that there must be some *inner experience that one goes by* in making one's judgement. However, in Gardner's (1987, p. 106) words:

Marbe found that, in judging weights, subjects reported no imaginal concepts as the basis of judgement: in other words, no images flitted through their introspective minds. Instead, counter to the Wundtian expectation, subjects reported that various vague attitudes passed through consciousness – attitudes like hesitation, doubt, waiting for an answer, feeling that the answer had arrived. Marbe was forced to conclude, 'The present data are quite sufficient to draw the conclusion that no psychological conditions of judgements exist.... Even... the observers concerned were extremely surprised to note the paucity of experiences that were connected with the judgmental process'. (Mandler & Mandler 1964, p. 143)

It is worth pausing a moment with this quotation, in order to feel the 'pull' of the Cartesian picture that makes us want to say: 'But there must have been a *feeling* of how heavy each weight was; it was surely that feeling on which the subjects based their judgements.' And yet there is no such 'feeling'; one simply has the ability to say that this weight is heavier than that.

Wittgenstein notes (1953/2009, §607) that we sometimes 'have a feeling' of what time it is, but having this feeling is not a matter of noticing anything 'inner': we *might* have an image of a clock face, or the words 'It's three o'clock' *might* come to mind, but neither of these is a feeling. Alternatively, nothing at all might go through our mind. In that case, *what did we go by* in saying it was three o'clock? 'Just by a feeling' – but we could equally well say there was *nothing* we went by; it was just a hunch. 'Feelings' of this kind are *fabrications* (ibid., §609), which nevertheless have a deep appeal for us.

Wittgenstein (1953/2009, 1982, 1992) often draws attention to the fact that our use of psychological language is not based on introspective observation. For example, when we say 'I'm in pain!' or 'My leg hurts!' we are not reporting an 'inner experience', since we are not engaged in *reporting* at all. These utterances are not reports but *expressions* of pain, on a par with crying out. Similarly, if someone says that they expect that it will rain tomorrow, this should not be construed as a report on an 'inner experience'; it is, rather, a way of saying that they would be surprised if it did not rain (Purton 2013a). An introspectionist psychologist might ask what *experiences* the person had, what experiences they *went by*, in making their judgement that it will rain. But the answer to this, as Marbe found, is likely to be 'Nothing much. There really weren't any experiences I went by. I just said it will rain because I think it will – I really would be surprised if it doesn't.' Wittgenstein often suggests that we can be misled by our pictures of how language works. One such picture suggests that what we say is usually a report on our experiencing, but in fact language is used in many other ways, for example to express, to question, to emphasize, to doubt, to pray, to encourage. 'Experience' itself can easily be misunderstood – we are inclined to picture it as something 'inner', as the introspectionists did, but the *actual* uses of the word are quite different. When someone agrees to tell us of their experiences as an inner-city police officer, for example, we expect to hear mainly about what they did, what happened to them, how they responded, and not about their inner imagery or sensations. I will discuss this point in more detail in Chapter 4, in connection with Carl Rogers' notion of 'experience'.

I think that in the end introspectionist psychology discovered something very important: that psychology is not about 'inner experiencing' but about human *living*. Psychology is concerned with what we feel, think and experience, certainly, but it needs to get away from the Cartesian picture which presents such things as feelings, thoughts and experiences as 'inner goings-on'. All this is important as a background to any discussion of behaviourist psychology which, I think, thoroughly 'took on board' the incoherence of a psychology based on 'the inner', but then replaced it with the equally Cartesian notion of a psychology based on 'the outer'. There are good reasons for saying that behaviourism was as incoherent as introspectionism, and it was in fact abandoned as a serious approach to psychology with the rise of cognitive science. However, as I will argue later, cognitive psychology tends to distance itself from behaviourism by bringing back 'the inner', though not in the form

Historical Prologue: Behaviourism and Behaviour Therapy

of introspectionist 'experiences'. In doing so I think it does not learn the basic lesson that can be learned from the failure of introspectionism: that while psychology is not about 'the outer' as the behaviourists held, nor is it about 'the inner'. 'Inner' and 'outer' both belong to the misleading picture that we have inherited from Descartes.

The behaviourist view, as found in the writings of John Watson, was that the fundamental difficulty with introspection as a method in psychology was that it is concerned with 'private inner events' that by definition are not open to study by the scientific community. This led to several rather different positions, although these were not always kept separate. One was the view that there is in fact no such thing as 'inner experience', only 'outer behaviour'. Another was that although we may speak of emotion, thought, memory and so on, what these terms actually refer to is behaviour; for example, people do of course feel sad, but some theorists held that 'feeling sad' *means* behaving in a particular way. There was also the view that although we do in fact have 'inner experiences' they cannot be made the objects of *scientific* study, since science can only study 'external behaviour'.

The behaviourist theory behind behavioural therapy was essentially a theory of learning that initially drew on Pavlov's work on what came to be known as 'classical conditioning'. The central idea was that while some behaviour is of the nature of a reflex or an inbuilt response (such as salivation) to a stimulus (such as presentation of food), other behaviour is learned through further stimuli (such as the sound of a bell) becoming associated with the original stimulus. Pavlov conceived of this conditioning process as something essentially mechanistic that could be explained in neurological terms. For him, 'stimulus' meant the excitation of nerve endings and 'response' meant some kind of bodily movement or other physical reaction. However, the term 'stimulus' was soon extended to mean something like 'perceived situation'. This confusing move was already made in Watson's (1925) writing, in which he construes situations as complex groups of stimuli. The move is confusing because a situation involves much more than mere stimuli, in Pavlov's sense of the word. 'Stimulus' is essentially a physiological concept, whereas 'situation' is essentially linked with a person's goals and their awareness of how things stand. Even in the case of Pavlov's dogs it seems plausible to understand their salivation on hearing the bell in terms of their hunger and their perception of the situation as one in which food can be expected. A simple mechanistic interpretation of the dog's behaviour as a conditioned response is implausible, if only because the response does not take place at all unless the dog is hungry (Hamlyn 1970, pp. 141, 145).

Some more recent studies seem to confirm that in human beings, at least, there is no such thing as 'classical conditioning', if that is taken to mean the acquisition of responses in a way that bypasses the person's *perception of their situation*. In a typical 'conditioning' experiment an experimenter turns on a light for a few seconds, and that is followed by a loud noise that triggers an emotional response in the subject. After a few repetitions the subject may begin to respond emotionally simply to the light. However, there is not *just* a conditioned response here: the subject *perceives* that the noise follows the light, and after a few repetitions they come to *expect* the noise – become 'prepared for the noise' – when they see the light. What is being called 'conditioning' here is the result of abstracting the behavioural aspect of the situation from the total context. Now in certain patients who have suffered damage to the hippocampus there is a split between their responses and their perception of their situation. In conditioning experiments they acquire the emotional response to the light but are unable to say why they are responding as they do (Bechara et al. 1995). Other patients, with damage to the amygdala, do not acquire the emotional response to the light but are aware of the connection between light and noise. However, in normal people with undamaged brains 'there is little or no convincing evidence that people can acquire Pavlovian conditioned responses in the absence of awareness' (McNally 2003, p. 32). The only circumstances in which anything like Pavlovian conditioning occurs in human beings are those of brain damage. All in all, it seems that the notion of Pavlovian conditioning is either an artificial abstraction from the full story of why the person is responding as they do or a pathological effect of brain dysfunction. It cannot therefore be used as a foundation for the understanding of learning.

Later in the history of behaviourism, B.F. Skinner and others did come to realize that Pavlovian conditioning is at best an artificial abstraction (Hamlyn 1970, p. 139). What Skinner puts in its place is the idea that animals are normally active in responding to their situations, that some of their responses lead to reward or 'reinforcement' and that those responses become established habits. For example, a pigeon pecks at various things in its environment, and some of them turn out to be edible; pecking at these things is then repeated, whereas pecking at inedible things is usually not. However, if pecking at a lever in a 'Skinner box' releases a pellet of food then *that* pecking response will be repeated, or 'stamped in'. Skinner called this 'operant conditioning', but clearly it is very different from classical conditioning. Here there is no mechanistic model in the background, as there was for Pavlov. We are no longer dealing with physical reactions to nerve stimulation but with how a motivated animal is responding to a perceived situation. That this is so becomes clear if we ask *what* the pigeon has learned: In classical conditioning what has been learned (conditioned) is a particular physical response that can be specified as a particular set of bodily movements, for example. By contrast, Skinner's pigeons learn to *do* something; the exact movements they make will vary, depending, for example, on where the food-release lever is placed. Skinner is concerned with the explanation of animal *action*, not animal *movement*.

The crucial point is that *doing something* can't be specified in terms of a particular set of bodily movements (Hamlyn 1953; Peters 1958; Melden 1961; Taylor 1964). This is obvious in the case of human beings: consider, for instance, the wide range of movements that can count as writing a letter, depending on whether the letter is written on a computer, by hand, by dictation and so on. It is not the bodily movements but the whole context that make it a case of 'writing a letter'. But, as gradually became clear in psychology, a similar point applies also in the case of animals. Tolman (1932, 1947), like many behaviourists, experimented on the learning abilities of rats in mazes. In one experiment he trained rats to swim through a maze. The theory was that the patterns of movement that led to reaching the food at the end of the maze would be 'stamped in' through reinforcement by the food reward. Tolman then removed the water, so that the rats needed to run in order to reach the food. But running requires different movements from swimming, so that according to conditioning theory the rats should have needed to relearn how to reach the food. In fact, no further learning was needed, and it seemed clear that the rats had not been conditioned to move in a particular way but had learned something about the maze situation and what was needed in order make their way through it. Tolman suggested that what they had learned was a 'mental map' of the maze that they could make use of whether they were swimming or running.

Tolman's experimental work has been seen (Gardner 1987, p. 110) as heralding the start of the 'cognitive revolution' in psychology, but with the benefit of hindsight I think it can be seen that the behaviourist approach to the explanation of behaviour was flawed from the outset. Ironically enough, behaviourism failed because the behaviourists were not clear about what counts as behaviour. They confused *behaviour* with patterns of *movement*. Further, they confused the notion of 'reacting to a stimulus', which can be understood in causal, physiological terms, with 'responding to a situation' which belongs to a very different conceptual framework.

They also failed to appreciate what is involved in giving *explanations* of behaviour. Understanding a person's (or animal's) response does not usually involve any knowledge of causality, in the sense of knowing general laws of behaviour; what it involves is the fitting of the person's or animal's response into a plausible account of what they want and how they see their situation. If we want to explain why Tolman's rats ran through the maze after the water had been removed, then it is not a matter of asking what 'caused them to run'. At least that form of the question would be odd in the way that it would be odd to ask of someone running for the bus 'What *causes* them to run?' We want to know *why* they are running, but that is not to ask for a cause in the way that we really might want to ask what caused them to blink, and be satisfied with the answer 'a puff of air'. That really *is* a causal explanation, but equally a reflex blink is not something one *does* in the full sense of 'does'. By contrast, running for the bus *is* something one does, and the natural form of explanation is in terms of the person's *wanting* to catch the bus in order to get home in good time, and their *perception of their situation* as one in which running is necessary for getting to the bus before it leaves. Similarly, to explain the running of Tolman's rats is a matter of pointing out that they want to get to the food and have learned where the food is.

Rejection of the behaviourist account of learning and behaviour does not entail rejection of everything that behaviourist psychology discovered. For example, one finding was that 'conditioning' was more effective if 'rewards' were used rather than 'punishments'. This, if understood as a fact about human learning, is well worth knowing. In the same sort of way 'animal behaviourists' or 'ethologists', who emphasized the prevalence of 'innate', rather than learned, forms of behaviour, discovered a kind of behaviour which had not previously been much remarked upon. Put in terms of their theory, there are situations in which the equal activation of competing 'drives' results in an animal being unable to perform either of the activities which it would normally perform. For example, a bird in which both flight and fight drives are activated may, instead of either fleeing or fighting, peck at the ground. The ethologists called this 'displacement behaviour', and one explanation was in terms of the energy associated with the two drives 'spilling over' into a seemingly irrelevant form of behaviour (Tinbergen 1951). On looking back at human behaviour with this in mind (Austin 1970, pp. 203–204) it seems clear that there is something similar in our own behaviour – for example, when, not knowing what to do, we sometimes twiddle our thumbs or scratch our head. It is not an entirely trivial matter that this kind of behaviour exists, since as I noted above, we are often concerned with the question of whether a person really *did* something in a full sense of 'doing'. The discovery of displacement behaviour could be taken as an addition to our inventory of the ways in which we may not *straightforwardly* be doing something: 'Yes, I know he was sitting there twiddling his thumbs during the most solemn part of the ceremony, but then he was, after all, in such a difficult situation, you know – he just didn't know whether to stay or leave.' It is worth knowing about displacement behaviour, but in adding this category to our list of ways of qualifying the fact that someone *did* something, we don't have to take on board the ethological theory of drives and energy-spills. We can ignore the theory while allowing our ordinary understanding of human behaviour to be enlarged by the discoveries of the ethologists. The same, I suggest, applies to the discoveries of behaviourist psychology.

In the first part of this chapter I discussed the kinds of procedures that were developed in the behavioural therapy that was derived from behaviourist psychology. We saw that it was possible to give an account of these procedures without delving into behaviourist conditioning theory, and there is today little discussion of that theory, since it has been so clearly recognized that the explanation of behaviour and of behavioural problems must invoke not 'stimulus' and 'response' but 'perceived situation' and 'action'. Nevertheless, the procedures that were developed in the context of the stimulus–response theory can be retained; they simply need to be re-described without the technical behaviourist terminology of 'stimuli', 'conditioning', 'reinforcement' and so on. My suggestion in connection with behavioural therapy is that we should let go of the theory and return to an everyday understanding of the ways in which behavioural procedures can be effective.

The theory and its dangers

Behaviourist theory brings with it a particular way of thinking about people. It is a way of thinking that explains what we do, not in terms of our considered view of what our situation is, and of what we see as valuable, but in terms of the schedules of conditioning to which we have been exposed. For behaviourists such as Skinner, talk of 'our view of the situation' or 'our values' is pre-scientific talk which makes reference to unobservable 'inner' entities, and it should therefore be rejected. The result of this rejection involved, for Skinner, a profound re-thinking of human life and society, which he outlined in his books *Science and Human Behavior* (1953) and *Beyond Freedom and Dignity* (1971a). He also wrote a novel, *Walden Two* (1976), in which he portrayed the kind of society which might be organized in conformity with behaviourist theory. It is a society in which a fairly benign control is exercised by its leaders. Skinner (1971b) wrote in connection with this: 'We must delegate control of the population as a whole to specialists – to police, priests, teachers, therapists and so on, with their specialized reinforcers and their codified contingencies.'

Other behaviourists did not follow up so consistently on the implications of their theory, but the basic principles of the theory do come through in such techniques as the 'token economy', which has been used to modify the behaviour of patients in psychiatric hospitals (Allyon & Azrin 1968). As John McLeod (2009, p. 131) points out, the effectiveness of such a system depends on the existence of a controlled social environment to ensure consistency in the direction in which patients' behaviour is modified. The system depends entirely on those running it having the power to control the patients' lives, and while those in charge might argue that this control is for the sake of the patients' own good, it nevertheless seems to involve a fundamental lack of respect for patients' own views and aims.

The central problem here is that to which Skinner himself draws attention: it seems that we have a choice between social arrangements and therapeutic procedures which emphasize such values as freedom and dignity, and those that emphasize social control. Skinner is prepared to relinquish freedom and dignity, as they are ordinarily understood, in favour of a society and a form of therapy that are structured according to schemes of reinforcement that lead to socially desirable behaviour.

It has sometimes been suggested that there is a fundamental incoherence in Skinner's position. He seems to want to convince us by rational argument that *his* approach to society and therapy is the correct one, but at the same time he is asserting that our choice is not based on reason: it is rather that we *will* adopt his way if we are suitably reinforced, conceivably by the appeal of his utopian community in *Walden Two*. This is not the place to enter a discussion of the matter; it may be better simply to say that behaviourist theory is deeply inconsistent with the spirit and practice of most counselling and psychotherapy. That spirit and practice involves encouraging people to find their own ways of relating to their problems and to their social situations. It is not at all a matter of the therapist setting up schemes of reinforcement that will modify client behaviour in a socially approved way. As I have already emphasized, this does not mean that therapy can't use behavioural techniques, but the context of such use will be that of the client's free choice to try out the technique. In other words, while the technique can be used, it will be used within an overall context of freedom and dignity.

We have seen that conditioning itself only exists in the wider context of a person's responses to their situation. There is no such thing as human conditioning in the mechanistic sense that is found in Pavlov's work, although people may come to respond to environmental factors in ways that go beyond mere intellectual registering of the factors. It is true that in a conditioning experiment the subject not only appreciates that the sound follows the light, but also *finds themself responding* to the light with an increase of muscle tension. What we can't do, however, is to take the physiological response out of context and 'explain' it in purely physiological terms. The response doesn't even *occur* out of context, except in cases of brain damage.

This, I think, is quite parallel to how things are in connection with the *application* of the theory. If we take behavioural techniques out of their human, relational context, we end up treating people as if they were things, or at best as animals that need to be trained. This seems unethical, and also likely to be ineffective, since being treated in such ways makes people very angry. If the techniques are to be used at all they need to be used within a human relational context, in which the client freely considers whether a particular technique might be helpful, and also decides on whether the technique *is* proving helpful to them. The danger of behaviourist theory is that it abstracts from the whole human context, and this opens the way to treating clients in ways that are not fully human.

Summary

Behaviour therapy constitutes one element in contemporary CBT, but the behaviourist theory in which it was originally embedded has long been abandoned. The practice of behaviour therapy has proved its worth, but this practice can be understood in a common-sense way that does not involve the abandoned theory. Nevertheless, it is worth examining this theory and its introspectionist predecessor because together they enable us to see something of the conceptual incoherencies that have haunted psychology and psychotherapy ever since. These incoherencies are inherent in the Cartesian picture of 'the external world' versus 'conscious experience' and it is this picture that is at the root of the difficulties which led to behaviourist *theory* being abandoned. So far as *practice* is concerned, behavioural techniques can be therapeutically valuable, but only so long as they are detached from the theory and relocated in a common-sense context of human action and perception.

Chapter 4

Person-Centred Therapy

In this chapter, and in most of the subsequent chapters devoted to individual therapeutic approaches, I will outline what I take to be the common-sense core of each approach and suggest that the practice of the approach is comprehensible without the associated theory. I will then discuss the confusions involved in the theory, and the dangers of taking the theory seriously.

The common-sense core

Carl Rogers had a *theory* of therapy (Rogers 1959) which I will discuss shortly, and also a characteristic way of working. Rogers held that what the therapist needs to do is to provide an interpersonal atmosphere in which the client can feel safe enough to explore their difficulties. Early in the development of his approach Rogers wrote (1942, p. 113) that it was an approach

> in which warmth of acceptance and absence of any form of coercion or personal pressure on the part of the counsellor permits the maximum expression of feelings, attitudes, and problems by the counsellee... In this unique experience of complete emotional freedom within a well-defined framework the client is free to recognise and understand his impulses and patterns, positive and negative, as in no other relationship.

Rogers gradually identified different aspects of this interpersonal 'atmosphere' in terms of therapist attitudes of 'acceptance', 'empathy' and 'genuineness' but was also inclined not to separate the aspects too sharply. He remarked in an interview late in his life (Baldwin 1987, p. 45):

> I am inclined to think that in my writing perhaps I have stressed too much the three basic conditions (congruence, unconditional positive regard and empathic understanding). Perhaps it is something around the edges of those conditions that is really the most important element of therapy – when myself is very clearly, obviously present.

And he had written much earlier that there is just a single condition that is required for effective therapy. He wrote (1961, p. 130) that he can 'state this assumed condition in one word... that the client experiences himself as being fully *received*'. The therapist does not need to make any judgements or interpretations in connection with what the client says but simply 'receive' the client.

However, there is of course the question of *how* the therapist is to provide the receptive, facilitative atmosphere that Rogers recommended, and what Rogers mainly *did* was to reflect back to the client what the client had said. One study (Merry 2000, p. 2) indicates that over 80% of Rogers' responses were of this reflective sort. Of course such 'reflection' is not a mere parroting of the client's words. It is often an attempt to express in brief form the essence of what the client has said. Rogers (1951, p. 28) wrote:

> Here is a client statement: 'I feel as though my mother is always watching me and criticizing what I do. It gets me all stirred up inside. I try not to let that happen, but you know, there are times when I feel her eagle eye on me that I just boil inwardly.'

> A response on the counselor's part might be: 'You resent her criticism.' This response may be given empathically, with the tone of voice such as would be used if it were worded 'If I understand you correctly, you feel pretty resentful toward her criticism. Is that right?' If this is the attitude and tone which is used, it would probably be experienced by the client as aiding him in further expression.

Rogers' own view of what he is doing is interesting. He writes (1986a, p. 37), 'I am *not* trying to "reflect feelings". I am trying to determine whether my understanding of the client's world is correct – whether I am seeing it as he or she is experiencing it at this moment.' Thus, for Rogers, reflection seems to be primarily a matter of checking whether he has understood, so that he can understand better. Then the client will feel more deeply understood, and so be freed to express themselves more adequately. But Rogers acknowledged that there is another aspect to reflection. One of his clients (Slack 1985, pp. 41–42) wrote:

> It was like Dr Rogers was a magical mirror. The process involved my sending rays towards that mirror. I looked into the mirror to get a glimpse of the reality that I am... This experience allowed me an opportunity to get a view of myself that was untainted by the perceptions of outside viewers.

In response to this Rogers wrote that 'in understanding the client's experience, we can realize that such responses do serve as a mirror', and in another paper written around the same time Rogers (1986b, p. 202) says, 'My response has the advantage of bringing fully into awareness her positive aims and goals. There is value in holding up a mirror to the client.'

I think that if we put all this together we might say that what Rogers is doing is, first, showing the client that he genuinely accepts them whatever they may tell him, and, second, that he is attempting with some success to understand what they say. These two things are crucially important in helping clients feel safe enough to express themselves further. Then there is the third point, that when clients hear back a version of what they have said, when clients 'see themselves in the mirror', they will be in a better position to judge whether they have expressed themselves adequately. If not, they will try again, the therapist will reflect again, and this process will continue until the client has found adequate expression for what they want to say.

This pattern of interaction between therapist and client was emphasized even more by Rogers' younger colleague Eugene Gendlin (1968, 1969, 1973, 1996). Gendlin had studied a large number of recorded therapy sessions with a view to determining what was distinctive about those sessions which lead to most therapeutic change. He concluded that sessions in which clients simply talk about events in their lives, or about their childhoods, or speculate about the reasons for their difficulties, or become submerged in their emotions, tend not to be very helpful sessions. In the more helpful sessions there was instead a pattern where the client expresses something, the therapist reflects it, the client says, 'It's not quite that – it's more like this', the therapist reflects the new way of putting it, the client says, 'Yes it is that, but also there's this other bit...', and this goes on until the client is satisfied that they have truly expressed what they wanted to say. Gendlin calls this attending to, and gradual articulation of, one's responses 'focusing' and holds that it is a very significant factor, not only in psychotherapy, but in many situations in which a person is trying to find the right way to express something. It is not a mysterious process, since all that it essentially involves is giving sustained attention to one's response to something unclear, and seeking ways of articulating that response.

The focusing process has a zigzag nature (Gendlin 1970) that complements the zigzag that I have discussed in connection with behaviour therapy. Clients go back and forth between what they feel, or how they find themselves responding, and their *articulation* of the response. For example, a client talks about being involved in a difficult situation and says that they found it embarrassing. They could just stick with that way of putting it, but then probably little more would happen. Instead, they give some attention to their felt response. They say, 'It makes me feel sort of *twisted*.' That is a linguistic form of the response – it begins to *articulate* the response. The therapist reflects what the client has said, and that may lead the client to wonder 'Is that quite the right way to express it? And is there more here that needs to be expressed?' The client attends again to their response. There is something twisted here but now it comes to them that what is so disturbing is not just their being twisted as their having been put into a situation where they can't but get twisted. The therapist reflects *that*. The client talks a bit about the features of the situation that make it like that, the therapist reflects, and the client attends again to what they have said. Is this the right way to put it? They try out 'being made to feel twisted', and experience a new response: putting it that way is in a way *releasing*, but it also makes them cringe. What is this *cringing*? It comes to them that perhaps they are embarrassed – or is it more *ashamed* – about allowing themselves to be twisted. They attend to the cringing and go back and forth between it and what they have just said. Yes, it is more 'ashamed' than 'embarrassed'... and so on, with a continual zigzagging between their response and the right way to articulate it. In time, their view of what is involved may settle down and become clear: 'Yes, that's what it is, I've once again let myself be too open to what other people want of me, and the result is that in the end I let them down', and they may notice a response of relief or release which follows from *that*.

This 'focusing' process can only work where the client maintains a sensitivity to what their actual felt response is. If the client says, 'I just felt embarrassed. That's how it is. Anyone would feel embarrassed in that situation', then this fixed, conventional expression provides no opportunity for change. For there to be change the client has to let go of their conventional utterance and allow what they say to become open to what they actually feel. They need to let their felt *response* gradually inform their *view* of how things are. Through the focusing 'zigzag' the client gradually approaches a point where their stated view of things is an adequate articulation of their response. 'Felt response' gradually impacts on 'view' here, in the same sort of way that in behaviour therapy 'view' gradually impacts on 'felt response'. In both cases the therapy process involves a loosening or softening of what was initially rigid, conventional or stereotyped. I will come back to the implications of this discussion of the zigzags between 'view' and 'response' later in the book, but for the present we need to return to the broader principles of person-centred therapy.

It seems clear enough how it is that the focusing process is helpful to the client. Through the process the client comes to formulate a view of their difficulty that is a wholehearted articulation of their response. They are no longer disturbed or confused about how they are responding, and now that they know that *this* is what it's all about, they can begin to consider what is to be done about it. Yet even before they take that further step they have, through 'focusing', *changed*. Their response to their situation now is different from what it was, in the sense that it is now a more specific, a more articulated, response. They may say to themselves, 'Well, it seems that things are much worse than I thought', but nevertheless feel the relief of having got to the truth of the matter (Gendlin 1973/1964, p. 454).

Gendlin elaborates on the *details* of what goes on when therapists reflect what clients say in the way Rogers recommended, but his 'focusing' procedure remains firmly within the person-centred approach (Purton 2004). It can only be effective if the therapist creates the conditions in which the client feels safe in expressing their feelings, or articulating their responses. Rogers own emphasis is on the conditions themselves, but his general view of why they are facilitative involves little by way of theory. His view is the common-sense one that human beings have a deep need for the love and respect of others, so that where a person has feelings that conflict with what others expect them to feel, there will be a tendency for the person to no longer express what they really feel but instead to engage in some form of self-deception. Then, if through fear of rejection a person has come to deceive themself about what they really think and feel, this is likely to result in anxiety and confusion. Such a person will find themselves behaving in ways that don't square with how they see themself, they will be taken aback by having feelings that they think they can't have, and they may have to engage in further self-deception in order to maintain the façade that they have acquired in relating to people. Rogers puts this by saying that our need for the approval of others leads to the introjection of 'conditions of worth', and that the receptive atmosphere of person-centred therapy is therapeutically facilitative through 'dissolving' the conditions of worth. However, it seems clear enough that this more technical way of putting things adds nothing to Rogers' basic account.

Variants of the person-centred approach

It has sometimes been suggested that there are two distinct variants of person-centred therapy. According to this view, one variant derives mainly from Rogers' early approach, which Barrett-Lennard (1998) has characterized as 'non-directive reflective therapy'. This is the variant of the approach (if we include its elaboration in focusing-oriented therapy) that I have so far been discussing. The other form of person-centred therapy derives more from Rogers' later emphasis on congruence and on relationship. It sees the therapeutic situation as one in which the therapist as a whole, authentic person provides a healing presence for the client simply by being with the client in an accepting and empathic way. There is less emphasis on reflection, or on skill in empathic responding, and the therapist has no specific goals in mind (such as facilitating client congruence). It is a therapy of 'being' rather than of 'doing'. Training in this approach strongly emphasizes personal development (Mearns 1997, p. 91), since becoming an effective therapist is held to be not so much a matter of developing skills as of becoming an authentic person.

The emphasis here is on the therapist being fully present to the client, or 'relating to the client in depth' (Mearns & Cooper, 2005). In terms of Rogers' 'conditions', it is 'congruence' that is most emphasized, although towards the end of his life Rogers (1980, p. 129) also wrote of the importance of therapist 'presence'. The most essential thing in therapy is held to be the relationship, or manner of interaction, between therapist and client, a view that has been quite strongly confirmed by research on the outcome of therapy (Cooper 2008, p. 103). However, while it clearly is important that there should be a good relationship between therapist and client, this is so seems to be very much a matter of common sense. It is hard to see much role for theory here, although more could be discovered about what exactly it is in the relationship that matters, and whether the relative importance of Rogers' 'conditions' is different for different people.

It is perhaps misleading to try to separate at all sharply the two traditions in person-centred therapy. The 'relating in-depth' dimension is certainly not absent in focusing-oriented therapy. For example, in some remarks at a conference presentation, Gendlin (1990, p. 205) said:

> The essence of working with another person is to be present as a living being... What matters is to be a human being with another human being, to recognise the other person as another being in there. Even if it is a cat or bird, if you are trying to help a wounded bird, the first thing you have to

know is that there is somebody in there, and that you have to wait for that 'person', that being in there, to be in contact with you.

This emphasis on the need for deep human contact is seen by Gendlin as being more basic in therapy than either reflective listening or focusing, and it runs through the whole of the person-centred tradition. Something of its importance is recognized even in contemporary cognitive therapy (Neenan & Dryden 2004, pp. 39–40), but it is in the second variant of person-centred therapy that it finds its fullest expression.

The 'core conditions' and common sense

There are perhaps the *beginnings* of a theory in the distinctions that Rogers makes between the well-known 'core conditions' of acceptance, empathy and what he usually calls 'congruence'. Yet from a common-sense point of view it is hard to see how these conditions could fail to be facilitative of increased self-expression and self-knowledge. Regarding acceptance, it seems to be just common sense to hold that clients will find it difficult to express themselves, or be clear about what they feel, if the therapist is rejecting or judgemental about their feelings. Then while it is not *essential* for self-expression that the therapist should empathize with the client (sometimes misunderstanding can actually help the client to clarify what they really mean), it is nevertheless much more difficult for the client to find the right words if the therapist has little idea of what the client is talking about. Where the therapist has little empathy with the client's view of things, they will be unable to respond in a way that encourages the client to go a bit further. The client will be distracted by the need to correct the therapist's understanding, and also may feel that what they are saying cannot be right, because it makes no sense to the therapist. The less the therapist's empathy, the more difficult the client will find it to express themself freely. I don't think we need any theory to account for why this is so.

Regarding congruence the situation is more complex. 'Congruence' is the condition that has given rise to most discussion in the person-centred approach (Haugh 2001; Purton 2013). I think this is partly because it is to some extent a theoretical concept for Rogers, but also because there are two different contexts in which Rogers uses the term. One is the context of the conditions for effective therapy, where 'congruence' means something like 'therapist genuineness'. The point here is that the therapist needs to be genuine (real, authentic) with the client, and especially in connection with their acceptance of, and empathy with, the client. Rogers rightly holds that therapy is unlikely to be effective if the therapist pretends to an acceptance or empathic understanding that they don't really have. Clients will pick this up, and the therapeutic process will be undermined. However, 'genuineness' for Rogers seems to cover more than deliberate deception; the therapeutic endeavour could also be undermined if the therapist were to deceive *themself* about their attitude to the client. Again, this is something that clients might well pick up, and hence realize that the therapist didn't really accept or understand them. 'Genuineness' seems a good word to cover both the case of deception and the case of self-deception.

However, we can't simply equate 'congruence' with this everyday sense of 'genuineness'. This is because Rogers also uses 'congruence' in the context of *clients* becoming more conscious of what they really feel. The process of therapy is seen as one in which clients become increasingly 'congruent', but what that means is that clients cease to deceive themselves about their feelings and attitudes. They come to realize what they actually feel, rather than what they have 'kidded themselves' that they feel. It is *only* self-deception that is involved here, and not also deception of others. Rogers, as a therapist, is not concerned with whether clients lie to others, but he is concerned with whether they lie to themselves. I think then that the right way to put Rogers' position is that the therapist needs to be genuine (as well as accepting and empathic) if the client is to become less self-deceived and therefore less troubled.

Self-deception

It could be said that this completes a basic common-sense account of what is involved in Rogers' approach, but the account has made significant use of the notion of self-deception. This is certainly an everyday notion, but it can seem rather puzzling and even paradoxical, since it can seem that when we deceive ourselves we both know and do *not* know something (Fingarette 1969). It might be suggested that we need something by way of theory if we are to understand what is involved in self-deception. Rogers' *theory* of incongruence (see below) and Freud's theory of the unconscious (Chapter 5) are possible candidates for the task of explaining what is involved, but both, I shall argue, are unsatisfactory. In fact, I think that a common-sense account of self-deception is quite possible, so that we do not stand in any *need* of the theories.

A common-sense account of self-deception can be set out as follows. We need first to consider the fact that there are things of which we are aware, but which are not in our explicit, *focal* consciousness. There is already a difference between the everyday use of the words 'aware' and 'conscious' (White 1964, pp. 41–60). For example, there is a difference between 'aware' as used in 'When they met last week, she was aware of what he had done, and I'm puzzled why she didn't ask him about it', and 'conscious' as in 'While she was speaking with him, she was very conscious of what he had done, but she didn't actually say anything'. The first means that at the time they met she knew what he had done, but did not necessarily think about it during their meeting, while the second means that as they were talking she kept thinking about, or being troubled by, what he had done. Similarly, while talking to someone while driving one may not be *conscious* of the road conditions, or of the familiar route one is taking, and at the end of the journey may not be able to remember much of what one saw during the drive. Nevertheless, one was *aware* of the road conditions, the change of the traffic lights and so on. One *took these things into account* (Fingarette 1998), but they were not at the centre of one's attention. Again, while watching a play one is *aware* that one is sitting in a theatre, but what one is *conscious* of what is happening in the play. While one is absorbed in the play it may be difficult for a companion to draw one's attention to features of the theatre's seating arrangements – that is not where one's attention is, that is not something one *wants* to attend to.

Given this everyday distinction between being aware of something and being conscious of something, cases of self-deception can be elucidated as cases where one is aware of one's jealousy, for example, but isn't conscious of it, and doesn't want to become conscious of it. One is aware of it in the way that, on the car journey, one is aware of the road conditions; one takes account of them, but they are not in one's consciousness. Similarly, a person's jealousy shows in what they do, and in how they take account of other people's actions, but they may not *attend to* what they are doing and so may not become conscious of it. I would not want to insist that the uses of the words 'aware' and 'conscious' are *always* distinguished in the way that I have suggested; it may be that the use of ordinary language here is a bit uncertain. In that case what I am doing is drawing attention to a distinction that *can* usefully be made, whether or not ordinary language consistently makes it. Common-sense and everyday language sometimes need refinement, but such refinement does not involve the introduction of theoretical notions.

Rogers' work is valuable in drawing our attention sharply to the pervasiveness of self-deception, or 'incongruence' in our lives, to the kind of troubled consequences it can have, and to what is most needed in helping us to become more congruent. Many person-centred therapists (Rogers 1959; Bozarth 1998, pp. 83–84) seem to believe that *all* psychological troubles arise from incongruence and the 'introjection of conditions of worth', and that therefore that *all* psychological therapy is a matter of eliminating these conditions of worth, through providing the atmosphere of acceptance, empathy and congruence that Rogers describes. However, as I have argued for many years (Purton 2002, 2004, pp. 39–41), this is extremely implausible: how, for example, do difficulties such as post-traumatic stress disorder (PTSD) or traumatic animal phobias fit that view? I will consider in later chapters how *other* kinds of therapeutic procedure may be better suited to difficulties such as these.

There is, nevertheless, a wide range of client troubles for which Rogers' approach will be helpful. In that approach the main aim of therapy is to help the client find ways of articulating their responses in an authentic or 'congruent' way. The process of therapy involves moving from speaking inauthentically, out of fear of being judged, to speaking authentically. The client no longer needs to hide, or pretend about, what they feel, and so is released into being more fully themselves. There is no longer a split between how they view things and how they actually respond to things, so that the therapeutic process is essentially a matter of *healing*, in the sense of being restored to wholeness.

This can be seen as a process analogous to that of a child, who, having initially absorbed their mother's anxious response to a situation, comes to realize that not everyone responds that way. The child comes to trust their *own* response more, comes to realize that their response is in fact shared by many others – that this is a better view of how things *are,* and perhaps eventually draws the mother into responding in a less anxious way. We can see the person-centred approach as encouraging a re-alignment of the client's view of things so that their view comes into line with how they actually respond. The client's 'trouble' is one in which they have lost touch with the reality of their own response. Having rediscovered what their response truly is, they *may* then wish to modify it, but that is a different story, which does not feature so prominently in person-centred therapy.

The theory and its confusions

'Experience' and 'incongruence'

Mearns and Thorne (1988, p. 5) once wrote that the person-centred approach 'travels light as far as theoretical concepts are concerned'. This is largely true, but Rogers does discuss his theoretical perspective in a paper 'Towards a science of the person' (Rogers 1964), and he also created an extensive theoretical structure in a long chapter that he contributed to Koch's three-volume work *Psychology: A Study of a Science* (Rogers 1959). In the rest of his writings Rogers was not so much concerned with developing theories, and even in his most theoretical paper of 1959, there is the remark that I quoted in Chapter 1 – that a theory is 'a fallible, changing attempt to construct a network of gossamer threads which will contain the solid facts' (1959, p. 191). Nevertheless, the 1959 paper is undeniably a significant exercise in theory construction, which follows a hypothetico-deductive method and employs the terminology of 'theoretical constructs' and 'functional relationships' that was characteristic of the logical empiricist philosophy of science that was dominant at the time.

Expressed in terms of this theory, Rogers' central idea is that people become troubled when their *self-concept* does not match their *experience,* and that this mis-match between self-concept and experience arises through the *introjection of conditions of worth.* 'Self-concept' here is a theoretical term: one does not encounter self-concepts in everyday life in the way one encounters people and their abilities to deceive themselves. Of course psychological terminology trickles down into everyday language so that today people say things such as 'I have a very poor self-concept' when they just mean they don't think much of themselves. However, for Rogers, 'self concept' is a defined theoretical term. In his 1959 paper he includes a long section (pp. 200–203) on 'the case history of a construct' which is the construct of the 'self' or 'self-concept'. These two terms don't mean quite the same in Rogers' theory (p. 200), but they are both *theoretical constructs* rather than descriptive terms. 'Experience' is also a theoretical term for Rogers, although this is a point that is often overlooked. By 'experience' Rogers doesn't mean something of which we are conscious. For Rogers, it includes '*events of which the individual is unaware,* as well as all the phenomena that are in consciousness' (p. 197; my italics). What Rogers has in mind is the idea, emphasized by Freud, that a person can be annoyed without being conscious of the fact that they are annoyed. In Rogers' terminology, such a person's *self-concept* is incongruent with what they *experience*, so that one can have experiences that one doesn't know one has, experiences of which one is not conscious. There are clearly difficulties with this concept of 'experience', as Rogers was to some extent aware. He writes:

> We are urgently in need of new and more ingenious tools of measurement...most urgently needed of all is a method whereby we might give operational definition to the construct *experience* in our theory, so that discrepancies between self-concept and experience, awareness and experience, etc. might be measured. This would permit the testing of some of the most crucial hypotheses of the theoretical system. (Rogers 1959, p. 250)

Here it is made explicit that 'experience' for Rogers is a theoretical construct, and also that there is a serious problem in knowing what, in *this* sense, a person's 'experience' is. What we have here, I think, is a conceptual problem very similar to that of how, in psychodynamic terms, we can know what is going on 'in the unconscious'. We might even say that it is the same problem, for although Rogers does not use Freud's terminology, his way of thinking is in the end not very different from Freud's (Ellingham 2001).

Rogers' theoretical idea is that being congruent is a matter of a matching between one's 'self-concept' and one's 'experience' (1959, p. 206):

> When self-experiences are accurately symbolised, and are included in the self-concept in accurately symbolised form, then the state is one of congruence of self and experience.

Rogers took the term 'congruence' from geometry (Kirschenbaum 1979, p. 196) where two triangles are said to be 'congruent' if they are of exactly the same shape and size, and hence match up with each other exactly. In order to see if the matching is accurate one has to observe closely the shape and size of each triangle in order to see whether they are the same. Rogers uses this as a *picture* of congruence, but it is hard to see how the picture can be used in practice, since while we can observe closely what people say about themselves – Rogers (1959, p. 202) used Stephenson's Q-sort technique in this connection – we can't observe their *experience*, and even they themselves can't observe the elements of their experience that are not in consciousness, which are precisely the ones that are of interest in connection with incongruence. I think that what causes the difficulty here is the picture of congruence as a matching of 'self-concept' (what the person says about themselves) with their 'experience'. However, the picture is a compelling one because it is an extension of the picture we have inherited from Cartesian philosophy, of 'the mind' as an inner arena which we can observe by introspection. (The extension is that in addition to the picture of 'looking inwards' at the mental arena, we now add that some things in the arena are *hidden*.)

The 'inner' and the 'outer'

Descartes pictured a human being as having both 'inner' and 'outer' aspects. The outer aspect is 'the body' and its movements; the inner aspect is what has variously been called 'consciousness', 'subjective experience', 'the experiential field', 'the phenomenal field' (Rogers 1959, p. 197). Rogers (1964, p. 110) writes:

> Within myself – from within my internal frame of reference – I may 'know' that I love, hate, sense, perceive, comprehend. I may believe or disbelieve, enjoy or dislike, be interested in or bored by. These are all hypotheses, which we often check, as Gendlin has shown, by using the ongoing flow of our preconceptual experiencing as a referent. So I may check my hypothesis by asking, 'Do I really hate him?'. As I refer to my experiencing I realize that it is envy rather than hate that I feel. Or I may wonder, 'Do I love her?' It is only by reference to the flow of feelings in me that I can begin to conceptualize an answer.

According to this picture, we turn our attention inwards to 'the flow of our preconceptual experiencing', and through making reference to that experiencing we can decide what it is that we are feeling. We can't know in the same way what *other* people are feeling, because we have no direct access to their 'inner experiencing'. All we can observe is their 'outer behaviour'.

This picture of 'the inner' is something to which Wittgenstein gives much critical attention. He writes (Wittgenstein 1992, p. 84):

> The 'inner' is a delusion. That is: the whole complex of ideas alluded to by this word is like a painted curtain drawn in front of the scene of actual word use.

He does not mean that *everyday* talk of 'the inner' involves a delusion. By a person's 'inner world' we may simply mean *what they are thinking and feeling*. Wittgenstein is objecting, rather, to the Cartesian picture of 'subjective experience' as *intrinsically* hidden from everyone apart from the person whose experience it is. Wittgenstein is not some sort of behaviourist, although that is a common misconception; it is rather that he thinks that the *philosophical picture* of 'inner events versus outer events' is misleading. This needs more explanation.

Consider an example of something that we might regard as a typical example of an 'inner event', such as a pain. The corresponding 'outer event' would be pain *behaviour*, such as screaming or writhing. According to the 'inner-outer' picture, the person who is writhing on the floor and crying out is also a person who has an essentially private, inner experience, unobservable by others, and that private, inner experience is what we call 'pain'. A behaviourist, by contrast, would say that this is wrong, and that it is the writhing and crying out that is the pain. However, there are difficulties with both accounts, since on either of them it is hard to account for how children learn to use the word 'pain'. They can't learn it by associating the word 'pain' with another's inner pain-event, precisely because that event is 'inner' and therefore 'hidden'. According to the picture, pain – unlike writhing and groaning – is not visible or audible. But nor do they learn that 'pain' means such things as writhing (the behaviourist error), since that would make it incomprehensible why we should feel that anything needs to be *done* when a person is in pain – as if one could say quite unproblematically, on looking into a room, 'Oh yes, Bruno is walking up and down, Charlie is writhing in pain, and Emma is looking out of the window.' Making pain into something 'inner' makes it invisible to others; making it into something 'outer' makes it an event with no implications for what needs to be done.

Wittgenstein suggests that we learn the use of the word 'pain' neither as a description of an 'inner' event nor as a description of an 'outer' form of behaviour. 'Pain' is not primarily used as a *description* at all. Rather, to say 'Charlie is in pain' is primarily an *expression of an attitude,* which might equally well be expressed by 'Poor Charlie!' and that linguistic expression is an extension of the natural impulse we have to relieve and comfort him (Wittgenstein 1953/2009, pp. 178, 187). Similarly, 'I am in pain' should not be construed as a description of an inner state; it is primarily an expression of the same sort as 'That hurts!' or 'Ouch!', and those expressions are linguistic *replacements* for non-linguistic responses such as groaning or screaming (ibid., §244).

Much the same applies in the case of emotions. Consider jealousy, for example: Jealousy is a common pattern in human life – we speak of someone being jealous in situations where, roughly, one person wants some special attention from another, but the other gives more attention to a third person. Such situations often arise in early childhood, for example when a mother gives attention to a sibling, and the other child becomes upset or angry, and tries to displace the sibling in order to get the mother's attention. In this sort of situation we see clearly that the child is jealous. Their jealousy is manifested in their behaviour in that particular kind of situation. Then, as the child begins to develop its linguistic capacity, parents may, instead of simply responding behaviourally, say 'You are jealous'. Later the child begins to recognize the situation and behaviour that is characteristic of jealousy and begins to say to their sibling 'Jealous!' or 'You are jealous!' And finally they learn to say 'Jealous!' or 'I'm jealous' instead of trying to get the mother's attention in the more primitive behavioural way. The utterance 'I'm jealous' is here a new form of behaviour that *replaces* the original behaviour. It does not *describe* 'external' behaviour, but nor is it a *report* of 'inner' events; it is not a description or report at all. It is an *expression*, the linguistic version of a form of behaviour that was initially manifested without language.

In *later* developments of language 'He is in pain (jealous)' and 'I am in pain (jealous)' *can* come to be used as descriptions or reports (Moyal-Sharock 2000). Whether they are being so used depends on the context. If I have hurt my arm rather badly and my friend says, 'What's wrong?' and I reply, 'I'm in *pain!*' that is expression, and the friend naturally responds with expressions of concern. But if I am having a medical examination and the doctor says, 'Are you in pain or is it more of an ache?' and I say, 'I'm in *pain*', then I am reporting something to the doctor, and might be said to be describing what I feel. But these later descriptive uses of the word 'pain' are built on the earlier expressive uses; they are reports of what in different circumstances I might naturally *express*. The words 'I am in pain' or 'He is in pain' are not used to describe 'inner states', and they are not *primarily* used to describe *at all*. That is why Wittgenstein says, 'The "inner" is a delusion.... like a painted curtain drawn in front of the scene of actual word use.'

A new way of thinking about incongruence

With this background we can approach the notion of incongruence in a new way. Imagine a situation in which Charlie has been aware of Anneka talking to and smiling at Theo, and that he strides up to them, and says rather impatiently to Anneka, 'Come on, it's late. We need to go. Goodbye, Theo.' Now fill in as much background as is needed to make it clear that Charlie is jealous, such as the fact that Charlie is attracted to Anneka but is unsure of her feelings for him, and so on. I take it that novelists, for example, can describe situations and behaviour in such a way that we might say, 'That clearly is a case of jealousy' or 'If that is not jealousy I don't know what jealousy is.' Then imagine that, having observed these events, we ask Charlie whether he is jealous. He says – and he is not *lying* about his feelings – 'No, I was just a bit anxious that it was getting late.' We regard Charlie as being incongruent, and I suggest that what this means is that we don't believe that his words are related to his feelings as an *expression* of those feelings; that is, we don't believe that in saying 'I'm just a bit anxious' Charlie is speaking in a spontaneous, expressive way. We think that he is saying this because he doesn't want to acknowledge that he is jealous, perhaps that he doesn't want to be seen as a jealous person. In short, what he is *doing* in saying 'I am anxious' is (among other things) trying to avoid criticism. Incongruence is present where it *seems* that we are expressing something but we are not: we are doing something else.

We can now return to the question that looks unanswerable if we remain, like Rogers (and Freud), within the picture of 'inner' states and 'outer' behaviour. The question was how a client – how anyone – can know that they are being incongruent. We can see now that the difficulty arises because we misconstrue the utterance 'I realise now that I am jealous' as a *report* on the person's inner state. We picture them as scrutinizing their inner world and realizing that they have mistaken a feeling of jealousy for a feeling of anxiety, and now they report this to us. But to say in this context 'OK, I'm jealous' is not to *report* anything; it is more in the nature of a confession. To confess is to express something that one had previously been unable or reluctant to express.

Our question now needs to be re-phrased as something like: 'How is it possible for someone to express something *now* that they were not able to express before?' Well, what actually happens in such situations? It will go something like this: After Charlie has denied that he is jealous we say to him:

> 'But look, you are clearly attracted to Anneka.'
> 'Well, yes I suppose that is true.'
> 'And were you not feeling a bit annoyed with Theo when you strode across?'
> 'Yes, now you mention it, he has started to annoy me. To be honest, I'd like to punch him!'
> 'And this *getting annoyed* seems to have begun when those two started meeting regularly?'
> 'Hmm. Yes... that's true'
> 'And in fact it was not really so late... you could easily have stayed and talked with them for another five minutes.'
> Charlie begins to look uncomfortable, and eventually says 'Ok... you are right... I *was* feeling jealous'.

What is going on here is that we are drawing Charlie's attention not to his 'inner state of jealousy' but to various aspects of the situation and his response to it.

It should perhaps be emphasized again that Wittgenstein is not denying that *all* talk of inner states involves philosophical confusion. That Charlie is jealous needs to be understood in terms of his situation and his responses, but among his responses might be such things as a felt tension, or the flashing through his mind of the thought 'I'd like to punch him!'. Wittgenstein is not denying the existence of such responses, or contesting our *everyday* talk of them as 'inner'. In such everyday talk, as contrasted with Cartesian talk, the events in question are not essentially private, for someone close to Charlie might well notice his tension, and even remark afterwards: 'I was a bit alarmed, because I could see him thinking, even before he said it, "I'd like to punch him." Using language in an ordinary way, we often 'see what people are thinking'; the Cartesian use of this phrase only arises when the picture of 'the inner' draws us into saying 'But one *can't* see what *another* person is thinking!' Wittgenstein's (1953/2009, §66) advice in such cases is 'Don't think, but look!' That is, don't think about what the picture says *can't* be so (e.g. that you can't see what another person is thinking), but look at what *is* so (that we often notice what people are thinking).

The essential point is that in helping Charlie to acknowledge that he is jealous we do not draw his attention to a Cartesian 'inner state', but instead draw his attention to certain aspects of his situation and of his responses. Such close attending to his situation and his responses is something that Charlie clearly had not already done himself, for if he *had* done so then he, being familiar with what jealousy is (with what 'jealousy' means), would already have said to himself 'Oh, my God – I'm *jealous!*'

How does a person come to see that they are being incongruent? Through their attention being drawn to the details of their situation and their response to it, and through their realizing that what they say does not articulate their response. Once they give sufficient attention to the situation and to their response they come to realize that, for example, 'I'm anxious about the time' is not an articulation of their response; their response can only be expressed linguistically by saying 'I'm jealous'.

There are many cases in which we express ourselves *without* giving attention to the details of our situation. In these cases we just use the words that, in our linguistic community, we have learned as replacements for, or extensions of, the relevant non-linguistic behaviour. We spontaneously say such things in the way we spontaneously cry out, or run away. However, there are also cases of the kind just discussed, where we can only express ourselves correctly if we first pause to consider the situation. Such cases are common in psychotherapy, a point that has been especially emphasized by Gendlin (1996, p. 33; 1997, p. 225).[1] As discussed above, a client says something, but then realizes that what they said does not articulate their response adequately. For example, they say 'I felt ashamed'. But when the therapist reflects this back they sense that 'ashamed' is not the right word. Then they pause, try again, and find a word that is better, perhaps 'embarrassed'.

The question for a theory of psychotherapy is: How do they do that? We need to set aside the picture of them looking at an inner state and seeing if the new word 'fits' that state better. What is really involved is something like this: they have learned the use of the word 'ashamed' in contexts of someone responding to having done something that they feel is unworthy of them – that is, they normally use the word as English speakers use it. But then, in the present circumstances, they realize that *this* is not a context of having done something unworthy of them, but of having done something socially inappropriate. They may notice this explicitly, but more often their linguistic training enables them to say that 'embarrassed' is a better word than 'ashamed', even though they can't say why. Someone who wasn't *at all* inclined to reject the word 'ashamed' after giving attention to the details of the embarrassing situation would thereby show an inadequate grasp of English (and similarly, of course for any other language). It *is part of knowing English* that one knows that 'embarrassed' and not 'ashamed' is the word to use in *this* kind of situation.

The above is an account of the context in which the words in question are initially learned in childhood, and hence of their *normal* contexts of use. However, psychotherapy often involves contexts in which people genuinely *feel* ashamed, for example, while realizing that the situation is one in which it would be appropriate to feel embarrassment, or they *feel* guilty while believing that they have done nothing wrong. These are cases where a person's *response* to their situation ('I feel guilty') is out of line with their considered *view* of the situation ('I have done nothing wrong'). I will suggest in Chapter 10 that much of psychotherapy involves helping clients to bring their 'response' into line with their 'view', or vice versa. In the case of person-centred therapy, the usual theme is that clients' responses have become distorted by conditions of worth, by *others*' views, and that when these conditions are dissolved the client's *own* view of the situation can come to inform their response. These are issues to which I will return.

I have so far considered the kind of case where the client – knowing a particular language – is able to find a word in that language that applies in the situation. However, it is quite often the case that there is no word in the language that seems quite right. In these circumstances a client may use a familiar word, but in a new way; in what we call a metaphorical way. For example, a client may say 'My life is an empty box!' or 'I am trapped!' The therapist reflects such an utterance back. When the client hears it back then either:

(a) It feels just right, and they are happy to say it again.
(b) It doesn't feel quite right, and they are no longer happy with saying it.

With metaphors we can't say that they are right or wrong, exactly. In that way they are different from non-metaphorical uses of words. We can say, for example, that a particular situation *just isn't* a situation for which 'ashamed' is the right word, but we can't say that a particular situation *just isn't* a situation for which 'empty box' is the right phrase. The question with metaphors is not whether the use of the word is correct but whether it is *apt*. But how does the client know whether 'trapped' or 'empty box' is an apt metaphor?

Consider a situation where the therapist reflects what the client is saying, using a metaphor that the client *rejects*. For example, suppose the therapist says 'You feel trapped', and the client says: 'No – it's more like paralysed.' The client may reject 'trapped' because 'trapped' is used in circumstances where a person or animal can move, but is restrained, whereas 'paralysed' is used in circumstances where one can't move. The client may not be explicitly aware of this, but if they know English they can use these words 'trapped' and 'paralysed' in the appropriate situations. With 'trapped' you can go on to ask, for example, 'What exactly is constraining you? What could be a way out?' But these questions don't fit with 'paralysed'. For 'trapped' to be an apt metaphor there needs to be something in the situation that could be seen as constraining, and it should make sense to ask about possible ways out – ways of getting rid of the constraint. The client knows (though may not be able to explain) the web of connections involved in 'trapped'. They also know (though may not be able to explain) that significant portions of this web don't exist in their situation, whereas much more of the web associated with 'paralysed' does exist. So again, the answer to the question 'How does the client know what to say?' can only be 'Because they have learned English'. An English speaker who gives attention to their situation isn't going to feel happy with the word 'trapped' when the situation is one to which the word 'paralysed' better applies.

This point about the finding of appropriate words and phrases can be extended to include more elaborate responses to situations. Indeed, when the client 'tells the story' of their difficulty, they are giving expression to how the situation is for them; they are trying to find a way of articulating their response to their situation. In telling their story they may make reference to other, shared, stories: for example, they might say 'Yes, I *am* jealous...but...I was thinking of *Anna Karenina*....I'm jealous in the sort of way that Dolly is jealous of the governess, not in the way that Karenin is jealous of Vronsky'. Narrative therapy (Angus & McLeod 2004; Dwivedi 1997; McLeod 1997) could be seen as elaborating on the point that a crucial role of the therapist is to help the client to find a way of articulating their situation in a way that does justice to it. Some stories – and frequently the story with which a client begins – ignore important features of the client's situation; then the therapist needs to help the client to look further into the situation. But this is not well put by saying that the client needs to look more deeply into their 'inner experiencing'; what they need to do is to reflect further on the *whole of their situation*, so as to find a better way of articulating their response to it.

To summarize, when a client is trying to find words to express their response in a situation it is misleading to say that they are consulting their Cartesian 'inner feelings', and trying to see which words 'match' the feelings, as if they had access to an inner screen on which their feelings are displayed. What they are doing is giving attention to their *situation* and seeking for words that will articulate their response. They are pausing and allowing the natural linguistic form of response to come. The response comes in the form it does because of the client's 'linguistic training', their immersion in a particular language-culture. The 'coming' may take a little time, since the client needs to give attention to the whole situation, and to sense what it is appropriate to say here. Someone for whom the words don't spontaneously come *at all* is to that extent not fully embedded in that culture, or is suffering from some kind of inhibition (perhaps of a kind with which psychotherapy deals), or is not sufficiently creative to find a suitable metaphor that will articulate their response.

What emerges from this Wittgensteinian analysis of congruence and incongruence is that the way in which Rogers frames the issue is confused. He pictures congruence as a matching of the 'outer' (the words the person utters) with the 'inner' (their 'experience'), but then runs into an insurmountable problem in the case of 'experiences' for which the person has no words, 'experiences' which the person does not experience. What a Wittgensteinian analysis shows is that the confusion here is part of a much wider confusion about 'the mind', a confusion that is rooted in the misleading picture of 'the inner'. Once we free ourselves from the spell of this picture we see that there is no problem about having feelings of which we are unconscious. To have the feelings is to be responding to a situation in a particular way, but we can respond without being able to articulate our response linguistically. That inability may be short-lived and due to our not having given sufficient attention to our situation. Or it may be longer-lasting, due to the fact that we don't *want* to attend to our situation, and instead of articulating our response we talk in other ways so as to conceal from ourselves what our response really is. That is what in common-sense terms is called 'self-deception'. Rogers was concerned with a particular kind of self-deception, in which what motivates our inability to articulate our feelings is our ubiquitous fear of the judgement of others that he called the 'introjection of conditions of worth'. His form of therapy works through providing a kind of antidote to the conditions of worth, in the form of the therapist's genuine acceptance and empathy. With a therapist who relates to the client in *that* sort of way, the fear of judgement and criticism is removed; the client no longer needs to pretend to be other than they are, and their associated confusion and anxiety fades away. I have little doubt that this is how in practice most person-centred therapists understand Rogers' form of therapy; my point is that such an understanding, far from requiring a grounding in Rogers' theory, is completely independent of the theory – which is just as well, since if my account is correct, the theory is in the end incoherent.

Memory and perception

Rogers' emphasis on what is 'subjective' or 'inner' has further consequences. In a late paper Rogers discusses the similarities and differences between his approach and that of the psychoanalyst Heinz Kohut. Kohut was interested in learning about the early childhood of his patients, but Rogers (1987, p. 185) comments:

> We can *never* know the past. All that exists is someone's current *perception* of the past. Even the most elaborate case history, or the most complete free association about the past, reveals only memories present *now*, 'facts' as perceived *now*. We can never *know* the individual's past. I pointed out earlier that 'the effective reality which influences behaviour is at all times the perceived reality'.

That we can *never know the past* is a clear example of a radical departure from common sense. It is a view that derives from the Cartesian picture in which people are never aware of events in the world, but only of the contents of their own minds, of their 'phenomenal field'. However, unless we distort the meanings of the words we use, people are normally aware of events *in the world*. If following a road accident the police ask me if I saw the car slow down, I may say 'Yes, I did see it slow down', but I might equally have said 'Yes, it did slow down'. The police are interested in what happened in the world, not in anything that went on in me. If I responded by saying 'I have no idea whether it really slowed down, but I did have a visual impression of it slowing down in my phenomenal field', this would be unintelligible to the police, or to anyone not captivated by a philosophical picture. Similarly, if a few weeks later in court I am asked whether I *remember* seeing the car slow down, and I say 'Yes, I clearly remember that it did', I am exercising a capacity to remember past events. I am remembering *those past events*, not attending to a *current* 'inner process' or 'memory image'. Again, what the court is interested in is not what is going on in me now, but what happened in the past. And one way of trying to establish what happened in the past is by asking people what they remember. Of course our memories are fallible, but in normal circumstance people are able to say a good deal about what happened yesterday, or a few weeks ago, especially if the events in question were of special interest to them. This is a basic capacity that people simply have. There are undoubtedly brain structures and processes that are involved in our having this capacity, but there need not be any inner *experiences* involved. When I am asked whether I remember seeing the car slow down, I may remember it clearly, but that does not mean that I consult, as it were, an inner screen on which my 'memory experiences' are displayed. I *may* experience images of the event, but equally I may not.

I think that one thing that feeds the misleading picture of remembering as 'having memory experiences' is that when we *mis*remember it is natural to say that we have a false memory. It seems to us that something happened, yet it did not. Then it is tempting to regard the 'seeming' as a kind of inner thing or process. Yet to seem to remember is not to have any particular inner experiences, in the sense of having certain thoughts or images. Such thoughts or images *may* be present, but they may not. It may just be – and I think it usually just is – that we are strongly inclined to say that something happened, when it didn't.

Rogers rightly connects his view of memory with his view of perception. In his view, which he shares with the cognitive therapists, what influences behaviour is not what happens but how we perceive what happens. There is a harmless, common-sense way of understanding that assertion (i.e. that we have to perceive the event for it to influence us), but Rogers' way of understanding it is not commonsensical or harmless. Rogers' view, following Descartes, is that we don't perceive the actual events in the world at all, but only our 'inner experiences' that are (we hope!) caused by the actual events. Each of us is locked inside a here-and-now subjective bubble, so that we cannot know external events. Again, what feeds this misleading picture is that we sometimes *mis*perceive things. We are subject at times to perceptual illusions, and much more rarely, to hallucinations. When we see the straight stick in the water as bent, there is something we see. What we *see* is a straight stick in water, though it looks bent to us. However, it is tempting to say that what we 'see', what is 'in our phenomenal field', is a bent stick. Then we may say that there exists both the real stick in the real (physical) world and the phenomenal stick in the phenomenal (mental) world. But this talk of 'the phenomenal world' is Cartesian picture-language that is unnecessary and misleading. Our ordinary way of putting the matter is perfectly adequate as it stands. We see the straight stick, but it looks bent to us; that is, if we didn't know it was straight we would say it was bent. We do not have to add to the presence of the stick, and how it looks to us, an 'inner entity' which is 'the look of the stick'.

The theory and its dangers

Of all the major forms of therapy it may seem that person-centred therapy is the least likely to be damaging to the client. At the heart of person-centred therapy is the practice of creating a genuine, understanding and respectful relationship with the client, through listening closely to what the client says, and responding in a way that imposes nothing on the client. Surely no one could be harmed by *that*? I think this is right in connection with the *practice*, if it is carried out in a common-sense kind of way. But there are ways in which the theory can interfere, leading to less happy results. According to the theory, what the therapist is trying to do is to help the client to attend to their 'experience', to their 'real feelings', as contrasted with the 'self-concept' that has been built up through the 'introjection of conditions of worth'. Then having found their real feelings they are encouraged to follow *them*. I have found that when clients realize that this is what they are being encouraged to do, they may have doubts about the procedure. They may remark that it is very nice to be able to follow your feelings, but what about the impact of this on others? Rogers' answer to this is that through being oneself, through finding and following one's feelings, one also becomes caring of others (e.g. Rogers 1990, pp. 183, 419). However, it is not clear whether this really is the case, or how it follows from Rogers' theory.

The theme has been much discussed in the person-centred literature (Thorne 1992, pp. 66–73; Mearns & Thorne 2000, pp. 177–186; Wilkins 2003, pp. 60–63). Gendlin (1959) suggests an alternative way of reading Rogers: he suggests that when Rogers speaks of 'following one's feelings', he does not mean that we should simply do what we feel like doing in the moment. Rather, we need to find a sense of our situation as a whole, taking *everything* into account, including what other people are likely to feel. In Gendlin's terminology, we should not simply follow our emotional responses but our wider 'felt sense' of what the situation requires. This seems plausible to me, but it is hardly consistent with Rogers' theory. What Gendlin is recommending is that we need to attend not just to our 'feelings' in the sense of our impulses and 'inner experiences' but to our whole *situation*. Gendlin himself has a misleading way of picturing the 'felt sense' of a situation as an inner bodily sensation (Purton 2013a), but what his suggestion really amounts to is that instead of 'introspecting' we should look at our situation and at how we are responding in it. That is quite compatible with person-centred *practice*: as our fear of the judgement of others fades, we will be more able to reflect clearly on what really would be best for us *and them*. But Rogers' *theory* will orient us instead to 'our own experience', to our 'real feelings' and the need to act on them; the feelings of others will not be seen as relevant *in themselves*, but only insofar as they generate feelings in us.

The difficulty here has been approached by Mearns and Thorne (2000) in terms of Rogers' notion of the 'actualizing tendency'. The 'actualizing tendency' is Rogers' term for the tendency of the organism to grow and fulfil its natural potential. In the case of human beings this translates into people finding ways of doing what they really want to do, independently of the conditions of worth that are laid on them by others. Mearns and Thorne suggest that in addition to this tendency, people are also concerned with preserving the viability of the social context within which they live (ibid., p. 182); they refer to this as a concern with 'social mediation'. They see such social mediation as a prudential rather than a moral issue, illustrating it by such client remarks as 'I could do more with my life, but I am scared to lose what I already have', 'I fought my way out of a relationship previously, and I lost more than I ever imagined' or 'I look at what other people have got and I want it like a child wants everything. But my child isn't going to make all my decisions'. The point seems to be that it is not prudential simply to attend to what one *immediately* wants and ignore the wider impact of 'following one's feelings'. But that does nothing to alleviate the worries of a client who feels that prudential concerns are not all that matters. Shouldn't one also allow oneself to be *affected by* what others want? Shouldn't one attend to *their* wishes, and open oneself to a way of responding that comes in part from *them*? As I will discuss in Chapter 11, the phenomenon of 'social referencing' that Stern describes in child–mother relationships seems to be built into the human situation: We *attend to* the feelings of others as well as to our own feelings, and our considered responses come only partly from our own feelings. Or to put it another way, through attending to the feelings of others our own feelings may change. Rogers' theory is very much focused on the kind of case where a person has lost track of their own feelings and needs help in finding them. Because of this focus it ignores the opposite kind of case where a person has lost track of the feelings of others and is not influenced much by how things look to them. Rogers' theory is centred around the theme of freeing people from immersion in the world of others, but it has little to say about freeing people from immersion in their own world. It can't *in principle* get to grips with this second kind of problem, because Rogers pictures human beings in a Cartesian way as individual centres of consciousness, each living within their own 'phenomenal field'. It has, indeed been a significant criticism of Rogers that his worldview is too individualistic (Holdstock 1993, 1996a, 1996b; Laungani 1999; Mearns & Thorne 2000, pp. 79–83).

Rogers' Cartesian way of thinking about memory and perception has other dangers. It can lead to a lack of concern with truth, or how things really are, or were. For Rogers, we can never know how things really are, or were. All we can know is our own 'subjective experiences'. Yet that is not, typically, what counselling clients – or most people apart from Cartesian philosophers – would say. A client may, for example, be deeply concerned about whether they really were abused as a child. This is surely a legitimate concern, and for a variety of reasons: it matters deeply in connection with their future relations with the putative abuser; it matters in connection with their perspective on other possible abuse by this person; it matters in connection with how other family members should relate to this person; and of course it has legal implications. To say in this connection that 'We can never know the past' is surely as bizarre as saying to the policeman 'I have no idea of whether the car *really* slowed down'. But it is not just bizarre; it conveys to the client – if they pick up how the therapist thinks about these things – that the client's concern for the truth is misplaced. Such ignoring of the client's concern would deeply conflict with Rogers' general principle of taking seriously what the client says.

It could also be argued that in one-sidedly supporting the client's felt responses (e.g. 'I want to leave this relationship') against the client's admittedly distorted broader view ('You can't break a promise'), the therapist does not respect the client's need to find their *own* balance between their felt responses and how others might see things. This issue arises often enough in cases where a client consults a therapist about their relationship with another person, but that other person does not accompany them to therapy. The temptation is then for the therapist to help the client simply 'find what they really feel', without also helping the client to consider how the *other* person sees the situation. In such cases, what the therapist does may simply reinforce feelings and attitudes in the client that are already out of step with a broader view of the situation.

Rogers emphasizes the importance of the therapist working within the 'client's frame of reference', but examples such as the recall of abuse suggest that the notion of 'the client's frame of reference' is easy to misinterpret. To speak of 'the client's frame of reference' is to speak of how the client perceives things, but it does not follow that there is no truth beyond the client's perceptions. We don't live in subjective phenomenal bubbles; we live in a shared world, under a common sky (Nuttall 1974). I suspect that in practice most person-centred therapists have a fairly robust, common-sense view of the past and would not be deflected by the theory when working in a pragmatic person-centred way with clients who are concerned to know more about their past. But that is to say that sound person-centred practice needs to be detached from Rogers' theory. The theory is not only confused but potentially damaging.

Summary

I have suggested that the practice of person-centred therapy makes good sense without bringing in Rogers' theory of congruence and incongruence. That theory is not needed since everything which needs to be said in that connection can be better expressed in terms of the common-sense notion of self-deception. In reaching this conclusion we have seen how Rogers' theoretical scheme involves the confusions that are inherent in the Cartesian picture of human beings and their capacities for memory and perception. But these confusions are not of purely academic interest; they have consequences for therapeutic practice, especially in connection with the individualistic worldview for which Rogers has often been criticized.

Note

1. I have discussed the implications of my ideas for Gendlin's 'focusing-oriented psychotherapy' elsewhere (Purton 2012, 2013a, 2014).

Chapter 5

Psychodynamic Therapy

Psychodynamic therapy is not the same as psychoanalysis, but the basic principles of these two forms of therapy are much the same; the difference seems to consist mainly in the fact that psychoanalysis involves 'long-term, daily session work' (Jacobs 1988, p. 4). Accounts of psychodynamic therapy are inevitably framed in terms of the basic concepts of psychoanalysis, such as those of 'the unconscious' and 'repression'. I will discuss these shortly, but first I will try to describe simply what psychodynamic therapists *do*, and consider to what extent their practices can be understood without appeal to the theoretical notions that lie in the background. This is not altogether an easy task; the philosopher Alistair MacIntyre (2004, p. 51) remarks in connection with psychoanalysis:

> Freud's own descriptions of the analytic process are all coloured by the fact that at the time that he was developing it he was also developing his own theoretical concepts; so that he rarely, if ever, gives a purely descriptive account of psychoanalysis.

The common-sense core

Nevertheless, it is worth trying to describe what in practice is *done* in psychoanalysis, and MacIntyre (p. 52) offers the following:

> In psychoanalysis the patient talks, saying whatever it occurs to him to say. In thus talking he will in fact tend to dwell on some subjects rather than on others, he will pass by some topics and continually return to others. When he dwells on some topic or when he displays great emotion the analyst will tend to suggest an interpretation to him of what he is saying. The more the analysis progresses the more the patient will pass from talk about adult life to talk about childhood, and incidents that had apparently been forgotten will be recalled. This recalling will in turn be accompanied by emotional release. Such emotional release will in turn be followed by a mitigation of the neurotic symptoms which were the occasion of undertaking psychoanalytic treatment.

Michael Jacobs (1988, p. 10) writes:

> The primary purpose in psychodynamic counselling is to help clients to make sense of current situations; of feelings and thoughts evoked by those situations; of memories associated with present experience, some of which readily spring to mind, others of which may rise to consciousness as the counselling develops; and of the images that appear in fantasies and dreams. From this wealth of material, all of which is important to the psychodynamic counsellor, counselling attempts to form a picture, representing not just the way in which the client relates, or wishes to relate to others, but also the way the client relates to him- or herself.

The aim of psychodynamic counselling is thus to help the client acquire insight into their feelings and relationships, and such insight, which often involves recall of childhood memories, leads to emotional release and an increased ability to live in a fulfilling way.

The basic techniques for achieving this end involve first of all close listening, both to the client's words and to 'the mood, the feeling, and the underlying messages that are conveyed through the actual words that the client chooses' (Jacobs 1988, p. 29). As in person-centred therapy the counsellor tries to gain an empathic understanding of the client and may reflect what the client says in order both to check that they have understood correctly and to help the client to proceed further. Other therapist responses may include attempts at clarification, for example through the use of open questions. In these respects, as Jacobs notes, what the psychodynamic therapist does is very similar to what is done in person-centred therapy. However, Jacobs (ibid., pp. 63–64) writes that a significant difference between the two approaches is that the psychodynamic counsellor makes *interpretations* of what the client says. The counsellor

> has his or her own ideas, drawn from seeing other clients, to which he or she pays attention, as well as listening carefully to the client's words and feelings.... The psychodynamic approach means that the counsellor listens not only to the client, but also to those ideas and constructions of the client's material which come to mind. When it seems appropriate, the counsellor suggests ideas, and tests them out with the client, to see if they make sense.

It is hard to say, however, whether this difference between the approaches really amounts to much. Person-centred counsellors, especially in the tradition of the later Rogers, may well bring their own thoughts and feelings to what the client has said, although they will not try to impose their views on the client, and will simply drop their suggestions if they are unhelpful to the client. I think that in both approaches the point of such interventions is mainly to stimulate the client into finding their *own* response, although there is the difference that the psychodynamic counsellor may have a definitely held (psychoanalytic) theory about what the client's trouble involves.

There is next the important point that the client may be to some extent unconscious of what they feel, or of what they are up to in their personal relationships. This idea is of course central to psychoanalytic theory, but in fact the notion of unconscious feelings predates Freud; it was a commonplace notion in the 19th century (Whyte 1967). More importantly, the notion of unconscious feelings is already contained in the everyday notion of self-deception. To say that someone is unconscious of their jealousy is the same as saying that they are self-deceived in thinking that they are not jealous. I have suggested a common-sense way of understanding self-deception in the previous chapter, and need not repeat it here, but I will elaborate on it shortly in connection with Freud's theory. Person-centred and psychodynamic therapies differ in their *terminology* for self-deception ('incongruence' vs 'unconscious feelings'), but it may be that the difference really *is* just one of terminology.

It has often been pointed out that there is in fact more to Freud's notion of 'the unconscious' than can be found in everyday, or pre-Freudian, talk of unconscious thoughts and feelings. For Freud (1915), 'the unconscious' is a dynamic reality underlying the everyday reality of 'consciousness'; it is a mental structure with its own 'laws of motion' that are very different from those of conscious mental processes. As I will discuss below, '[w]hat distinguished Freud's contribution is that he gave to the term "unconscious" a substantive status' (Jacobs 2003, p. 34). In other words, Freud turned the everyday use of 'unconscious' as an adjective or adverb into a *noun*, and so set up the hypothesis of the unconscious as an *entity*. It is this notion of '*the* unconscious' that is central to Freudian *theory*, but it is important to realize that we can set it aside, while still accepting that in common-sense terms we may not always be conscious of what we are feeling or doing. As Alasdair McIntyre put it: '... what the psychoanalyst is really relying on is a compound of empirical know-how and skill in detecting deception... And that this would agree with what we should expect on commonsense grounds anyway is perhaps not a point against it' (McIntyre 1958, pp. 83–84).

In practice the issue of 'unconscious feelings' is the issue that clients may not always be conscious of what they are feeling and doing. One can be jealous without being conscious of one's jealousy, and one can be trying to undermine someone's position without being conscious of what one is doing. An important aspect of psychodynamic therapy is that the therapist may try to draw the client's attention to what they are unconsciously feeling or doing. That is not a matter of encouraging the client to engage in deep introspection, but rather of pointing out aspects of the client's situation and behaviour that don't fit with what the client has said.

> In drawing attention to (or technically 'confronting') these patterns, a counsellor is aware that what he or she has to say to the client may come as a shock, be experienced as painful, and be taken as criticism. Confrontation is thus a skill in itself, requiring attention to its possible effect on the client. Well expressed, and calmly put across, good confrontation may temporarily sting, but at the same time bring relief to the client. The effort of denying

(consciously or unconsciously) thoughts and feelings can create considerable inner tension, which is eased following the acknowledgement of any material previously denied access to consciousness or communication. (Jacobs 1988, pp. 77–78)

The reference to 'material denied access to consciousness' brings with it something of Freud's picture of 'materials in *the unconscious*', but there is no need to take that picture seriously. What Jacobs is saying here about the procedure of 'confrontation' seems to be perfectly understandable in terms of trying to draw clients' attention to what they are really feeling, or what they are really up to. This is something we frequently do in everyday life without any need to refer to Freudian theory.

The same sort of point can be made in connection with the psychodynamic practices of 'working with defences' or 'working with the transference'. Defences are strategies of self-deception which one employs in order to avoid facing aspects of oneself, or of one's relationships with others, that one would rather not face. They are ways in which we manage not to be conscious of what we do nevertheless know. Psychoanalysis has developed a classification scheme for defences, such as 'projection', 'introjection', 'displacement', and I think this is valuable in providing a more detailed account of the kinds of ways in which we can deceive ourselves. This is a case of *extending*, or *further specifying*, our common-sense view of things, but the extension can be made without introducing any theoretical terms. (It may also be true, as the psychoanalyst Fenichel (1946, p. 153) remarked, 'There are no sharp lines of demarcation between the various forms of defence.')

'Working with the transference' is the special case of working with clients who see and respond to the therapist in ways that derive from earlier ways of relating to parents or lovers. The self-deception involved here is that the client really does know what the therapist's role is, yet begins to think of them as an authority figure, or a 'special friend'. The psychoanalytic view is that in working with this difficulty the client may well come to see how in other relationships they tend to deceive themselves in similar ways, and how their tendency to endow people with the characteristics of 'authorities' or 'potential lovers' can interfere with their genuine relationships with people. That is not to say that other people can never come into our lives as genuine authorities or special friends; it is just that therapy can help us to distinguish where such relationships are real and where they are not.

It is of course valuable to realize that we can misperceive people in various ways, due to our past experiences of relating to others, and it may well be true that psychoanalysis has helped us to see more clearly how widespread such misperceptions are. Yet it is hard to see a necessary role for psychoanalytical *theory* in all this; it seems rather that Freud has helped us to see in more detail the ways in which we can deceive ourselves. It is perhaps this that has sustained psychoanalysis over the hundred years or so of its history, in the face of overwhelming objections that can be made against Freud's *theory*.

The theory and its confusions

Psychoanalysis has by now a long history, and there is not just one psychoanalytic theory but a whole range of theories, developed over more than a hundred years, that are related to each other in complex ways. There are significant disagreements between the various psychoanalytic schools, such as the Freudian, Jungian, Adlerian, and also *within* the schools. For example, there are psychoanalysts who fall within the classical Freudian tradition, others who follow the thought of Melanie Klein, and still others – uncommon in the United Kingdom, but the most numerous worldwide – who follow the very different perspective of Lacan. Similarly, there is a Jungian school that has absorbed many of Klein's ideas, and a Jungian school that sees itself as remaining closer to Jung's own thinking and practice. It is thus not easy to say what constitutes 'psychoanalytic theory', or what version of the theory might prove most useful in psychodynamic practice. Freud's own account of the 'structure of the mind' was formulated rather differently at different times in his life (Frosh 2012, pp. 69–75). The version I will be concerned with here is that which involves distinguishing the 'conscious', 'preconscious' and 'unconscious' parts of the mind. In his later writings, Freud also distinguishes 'ego', 'id' and 'superego', which is a scheme that only partly overlaps with the earlier scheme. As I will suggest in Chapter 11, the *later* scheme connects with a number of other accounts of human personality, which go back as far as Plato, but I will not be discussing it in the present chapter.

The theories of Freud and his successors have been widely criticized, for example in a 762-page historical study by Malcolm Macmillan, who concludes that 'psychoanalysis as a theory of personality has little to recommend it' (Macmillan 1997, p. 561). It has been argued that Freudian theory is unscientific, as claimed by the psychologist Hans Eysenck (1985) and the philosopher of science Karl Popper (1959); falsified, as claimed by the philosopher Adolf Grünbaum (1984); and 'mystical', as claimed by the anthropologist Ernest Gellner (1985). This widespread scholarly criticism, together with the wide diversity of theoretical ideas within psychoanalysis, raises some doubt about whether it is wise to seek a grounding for therapeutic practice in psychoanalytic theory. It is difficult for anyone who is not a specialist in the field to assess psychoanalytic theory adequately, but when at least some scholars, who have studied it impartially over many years, conclude that it is fundamentally flawed, therapists should surely take note of this.

On the other hand, the situation in relation to psychoanalytic theory is different from that in relation to behaviourist theory. There are no longer any real 'believers' in behaviourism, but there are numerous writers who would still see themselves as believing in at least the central ideas of psychoanalysis. Psychodynamic theorists belong to this group, and what I will be concerned with in this chapter is the version of psychoanalytic theory that is to be found in the writings of psychodynamic counsellors such as Michael Jacobs (1988, 2003). To what extent the criticisms that can be made of this version will also apply to other versions of the theory I will leave as an open question.

Jacobs (2003, p. 33) quotes an encyclopaedia article by Freud in which Freud lists the 'corner-stones' of psychoanalytic theory as:

> the assumption that there are unconscious processes, the recognition of the theory of resistance and repression, the appreciation of the importance of sexuality and of the Oedipus complex – these constitute the principal subject-matter of psychoanalysis and the foundations of its theory. No one who cannot accept them all should count himself as a psychoanalyst.

In Jacobs' book *Psychodynamic Counselling in Action* (1988), which is, as it were, a scaled-down version of psychoanalysis for counsellors, the corner-stones of 'the unconscious', resistance and repression, and sexuality are prominent, though the Oedipus complex is not. For my purposes here, it may be sufficient to confine attention to 'the unconscious' and 'resistance/repression', since these theoretical notions do seem central to any form of psychoanalysis or psychodynamic therapy. For example, when Jeffrey Masson was dismissed from his post of Project Director of the Freud Archives, because of his criticisms of Freud, one of the accusations made against him was that he 'no longer believe[d] in repression or the unconscious' (Masson 1992, p. 199).

As I remarked above, Freud's account of the 'structure of the mind' was formulated differently at different times in his life, but in one well-known version the structure involves the following three elements or 'systems'. There is first *consciousness*, or what Freud called the 'system Cs', then there is the *preconscious* or 'system Pcs', and finally the *unconscious* or 'system Ucs'. In everyday terms, 'the system Cs' refers to what we are conscious of, to 'what is present in our mind at the moment'. For example, one might be conscious of being tired, or of someone else's sadness, or of a tapping noise outside the window. What is in 'consciousness' or 'the system Cs' is what we are noticing or attending to. The 'system Pcs' is Freud's way of referring to what we are not currently attending to, but which we might attend to if circumstances required it, or if someone asked. To take an example from the previous chapter, when we are absorbed in a play at the theatre we are not conscious of the seating arrangements, but we could easily become conscious of them. Similarly, while absorbed in the play we may not be conscious of how tired we are, but later our attention may be drawn to this, as we find ourselves yawning. The 'system Ucs' is Freud's way of referring to cases where we have certain feelings or thoughts, yet *don't* become conscious of them even when our attention is directed to the question of what we are feeling or thinking. For example, we can be angry or jealous, yet deny that we have these feelings. In common-sense terms this seems to be the territory of self-deception that I discussed earlier.

Freud often pictures the three 'systems' as 'chambers of the mind', although sometimes consciousness is not so much a 'chamber' as a spectator that can see into the chamber of the preconscious but not into that of the unconscious. He also refers to a mental function that he calls 'the censor', which acts like a doorkeeper of the unconscious, and decides whether or not unconscious thoughts and feelings should be allowed through into consciousness. This is of course metaphorical picture-language, but Freud (1915, p. 104) writes:

> I should like to assure you that these crude hypotheses, the two chambers, the doorkeeper on the threshold between the two, and consciousness as a spectator at the end of the second room, must indicate an extensive approximation to the actual reality.

There is not necessarily anything wrong with a picture of this sort, but we need to consider how it is to be used in practice, and whether it can in some ways mislead us. One feature of the picture is that it presents each part of the mind as a kind of *thing*, or as a structure with various contents. This is an elaboration on the Cartesian idea that the *mind* is a kind of thing, though a non-physical kind of thing. For Descartes, thoughts, emotions, beliefs and so on are to be found 'in the mind', much as blood vessels, bones and nerve cells are to be found in the body.

As mentioned earlier, Freud moves from the everyday way of talking about 'unconscious thoughts and feelings', where 'unconscious' is used as an adjective to his own way of talking about 'the unconscious', where the word is used as a noun. For example, Jacobs (2003, p. 34) writes:

> What distinguished Freud's contribution is that he gave to the term 'unconscious' a substantive status, seen in the title of his longest paper on metapsychology *The Unconscious* (1915). Summarizing his thinking to date in the *Introductory Lectures* Freud writes: ' "Unconscious" is no longer the name of what is latent at the moment; the unconscious is a particular realm of the mind with its own wishful impulses, its own mode of expression and its particular mental mechanisms which are not in force elsewhere' (1916–17: 249).... Freud felt there had to be a place where what was unacceptable to the conscious mind was repressed and held, and from which the repressed emerged from time to time, in one form or another, back into consciousness.

However, it seems clear that Freud did not give only the term 'unconscious' a substantive status; the same applies to 'the preconscious' and to the contents, at least, of 'the conscious'. As Bouveresse (1995, p. 22) writes:

> Freud has been credited, if not with an actual 'discovery' of the unconscious (which he had the wisdom not to claim entirely for himself), at least with the introduction of a revolutionary idea of its nature and function. It is less frequently noticed, however, that his vision of consciousness remained utterly traditional and bound to the idea of consciousness as the internal perception of 'objects' of a certain type.

The 'traditional vision' of thoughts and feelings as 'internal objects' is the view I have already criticized to some extent in Chapters 3 and 4. In Chapter 3 we saw how the introspectionist school of psychology failed largely because it could not find the 'inner objects', and in Chapter 4 we saw that it is a mistake to try to understand a term such as 'jealousy' in terms of a Cartesian 'inner state'. Jealousy is rather a matter of responding in a particular kind of way in a particular kind of situation. The response may involve behaviour, a bodily 'pang', the flashing into one's mind of particular thoughts or feelings, but none of these *are* jealousy. Jealousy is a context-related notion: one can't 'have a jealous feeling' independently of a social context, and one's perception of that context. And giving attention to one's feelings in order to determine whether one is jealous is not a matter of 'looking within' but of attending to the details of the situation one is in, and how one is responding to it. To think of 'the conscious' as an inner system or entity, with contents that capture our attention, is to make use of a misleading picture.

To say that a person's feeling of jealousy is 'in their *preconscious*' seems to be to say that the person would notice that they are jealous if something or someone drew their attention to what they are feeling. The same general point applies in the case of 'the unconscious': to say that a person's feeling of jealousy is 'in their unconscious' is to say that the person would *not* notice that they were jealous even if someone tried to draw their attention to what they are feeling. The everyday way of putting this is to say that the person is self-deceived. They *are* jealous, but they deceive themselves that they are not.

The notion of self-deception is one that I have already discussed in connection with the person-centred notion of 'incongruence'. I think that much of what I said there applies, with appropriate changes of terminology, to Freud's notion of 'the unconscious'. To take again my example of Charlie and his jealousy, the Freudian way of describing the situation is that Charlie has jealous feelings, but that they exist in the unconscious part of his mind, not in the conscious or preconscious part. When queried about his feelings he denies that he is jealous, and this is because his jealousy is *repressed*; that is, it is kept (by the censor) in the unconscious because if it was allowed into the conscious it would make Charlie very anxious. The *repressing* of the jealous feelings also goes on in the unconscious. However, this seems at best a picturesque, and at worst an incoherent, way of saying what can better be said in everyday language. That is, Charlie is jealous but, for reasons that might well be explored, he does not give any attention to his jealousy, and so is not conscious of it.

It might still be felt that in reformulating talk about the unconscious and repression in terms of the familiar notion of self-deception, we haven't done justice to the kinds of case which Freud uses when he is trying to convince us of the existence of the unconscious. Some of these cases do seem to be of a different order of puzzlement from that of Charlie's unconscious jealousy. In a recent balanced assessment of psychoanalysis, Stephen Frosh uses the following example, taken from Freud, as an introduction to his chapter on 'The Freudian unconscious', in which he is trying to convey the kind of 'evidence' that Freud sees as supporting his theory (Frosh 2012, pp. 38–40). I take it that Frosh chooses *this* story because it is one of the most convincing stories that can be told in support of Freud's account. It is a story, from a culture that already seems rather remote, in which a female patient was troubled by the fact that she found herself performing the following obsessional action several times a day.

> She ran from her room into another neighbouring one, took up a particular position there beside a table that stood in the middle, rang the bell for her

housemaid, sent her off on some indifferent errand or let her go without one, and then ran back into her own room.

The patient could not explain why she did this, until one day during her sessions with Freud 'she suddenly knew the answer':

> More than ten years before, she had married a man very much older than herself, and on the wedding-night he was impotent. Many times during the night he had come running from his room into hers to try once more, but every time without success. Next morning he had said angrily: 'I should feel ashamed in front of the housemaid when she makes the bed,' took up a bottle of red ink that happened to be in the room and poured its contents over the sheet, but not on the exact place where a stain would have been appropriate. I could not understand at first what this recollection had to do with the obsessional action in question; the only resemblance I could find was in the repeated running from one room into the other, and perhaps also in the entrance of the housemaid. My patient then led me up to the table in the second room and showed me a big stain on the tablecloth. She further explained that she took up her position in relation to the table in such a way that the maid who had been sent for could not fail to see the stain. There could no longer be any doubt of the intimate connection between the scene on her wedding-night and her present obsessional action.

Freud suggests that in her compulsive action the patient was identifying with the husband and replaying the wedding-night incident in such a way that would make it no longer so painful:

> We see, therefore, that she was not simply repeating the scene, she was continuing it and at the same time correcting it; she was putting it right. But by this she was also correcting the other thing, which had been so distressing that night and had made the expedient with the red ink necessary – his impotence. So the obsessional action was saying 'No, it's not true. He had no reason to feel ashamed in front of the housemaid; he was not impotent.' It represented this wish, in the manner of a dream, as fulfilled in a present-day action; it served the purpose of making her husband superior to his past mishap.

We can easily appreciate the appeal of the idea that in this case the patient's action arose from a powerful desire that was outside her consciousness. The desire was very clearly there, but it was not a conscious desire of hers; it existed in her unconscious. One might even suggest that here we can almost 'see' the two entities of the conscious and unconscious minds in action; one of them is her conscious self that runs between the rooms, while the other is the unconscious self that is trying to remove the pain of the wedding-night. Some therapists might put this in terms of two distinct sub-personalities; there are excellent dramatic possibilities in this way of thinking.

However, while some people will be persuaded by Freud, others will not. It is not obvious that there would be any conclusive way of refuting someone who said:

> This is just fanciful nonsense. The patient, and Freud, choose to see the similarity between the husband's running on the wedding-night and the patient's compulsive running as significant, but it could just be a matter of coincidence. And the similarities are not *so* great: in one case it is the husband who runs, in the other the patient; in one case it is an ink stain on a bed-sheet, in the other a food-stain (presumably) on a table-cloth. There *could* be some sort of connection here, but Freud hasn't *shown* that there is. He assumes that the connection lies in the patient's unconscious, but that by definition is inaccessible to us.

On the other hand, the story is a striking one, and I think most people would feel that there may be *something* in what Freud says. Why should we feel this? I think it is because we sense that Freud's account is not very far from accounts of people's behaviour that we *do* find acceptable. For example, when we have experienced something very painful, we may go over it again and again in our minds, but also we may replay the scene in our mind in such a way that things come out well for us. A child might respond to a painful event by playing out a benign version with their toys, or in a therapist's sand-tray. Or they might act out the benign version. Freud himself explains that the patient was 'not simply repeating the scene, she was continuing it and at the same time correcting it; she was putting it right'. It is not so implausible that that *is* what she was doing, but of course we have to add that she was not conscious of what she was doing, and in a stronger sense of 'unconscious' than that in which one can unconsciously twiddle one's thumbs. In Freud's terminology her intention was in her unconscious, not her preconscious mind, but as we have seen, all that amounts to is that she resisted turning her attention to what she was doing until something in her sessions with Freud weakened the resistance. Then, if I understand Freud's account correctly, she did acknowledge what she had been doing, that is, she came to be able to articulate a response that had previously been inarticulate. At that point, we are no longer concerned with *interpretation*; the crucial thing is that the patient *expresses* their response linguistically, rather than saying that Freud's interpretation must be right. It seems then that there is after all no very significant difference between this case and that of Charlie's unconscious jealousy.

One way of understanding some of Freud's claims may be to say that they are analogous to claims about how one should interpret a work of art. It is not at all a question of having discovered the cause of the behaviour in a hidden region of the mind but of reflecting on the whole context of the behaviour, comparing it with other kinds of behaviour that seem in some way analogous, drawing attention to this feature rather than that. Then, at least sometimes, the whole picture falls into place and we see it like *that*. It is in other words more like an exercise in aesthetic appreciation than a seeking of causal mechanisms (Bouveresse 1995), although in psychoanalysis there is the additional point that for an interpretation to count as valid the *client* needs to 'see it like that'; it is not enough that the therapist does so. Some theorists, as discussed by Macmillan (1997, pp. 614–617) and Frosh (2012, p. 32), put this by saying that we should understand psychoanalysis as a 'mode of hermeneutics', but, as Frosh notes, it is clear that such an understanding is not Freud's.

Freud himself regarded unconscious mental states as real entities that are the *causes* of neurotic behaviour. In his early writings (Freud 1895) he had hoped to develop a *physiological* explanation of mental disorder, and to the end of his life hoped that this would eventually be possible. Then his *mental* systems would find their *physical* embodiment: 'Our psychical topography has *for the present* nothing to do with anatomy; it has reference not to anatomical localities, but to regions in the mental apparatus, wherever they may be situated in the body' (Freud 1915, p. 177; Freud's italics). Recently, some psychoanalytic theorists with an interest in neuroscience have picked up this idea. For Ornstein (1997) and Schore (2003), the right hemisphere of the brain is the anatomical location of the unconscious. I will discuss this suggestion briefly in Chapter 9, but mention it here simply to emphasize that in psychoanalytical and psychodynamic thinking, the unconscious is a 'realm' or a 'system', and not simply a 'latency'.

One thing that may tempt us into thinking in Freud's way is the consideration that there can't be a latency without there being something substantive there that *explains* the latency. If a person is disposed to angry behaviour, yet not aware of their disposition, it may seem that there must be something in them corresponding to the disposition, perhaps a brain state, or perhaps an unconscious mental state, that *is* the unconscious anger. However, in the case of the hypothesized brain state, that would *be* just a hypothesis. It is not as obvious as it seems that there are specific brain states corresponding to specific emotions. We speak of anger in certain *contexts*, for example in a context where someone has been unjustly treated, but clearly the *physical* contexts embodying unjust treatment will be highly various. Why then should these very different physical contexts result in the same brain state? One answer would be that in spite of the different physical contexts there is the same *mental* state of anger, and to that particular mental state must correspond a particular physical state.

The notion of anger as a 'mental state' is crucial to this argument, and that notion is not one that Freud ever questions. So far as what is 'in consciousness' is concerned, Freud accepts fully the picture of 'mental states and events' that comes to us from Cartesian philosophy. He only disagrees with Descartes on the matter of whether all mental states or events are conscious. However, as I have been arguing, talk of 'mental states' can be highly misleading. We are misled partly by the appeal of the Cartesian picture of 'the inner', and partly by the idea that nouns such as 'anger', 'fear', 'expectation' must be names of things, or events or processes. There must be 'something there' to which they refer. What is confusing is that in one (trivial) sense, when we speak of 'anger' we are obviously referring to anger. In another (Cartesian) sense we picture the anger as being 'something there' – for the behaviourists the 'something' was behaviour, for the introspectionists the 'something' was a private, subjective experience. We have a picture of language as lining up words with things, and also of the meaning of a word being the thing to which it refers. Wittgenstein himself was captivated by this picture in his early book, the *Tractatus Logico-Philosophicus* (1921/1963), but he spent much of the rest of his life fighting his way out of it.

Wittgenstein's way out involves appreciating that in explaining what a word means we do not simply present the 'thing' to which it refers; what we do is to explain how the word is used. In Chapter 1, I made some reference to the notion of truth and suggested that we should stick to its everyday meaning. It may be tempting to imagine that there is such a 'thing' or 'relation' called 'truth', to which our attention can be drawn, but this imaginative picture is just that; it doesn't help us in explaining what 'truth' means. Instead of staying with the picture of truth as some kind of thing to which the word 'truth' corresponds, Wittgenstein would say that we need to ask how the word is actually used. And then, as I suggested, the answer will be that we say that something is true in contexts where we have no real doubts about it, where we place our trust in what is said. The crucial shift is from the traditional philosophical question 'What is Truth?' to the more mundane question 'In what contexts do we use the word "truth"?'

Similarly, as I discussed in the previous chapter, it is misleading to think of words such as 'pain' or 'jealousy' as names of states or processes. Exclaiming that one is in pain is something that develops out of non-linguistic responses such as crying out, in a context of bodily injury or discomfort. The utterance 'I'm in pain!' is, as Fogelin (1987, p. 170) puts it, an 'articulated crying', or at least it is out of such crying that talk of pain develops. Similarly, exclaiming that someone else is in pain is an utterance that is, or grows out of, an articulated expression of concern.

In the case of emotions, the *context* of the response plays a larger role in what the words mean. We speak of fear in situations where there is danger; we speak of pride in situations where the person is pleased with having done something good; and we speak of embarrassment where there is social ineptitude. At least, it is in such situations that the talk of emotions *originates*; it is in connection with such situations that children begin to learn the emotion words. Later, 'extra joints' may be added to the language-game: for example, the child *later* learns that there *can be* circumstances where someone is afraid yet there is no danger, but the *normal* connection between fear and danger is still there. Similarly, the child later grasps that there can be situations where a person is being socially inept but *doesn't* feel embarrassed – they just don't care about their ineptitude; but that is not the normal case, that is not where the language-game *begins*.

Each emotion involves a little 'story': in jealousy we have a story about three people, one of whom shows a preference for the second over the third, and so on. But these are just the simplest story outlines; in *Anna Karenina* the jealousy – if that is what it is – which Anna's husband feels in connection with Vronsky is not the *same* as the jealousy which Dolly feels in connection with her husband's affair with the governess. This is because Karenin's marriage, and the way in which it is perturbed by Anna's affair is different from Dolly's marriage and the way it is perturbed. The emotions here are different, but there are no single words that catch the difference; we have to consider the whole story.

It is true that a person needs in some way to be *moved* by their situation in order to count as feeling an emotion, but the way in which they are moved can be various. A person who runs from a charging bull is moved in a very straightforward way, and we say they are afraid. Another person may not run, but be rooted to the spot, and tremble all over. A third may be afraid of bulls in the sense that when they see a bull their mind is filled with thoughts of being chased and gored. The emotion of fear may show in what a person does, in the physical responses they have, in the images or thoughts that come to them; the responses are variable, but the context of danger runs through all cases of fear, including those where the danger is illusory.

What I want to convey by all this is that it is misleading to talk of pains or emotions, for example, as if they were Cartesian inner states that one can identify through 'looking into one's mind'. There is nothing wrong with the idea of *looking into* the question of whether one is jealous, but this 'looking into' is badly pictured as 'turning one's attention inward'. It is also misleading to talk about emotions as *states* at all, although in some cases there may be *bodily* states (such as increased heart rate, muscle tensions, raised blood pressure) associated with them. However, Freud takes it for granted that emotions are states at which one can look by turning one's attention inward. His position is the same as that of the introspectionist psychologists, who held that we know what we are feeling by 'looking within' and observing the 'experiences' that are there. Thus Freudian theory does not get off to a good start, but as I have tried to show, the confusions multiply once we begin to talk about *unconscious* mental states.

The theory and its dangers

One important aspect of the notion of the 'unconscious mind' is that memories can not only fade and be unreliable, but that they can be *repressed*. The inability to remember highly significant events is part and parcel of Freud's idea that therapy is a matter of 'making the unconscious conscious'. Motivated failure of memory is clearly a very different thing from ordinary difficulties in remembering. In the ordinary cases we may not have given sufficient attention to the relevant events in order to remember them clearly, or the passage of time and our changing circumstances and interests may make it hard to recall what happened many years ago. In addition, as psychologists have repeatedly demonstrated, our memories are liable to be influenced by how we would *like* to remember things, or by what we now take to be the facts of the remembered situation. Psychologists have known for a long time that autobiographical memory is not a straightforward reproductive process (Bartlett 1932/1995). As McNally (2003, p. 35) puts it: 'Recalling one's life is not like replaying a videotape of one's life in working memory.' McNally discusses how this misleading picture of the videotape gained popular credence partly from the work of Wilder Penfield, a neurosurgeon best known for his work in mapping the regions of the brain that are typically related to different functions. Penfield

> in the 1950s claimed to have discovered the 'anatomical record of the stream of consciousness' (1955: 68). Prior to performing surgery on epilepsy patients to cure their intractable seizures, he electrically stimulated their temporal cortex to identify where their convulsions originated. Much to his surprise, some of his patients reported remarkably vivid 'experiential flashbacks from the past' (1969: 150). He concluded that the brain contains a neuronal record akin to 'a strip of cinematographic film, on which are registered all those things of which the individual was once aware' (1955: p. 68).
>
> (McNally 2003, p. 37)

However, Penfield exaggerated his claims (McNally 2003, ibid.). Less than 10% of his patients reported any experiential responses. The rest reported sensory fragments such as hearing someone talking, a dog barking or a toilet flushing. 'Penfield thought these events were "reproductions of past experience" (Penfield & Perot 1963, p. 686), and because they were so trivial, he concluded that the brain must retain everything that was once in awareness.' Yet some 'remembered scenes' could not possibly have happened as they were described. For example, one woman saw herself as a 7-year-old girl walking through grass, but this was *from the perspective of an observer*. Penfield himself acknowledged that genuine autobiographical memory does not function like a cine film or video recorder, but he did maintain, with very little evidence, that there was a permanent, accurate and unchangeable record of conscious experience in the brain. His view was that conscious recall amounted to a selective reconstruction of what had been stored (McNally 2003, p. 37).

The picture of memories as being *stored* in the mind or brain draws its power from the wider picture of 'experiences' taking place 'in the mind'. We have already seen how misleading this picture is in the case of emotions, and in the next chapter I will discuss how much the same applies in the case of thoughts. So far as memory is concerned, the ordinary notion of 'memory' is that of a *retained ability* (Bennett & Hacker 2003, pp. 154–171). That ability *may* be associated with certain thoughts or images coming into one's mind, but one can remember without having any particular thoughts or images in one's mind. One has a certain experience, and then to a greater or less extent one retains the ability to say, or picture, what happened.

Neuroscientists have learned something of which brain systems, such as the amygdala, are involved in having this capacity (or rather capacities, since different systems may in involved in, say, short-term vs long-term memory). There are modern neuro-imaging studies that attempt to correlate brain activity with audio-taped scripts narrating traumatic events that patients suffered but

> interpreting this literature is not easy... results vary from study to study. Other than making general predictions regarding the activation of limbic

(emotional) regions of the brain, researchers have seldom been specific about the implications of their findings... It is a new field fraught with complex findings that are often not replicated and are difficult to interpret (see Uttal 2001). This is especially true when the investigations concern higher-level cognitive and emotional processes, such as remembering trauma. (McNally 2003, p. 152)

Altogether there seems little evidence for any *simple* correlation between what people remember and what goes on in their brains. But this should not be a surprise: remembering is the exercise of an ability, not the inspection of a stored image. The whole idea of *experiences* being *stored* comes from the background picture of experiences as mental events 'in the mind', which are then 'put away' in the preconscious, or repressed into the unconscious. Then this picture becomes further confused by the suggestion that the stored images in the mind have a physiological substratum in the brain. Just what the connections are between having the ability to remember something and the neurophysiological conditions which make it possible is something that remains to be established, but what does seem clear is that a plausible account of the connections won't involve anything like Penfield's 'cinematograph film in the brain'.

All this is very relevant to the question of the recall of traumatic memories. The popular picture of such recall is that memories have been laid down in the mind or brain, but that because they are intensely painful they are *repressed*, and are therefore inaccessible. In Freudian terms, they exist in the unconscious rather than in the preconscious, and can only be retrieved through therapy. It is held that in the course of therapy the memories come back in vivid, accurate detail. This is, of course, the video-recorder picture again, which we have seen can be highly misleading. Memories, according to everything that psychologists have learned, are *not* detailed, stored representations of past events. They are strongly influenced by current interests, wishful thinking and so on. Unless traumatic memories are a quite distinctive kind of memory, the images that come during the process of 'recall' can't be taken at face value to *be* memories. They *may* have some connection with past experiences, but they may well not.

The doubts we may reasonably have here have implications for some forms of therapy. Large numbers of psychological experiments show that it is disturbingly easy to instil *false* memories in experimental subjects (McNally 2003, pp. 72–77). Then the history of 'recovered memory therapy' in the 1980s and 1990s has led to serious doubts about whether many 'recovered memories' of child sexual abuse are genuine memories. In the *Brandon Report*, a set of training, practice, research and professional development recommendations, the United Kingdom's Royal College of Psychiatrists advised psychiatrists to avoid the use of any 'memory recovery techniques', citing a lack of evidence to support the accuracy of memories recovered in this way (Brandon et al. 1997).

Recovered memory therapy involves such procedures as hypnosis, guided imagery, dream work, body work (McNally 2003, pp. 6, 21), but it is just such procedures as these that are effective in generating false memories. This is a large and controversial area, with strong feelings on both sides, but several factors have contributed to increasing scepticism about 'recovered memories'. One is that following the earlier reports of such 'memories' of early sexual abuse, an increasing number of clients began to report incidents of abuse by satanic cults. Such abuse was not solely sexual; it often involved being forced to consume urine, blood and faeces, to worship the devil and even to participate in human sacrifices (ibid., p. 234). A prominent psychologist in the field of dissociative disorders, Corydon Hammond, developed a theory of multiple personality disorder according to which this syndrome often originates from ritual abuse (ibid., pp. 235–237).

A further development has been that of clients who report having been abducted and sometimes abused by space aliens. The Harvard psychiatrist John Mack (1994), in his study of this phenomenon, notes that most of the clients involved recover their memories under hypnosis, or other quasi-hypnotic processes of the same kind as those used in standard recovered memory therapy. It may seem incredible that significant numbers of people recover 'memories' of abduction, but the phenomenon becomes less surprising when we consider that false memories are inevitably related to the context of a client's beliefs, or of what they consider plausible. Polls in 1997 and 2000 revealed that 43% of Americans believe that unidentified flying objects (UFOs) are real, rather than products of the imagination; 30% believe that intelligent beings from other planets have visited the earth; and 17% believe that aliens have abducted human beings (Barkun 2003, p. 81). That part of the required belief-context is already in place. But the other element required is that clients need to believe that in the course of the therapeutic procedure images may come to them that constitute *memories* of abduction. Without the idea that the images must come from a memory store in the unconscious, and so can plausibly be taken *as* memories, the procedure could not work.

A third kind of context in which clients seem to recover questionable memories of past events is that of 'past life therapy'. The techniques for the recovery of such memories are the same as employed by other recovered-memory therapists, that is, hypnosis or the inducement of states of deep relaxation. My limited experience of this procedure suggests that almost anyone will produce 'memories of past lives' if guided appropriately towards remembering what happened before their birth. However, the psychiatrist Ian Stevenson, who devoted much of his life to the study of *spontaneous* cases of past-life recall (Stevenson 1973; Schroder 1999), was very sceptical about relying on recovered memory procedures, and never included such cases in his studies of 'past-life memories'. The Jungian analyst Roger Woolger (1988) was more sympathetic to the use of such procedures, but had an open mind as to whether such 'recovered memories' were genuine *memories,* rather than imaginative constructions that were therapeutically valuable for the client. For many people (e.g. McNally 2003, p. 245) the past-life cases of 'recovered memory' provide extra evidence of the fatuity of trusting 'memories' that arise during these forms of therapy, but as in the cases of sexual abuse and satanic abuse, the crucial point is that one simply can't judge from the images that come to the client, whether these are a *memory phenomenon* or not. One's judgement of whether they could be, in some cases, genuine memories has to depend on other considerations of how plausible the claims are, and not on the vividness, or felt convincingness, of the imagery. However, what has to be kept in mind is that while some 'recovered memories' could be genuine, it is an established fact that what seem to be memories can very easily be generated by the procedures used by the recovered-memory therapists.

What gives recovered memory therapy more plausibility than it deserves is the picture we have of repressed memories stored in the 'video recorder of the unconscious', and it is above all psychoanalytic theory, with its notion of the dynamic repression of unconscious contents that supports the picture. The theory, at least in its broad outline, is so familiar that many therapists will find it hard to suppose that it may be fundamentally flawed. Yet there seem to be good reasons for saying that that there is no such thing as 'repression' as understood in psychoanalysis. Sometimes we deceive ourselves, through making sure we don't give conscious attention to things that we nevertheless know. Sometimes we misremember things in ways that ensure that our memories fit better with what we want or believe. But there is no evidence that, after a traumatic event, images of the event, exactly as it occurred, are repressed into the unconscious, to remain there until, during therapy, they are drawn out again. Such recording of images in the mind or brain is just not the sort of thing that memory is. Clients themselves sometimes come to have doubts about their recovered 'memories'. Ost, Costall and Bull (2002), in a study of 20 people who later retracted their sexual abuse claims, report that the recovered memories usually seem 'different' from ordinary memories, and from memories of abuse which they already had. 'Some noted that recovered memories were abnormally clear and vivid and became more so with time, unlike normal memories that tend to fade with time' (McNally 2003, p. 258).

My conclusion is that the psychodynamic theory of the unconscious and of repression can lead to damaging therapeutic practice. It could be said that eliciting 'memories' of abduction by aliens is bizarre rather than damaging, but in the case of 'memories' of sexual abuse the situation is very different. There can be no doubt that child sexual abuse is distressingly common, but there is also no doubt that even subtle suggestions by therapists can result in clients seeming to remember things that never happened. Unlike the memories of alien abduction and ritual satanic abuse, some recovered memories of childhood abuse do emerge without the suggestions of therapists (ibid., p. 258), but that is not surprising, given the pervasiveness of the belief in the unconscious and repression. What does seem clear is that the explicit or implicit suggestions of the therapist, or simply the client's awareness of what the therapist believes, can play a significant role in the elicitation of false memories.

This is a serious matter, since in spite of what is sometimes said, it makes a big difference whether the memories are true or not. It makes a big difference to how the client relates to their alleged abuser, who is often a family member, and of course it has a huge impact on that family member. In the United States a group of accused parents set up the False Memory Syndrome Foundation

(FMSF) in 1992, and a similar organization, the British False Memory Society, was established a year later. These organizations provide support and advice to accused family members, and while some victims have filed legal suits against alleged abusers, others have initiated litigation against their former therapists (ibid., p. 257). An immense amount of pain is involved in all this, and at least some of the blame must be laid at the door of therapists who implicitly or explicitly convey to their clients that therapy involves retrieving repressed memories from the unconscious. Of course it is not the intention of these therapists to harm their clients; they say what they do because of their belief in the theory. Yet it is hard not to conclude that their belief in the theory may render them as deluded as those who have the misfortune to be their clients.

Summary

As in the case of person-centred therapy there is a common-sense core to psychodynamic practice that makes good sense without the elaborate structures of psychodynamic theory. In fact, there is a wide range of psychodynamic theories, associated with the different schools of psychoanalysis, but at their heart are Freud's notion of 'the unconscious' and of 'repression'.

However, these notions involve significant conceptual incoherence which parallels the incoherence found in Rogers' notion of 'incongruence'. Freud employs an essentially Cartesian notion of 'the mind', and his introduction of the notion of 'the unconscious mind' only adds to the confusion. As in the case of Rogers' theory these confusions are not merely of academic interest; they can lead to forms of practice, such as 'recovered memory therapy' which can be damaging to clients.

Chapter 6

Cognitive-Behavioural Therapy

Cognitive-behavioural therapy (CBT), as distinct from the earlier behaviour therapy discussed in Chapter 3, evolved through the incorporation of 'cognitive procedures' into psychotherapy. This development (sometimes referred to as 'second wave' CBT, as contrasted with the 'first wave' of behaviour therapy) occurred at roughly the same time as the consolidation of the 'cognitive revolution' in psychology, although the originators of cognitive therapy, Aaron Beck and Albert Ellis, did not come from a background in cognitive psychology; they were both trained in the psychoanalytic tradition. Ellis was influenced by Stoic philosophy, but there is also a strong common-sense aspect to their writings. Hofmann (2012, p. 4) remarks: 'Although Beck and Ellis are rightly credited for their pioneering work, the basic idea that gave rise to the new approach to psychotherapy is certainly not new. It could even be argued that it is simply common sense turned into practice.'

The central idea in the 'new approach' is that emotional disturbance arises from maladaptive thinking, so that if a client can change the way they think about their situation, therapeutic changes in feeling and behaviour will follow. The application of this idea in therapy leads to very different procedures from those employed in behaviour therapy, and CBT can probably best be seen as a loose combination of two approaches that are in themselves quite distinct.

The cognitive procedures of CBT

In the following brief account of CBT's cognitive techniques, I will draw mainly on the 'CT Practice' sections of Neenan and Dryden's book *Cognitive Therapy* (2004, pp. 47–219). Cognitive therapy typically begins with the client saying a little about their difficulties, and the therapist explaining roughly what the pattern of the sessions will be. The client is asked to list their problems, and the therapist discusses with them which problems should be prioritized. The therapist then suggests a re-framing of the problems in terms of more specific goals. For example, if the client's problem is that 'I feel disconnected from myself', the therapist will ask what would count in practice as 'being more connected', and the client might then say that they 'want to be more assertive at home in speaking up for what I want' (ibid., p. 65).

Much of cognitive therapy involves detailed exploration of how the client thinks about their situation, and the identification of places where their beliefs are unreasonable. The therapist may help the client to weigh the evidence for their beliefs; to consider alternative explanations of situations that the client has found to be distressing; to notice where their thinking is of an exaggerated or 'all-or-nothing' nature; or to examine to what extent their failures are due to circumstances, and to what extent they themself played a significant role in the outcome. To a large extent, one could say, cognitive therapy 'works' by challenging clients' beliefs, but that can't be quite the right way to put it. After all, as I will discuss in more detail later, it is quite possible to realize that one's beliefs are unreasonable while still feeling and responding in the same way as before. There is a difficulty with the *theory* here, but in practice I think that cognitive therapy evades the difficulty through mixing its rational examination of client beliefs with procedures that are familiar from behavioural therapy.

We can see that the cognitive procedures are not really employed on their own in examples such as the following (Beck 1976, p. 250):

Patient: I have to give a talk before my class tomorrow and I'm scared stiff.
Therapist: What are you afraid of?
P: I think I'll make a fool of myself.
T: Suppose you do ... make a fool of yourself ... why is that so bad?
P: I'll never live it down.
T: 'Never' is a long time ... Now look here, suppose they ridicule you. Can you die from it?
P: Of course not.
T: Suppose they decide you're the worst speaker that ever lived ... Will this ruin your future career?
P: No, but it would be nice if I could be a good speaker.

Thus far, the discussion follows purely rational lines, but it is not obvious that such a discussion will make any difference to what the client feels and does.

The session continues:

Therapist: So you're scaring yourself just as though your fate hangs in the balance.
Patient: That's right. It does feel as though my whole future is at stake.
Therapist: Now somewhere along the line, your thinking got fouled up ... and you tend to regard any failure as though it's the end of the world ... What you have to do is get your failures labelled correctly – as a failure to reach a goal, not as disaster. You have to start to challenge your wrong premises.

This is the point at which the therapist draws the client's attention to the 'cognitive model', but again it seems doubtful whether this 'information' will have any immediate impact on the client.

The student then proceeds to give his talk before the class; it is not a pleasant experience, but he survives. The therapist then coaches him 'in changing his notion that a failure is a catastrophe', and in the next session the student agrees that he had attached too much importance to what the reactions of his classmates might be. The session continues:

Patient: I felt much better during my last speech...I guess it's a matter of experience.
Therapist: Did you get some glimmer of the notion that it really isn't vital for the most part what people think of you
Patient: If I'm going to be a doctor, I've got to make a good impression on my patients.
Therapist: Whether you're a good doctor depends on how well you diagnose and treat your patients, not on how good you are at public speaking.
Patient: Well, I know I'm good with patients – and I guess that's what counts.

Part of what is going on here seems little different from what goes on in behavioural therapy. Through his early discussion with the therapist the student's fear of speaking in front of the class probably diminishes a little, partly perhaps from experiencing the sympathy and support of the therapist, and partly perhaps from attending to aspects of his response that are usually swamped by his fear; he comes to acknowledge, for example, that he won't die or have his career ruined by a poor performance. It is hard here to distinguish between his responses and his view of things; they are bound up with one another. He says, 'It does feel as though my whole future is at stake', yet if closely questioned would no doubt deny that he 'really' believes this. Beck says that 'Somewhere along the line, your thinking got fouled up', but it seems more plausible to say that somewhere along the line the student's emotional responses came to deviate from his beliefs. As in the case of the person who is scared of spiders, the student finds himself responding in a way that, on reflection, he thinks is irrational. I will discuss this kind of point further below, but I don't think that our understanding of what is happening in Beck's example depends crucially on whether we see emotional response as arising from beliefs, or whether we see the beliefs as an articulated expression of emotional response. And the student's own remark 'I guess it's a matter of experience' seems to be a better account of what has been helpful than any account which sees the change as being due to a change in beliefs.

The common-sense core

Without delving into theory I think we might understand what is happening in this sort of situation in the following way:

First, the therapist helps the client to clarify what exactly he is afraid of; this part of the procedure is not very different from what would be done in person-centred therapy. A blank terror of speaking in class comes to be articulated as a fear of being ridiculed (and then following this realization, the student might be able to act differently, perhaps through deliberately including some jokes in his presentation).

Second, the student allows himself to experience the frightening situation and, encountering no ridicule, finds his fear diminished to some extent. We can understand this part of the example in the way that we understand behavioural procedures, but we can also see the verbal interaction with the therapist in a similar way: the student's response to the prospect of the class presentation is one of fear of an extremely dangerous situation, but the therapist presents the situation in a different light, which the student shares to some extent. In effect, they agree that the reality is that nothing very drastic will happen, and that the student's reaction is an irrational one – 'somewhere along the line something got fouled up'. Part of what is happening here is that the therapist is exposing the student to the reality of the situation, and this exposure continues when the student gives his talk. If someone should ask 'Why should exposure to the reality of things make a difference to how one responds?' it would be hard to find an answer. This is something that seems to be very deeply rooted in our ordinary understanding of things. Perhaps all that can be said is that beings whose responses were not normally affected by the realities they encounter would be very different from us.

It seems then that in CBT there may often be two things going on. To some extent it is a matter of helping the client to clarify and articulate what their responses really are (e.g. 'I'm really scared of something...I'm scared of...ridicule...that's what it is'), as is done in person-centred therapy, in focusing-oriented therapy and also in psychodynamic therapy when a therapist makes a tentative interpretation of what a client really feels. However, the other element in CBT is that of helping the client to *respond* differently in the situation, through facilitating exposure to what client and therapist agree to be the reality of the situation. That element in CBT belongs with the procedures of behavioural therapy.

It may nevertheless be a mistake to try to separate the 'cognitive' and 'affective'/'behavioural' aspects of CBT too sharply. What often seems to be involved is that the therapist helps the client to engage and grapple with their situation, whether this is done through the effort to articulate their felt response (as in person-centred therapy) or to respond to their situation in a way that is appropriate to their articulation of it (as in behaviour therapy). At one end of the spectrum are cases where, for example, a client first comes to acknowledge that they tend to be 'pushy' with people, and then further articulates their 'pushy' responses as 'wanting people to notice them more'; then following that realization they become able to act in a way that achieves their aim more effectively. At the other end are cases where, for example, the client first *acts* differently by bringing themselves to touch a model of a spider, and then finds themselves more able to say wholeheartedly, 'spiders are not dangerous'. What CBT fundamentally involves, I suggest, is the effort to help the client integrate their felt responses with their view of how they are in their situation. A wholehearted engagement with one's situations involves healing the split between 'how I feel' and 'how things are', but in some cases it is more a matter of adapting one's felt response to one's view of the way things really are (increased attention to one's view that 'spiders are not really dangerous' helps one to approach them), while in other cases it is more a matter of adapting one's view of how things are to the reality of one's felt responses (increased attention to one's pushiness helps one to articulate it first *as* 'pushiness' and then as 'wanting people to notice me more'). I will discuss further the notion of 'integrating response with view' in Chapter 11; for the moment I would simply suggest that it is a notion that does not go far beyond common sense.

My discussion has for simplicity centred on 'classical' or 'second wave' CBT. However, modern forms (the so-called 'third wave') of CBT (Neenan & Dryden 2004; Hofmann 2012) have incorporated much of person-centred practice, so that now in addition to the earlier techniques there is a strong emphasis on listening, empathy and generally relating to the client in a warm and personal way. The 'third wave' also includes variants of CBT that emphasize giving attention to one's responses in a mindful way (Segal et al. 2002), rather as is done in focusing-oriented therapy, and also variants that explicitly focus on the therapeutic relationship (Swales & Heard 2008), as is characteristic of the psychodynamic and (later) person-centred schools. As Hofmann (2012, p. 12) remarks: 'Today, CBT is an umbrella term that includes many different empirically supported therapies.' This seems to me to be a welcome development that fits well with common sense, although it takes CBT a long way from its theoretical roots in behavioural learning theory and cognitive psychology. The current developments also make it increasingly hard both to criticize and to defend 'CBT' effectively: it is no longer clear just what it is that one is criticizing or defending.

The combination of cognitive and behavioural elements in CBT also makes it difficult to speak about 'CBT theory', since there are *two* theories in the background of the approach, and these theories are very different from one another. I have already discussed behaviourist theory in Chapter 3, so it remains now to consider cognitive theory.

Cognitive theory and its confusions

Cognition: Beliefs, thoughts and perceptions

A few remarks are necessary first about 'cognition'. This is more of a psychologist's or philosopher's term than a word used in everyday contexts, but it is clearly linked with cognizing or knowing. The *Shorter Oxford English Dictionary* defines the word as 'the action or faculty of knowing'. Perhaps the central idea in cognitive therapy is that human emotion and behaviour have a cognitive dimension. This fits with what I have said earlier (in Chapters 4 and 5) – that to experience an emotion is not essentially a matter of having bodily feelings, though these may be present; it is more a matter of seeing one's situation in a certain way, as when in being jealous one sees someone else being preferred to oneself, or in feeling proud one sees oneself as having done something good. But one can only see oneself in a certain way if one has the concepts that are involved in seeing things that way. One couldn't be jealous without having some concepts of human relationship and of preferment. 'Concept' – at least in this sense – is another word that perhaps belongs more to psychology and philosophy than to everyday speech, but I think it would not be a departure from everyday language to say that a person having the concept of something – say, *preferment* – is a way of saying that they know what preferment is; they can recognize it when they come across it, they can draw attention to it, they can reflect on whether *this* is a case of it or not.

It seems to be incontestable that cognition (having concepts, knowing what things are) runs through much of human life. Emotion involves cognition; so, obviously, do belief and thought. So does perception, at least in the case of seeing something *as* something. One can't be said to see something as a wind-sock, or as an intrusion, or as a mistake, unless one knows what wind-socks, intrusions or mistakes are. 'Cognition' needs to be understood as meaning *having knowledge*, and especially the kind of knowledge that is involved in having concepts, the knowing of what's what.

This is a little different from how cognitive theory understands cognition, and I think some confusion can arise from not appreciating the difference. Ellis and Beck hold that the essential idea in cognitive theory is that found in the thought of the Stoic philosopher Epictetus: 'It is not how things are that are important for us, but how we see them.' Cognitive theory develops this idea by suggesting that troubled behaviour arises from our not seeing things straight, or from our having irrational thoughts and beliefs, so that if our way of seeing things can be straightened out, or if we can reframe our irrational thoughts and beliefs, then we will no longer be troubled. However, if it is put like that, it seems that there is already a difficulty: is it what we *believe* that is crucial, or what we *think*, or how we *see* things? These notions are different, and as I will try to show, the differences are critical for a cognitive theory of therapy.

Cognitive theory proposes that emotional disturbance arises from ways of thinking that are in some way distorted or irrational. Three levels of thinking are often distinguished (Neenan & Dryden 2004). There is first the level of *negative automatic thoughts*. These are thoughts that go through a person's mind when they are distressed, such as 'I'm clumsy', 'I'm always late'. These thoughts are often formulated in words, though Beck (1976, pp. 37–38) holds that emotional distress may also involve mental *imagery*. A client's attention can be brought to such thoughts by asking 'What was going through your mind at the time?' Next there is the level of *underlying assumptions* such as 'I'm nothing if I am not loved' or 'I can't ask for help'. Finally, there are *core beliefs* which are very general and unconditional. Examples would be 'Everything is against me', 'I'm worthless'. The central idea of cognitive therapy is that what needs to change is the client's core beliefs. The therapist attempts to bring about the change by first drawing the client's attention to their negative automatic thoughts. When these have been challenged and the client has accepted that they are irrational, the therapist helps the client to appreciate that the thoughts arise from unreasonable assumptions, and that those assumptions are embedded in core beliefs that are themselves highly questionable. Once the client can begin to reformulate their core beliefs, their underlying assumptions will change, and their emotional distress will be relieved.

As McEachrane (2009) points out, one difficulty with this analysis is that it identifies *what a person thinks* with certain thoughts that go through their mind. Yet to think that one is worthless, for example, is not essentially a matter of having the thought 'I'm worthless' go through one's mind. It is rather a matter of one's whole way of responding to situations. McEachrane quotes an example from Judith Beck of a student client who feels upset while walking to her class that morning. The therapist asks what was going through her mind at that moment, and the client says she had been looking at the other students talking, playing frisbee, hanging out on the lawn and that what went through her mind was 'I'll never be like them'. The therapist then identifies this as an automatic thought, and continues:

> What we'll do is to teach you to identify your automatic thoughts and then to evaluate them to see just how accurate they are. For example, in a minute we'll evaluate the thought, 'I'll never be like those students'. What do you think would happen to your emotions if you discovered that your thought wasn't true – that when your depression lifts you'll realise that you *are* like the other students? (Beck, J.S. 1995, p. 78)

One thing that can be confusing here is that when the therapist asks the client what was going through her mind, and the client says 'I'll never be like them', it may well not have been true that *that thought*, formulated in words or images, went through her mind at the time. When she says that this was what 'went through her mind', she is more likely to be expressing a feeling of sadness and resignation: that was how it *felt to her* at that moment.

To *think that I will never be like them* is not essentially a matter of having that thought go through one's mind; it is a matter of feeling and responding in a certain way. We have seen in earlier chapters that to have an emotion is not a matter of having any particular inner experience, but the same applies to thinking, realizing and recognizing. The philosopher Norman Malcolm (1977, p. 52) writes:

> You and I notice, for example, that Robinson is walking in a gingerly way, and you ask why. I reply, 'Because he realises that the path is slippery.' I do not imply that the proposition 'This path is slippery' crossed his mind. Another example: I wave at a man across the quad. Later on I may say to someone, 'I saw Kasper today'. It may be true that I recognised Kasper, but not true that I thought to myself, 'That is Kasper'.

Realizing, recognizing and thinking are not a matter of having thoughts in one's mind, in the sense of being aware of particular words or images. As Malcolm puts it, we need to distinguish 'thinking that' from 'having thoughts'. A self-confident person can *think that they are great* without having the thought 'I am great' pass through their mind. Hence insofar as cognitive therapy directs its attention to negative thoughts, it seems to be aiming at the wrong target. What is important is 'what the client thinks' (e.g. that they are worthless), and not what thoughts they have, that is what words or images pass through their mind.

A second source of confusion here is that in everyday usage there is little difference between 'thinking I am worthless' and 'feeling I am worthless'. These both express an attitude to oneself, a way of being in the world. Neither can be elucidated in terms of words or images passing through the mind, or in terms of sensations felt in the body. Thinking that it will rain tomorrow amounts to much the same as feeling that it will rain, sensing that it will rain, having a hunch that it will rain, and what all these involve is an attitude towards the weather tomorrow, and certain inclinations to behave in ways that are seen as appropriate to a rainy day. It is a matter of how one is *responding* to the situation. *Believing* that it will rain tomorrow is different: it *could* perhaps be taken as equivalent to thinking/feeling/sensing that it will rain, but more typically, if someone says that they *believe* that it will rain they are not expressing an attitude, but asserting something for which they will normally be prepared to give reasons. Then the question can arise of whether their reasons are good reasons, and if they are not, then the belief will be seen as unreasonable. By contrast, to think, feel, sense, have a hunch that it will rain does not open one to questions about what is reasonable, since one is simply expressing one's response: If challenged, one might say 'Well, it's just a thought (impression, feeling, hunch)'. One couldn't in the same way say 'It's just a belief that I have'. Responses such as feelings, impressions and hunches may be said to be *irrational*, but that is not to say that the person's reasons are inadequate; it is to say that reasoning is not involved.

There is a big difference between an irrational response and an unreasonable belief (Hacker 2007, p. 200). We could speak of an unreasonable belief if a client said something like

> I know that there are no native species of poisonous spiders in Britain, but sometimes poisonous spiders from abroad are brought to this country on ships, and it is hard to know whether any particular spider is one of these. And even if this is not one of the known poisonous ones, there are almost certainly poisonous spider species that have not yet been identified, so one really can't be sure.

This argument doesn't seem very reasonable, and the appropriate way of responding would be to point out how weak the reasoning is; for example, by drawing attention to the statistics on poisonous spiders reaching Britain, or the improbability of there being totally unknown and poisonous species among these. Such a conversation would involve a debate about the reasonableness of the client's beliefs; it would involve the therapist arguing with the client and trying to convince them that they were wrong. But that is not at all how it is with a client who has a spider phobia; they don't have an unreasonable belief that can be argued with. Their *beliefs* are reasonable – they know very well that spiders in Britain are not dangerous – but they do have an irrational response.

How we perceive or respond to things may *clash* with what we believe, as is obvious in the case of visual perception. In the visual illusion known as the Müller-Lyer we see, or spontaneously respond to, the two main lines of the figures as unequal in length, but once we have measured them we come to believe that they are equal. Yet, importantly, coming to believe that they are equal does nothing to change how we perceive them, or our spontaneous response to them. Similarly, coming to believe that spiders are not dangerous may do nothing to change one's *perception* of them as dangerous.

In the example above, in which the client 'thinks that she will never be like them', the therapist proposes to target this 'automatic thought', to evaluate it for its reasonableness. However, in much cognitive therapy it seems to be not so much automatic thoughts that are the primary target of therapy, but rather the underlying assumptions or 'core beliefs'. A cognitive therapist might agree that the client who 'thinks she will never be like them' need never have that thought in her mind, but does she not *believe* that she will never be like them? Suppose we ask her whether she really believes it, and she replies 'I don't know – but that's how it feels.' A therapist like Ellis would challenge her way of expressing herself. For example, in the case of a man who says he 'feels that there is something rotten about himself', Ellis (1994, pp. 32–33) tries to get him to say that this is what he *believes*, but the client resists:

> I know I'm doing better of course, and I'm sure it's because of what's gone on here in these sessions. And I'm pleased and grateful to you. But I still basically feel the same way – that there's something really rotten about me, something I can't do anything about, and that the others are able to see. And I don't know what to do about this feeling.
>
> 'But this "feeling" as you call it, is largely your *belief* – do you see that?'
>
> 'How can my feeling be a belief? I really – uh – *feel* it. That's all I can describe it as, a feeling.'

Ellis seems not to consider the possibility that there is a real difference between *feeling* that one is rotten and *believing* that one is rotten, and that the client is perfectly well able to make this distinction. Likewise, Beck has a policy of trying to get clients to substitute 'I believe ... ' for 'I feel ... : "It is desirable for the cognitive therapist to get an early start in making appropriate translations of 'I feel' into 'You believe'" (Beck et al. 1979, p. 37).

I think that clients are right to resist such 'translations'; their sense of how the language works here is in fact better than that of the cognitive therapists. (This is not really surprising, since the client is simply using language in an ordinary way, whereas the therapist's use of language is likely to be contaminated by their theory.) There *is* an important distinction between feeling that one is a rotten person and believing that one is a rotten person. It is this distinction that Ellis' client rightly wants to make. Ellis' session with the client continues as follows:

> 'How can my feeling be a belief? I really – uh – feel it. That's all I can describe it as, a feeling?'

'Yes, but you feel it *because* you believe it. If you believed, for example, really believed you were a fine person, in spite of all the mistakes you have made and may still make in life, and in spite of anyone else, such as your parents, thinking that you were not so fine; if you really *believed* this, would you then feel fundamentally rotten?'

'Oh. Hmm. No, I guess you're right; I guess I then wouldn't feel that way.'

The client doesn't sound altogether convinced by what the therapist says. When clients say 'I guess you're right', this is often client-speak for 'You're wrong, but I'm not sure why'. Nevertheless, we can understand why the client hesitates. There does seem to be *something* in the suggestion that if the client really believed that he was a fine person, then he wouldn't feel fundamentally rotten. But I think this is because the therapist says 'if you *really* believed this'. 'Really believing' is often used in contexts where one not only believes something but is prepared to act on it. The spider phobic *believes* that spiders are not dangerous (that is a view that they would assert, and argue for), but if pressed to say whether they *really* believe it, they might hesitate. They might say that they believe it in an intellectual way, but don't wholeheartedly believe it. In the normal course of events, what I have been calling our *view* and our *response* coincide, but in therapeutic contexts the two can come apart. Hence it is unsurprising that in these contexts we may not quite know what to say. The therapy context often requires us to distinguish between *view* and *response*, but everyday language is oriented towards the normal case where they are not separate. Yet we do have everyday linguistic resources for this sort of situation: for example, we may distinguish between 'intellectually believing' and 'really believing', or between 'believing that' and 'merely feeling that'.

It may be true that if Ellis' client *really* believed he was a fine person he would not feel that he was a rotten person, but that is because '*really* believing that one is a fine person' *includes* having a particular sort of attitude or response, a particular way of engaging with life; a way that is clearly incompatible with 'feeling that one is a rotten person'. I think that in the extracts quoted above, Ellis shifts from the notion of 'believing' to '*really* believing'. In the first extract, the therapist speaks of believing: 'But this "feeling" as you call it is largely your *belief* [this intellectual belief that you have, that you are a rotten person] – do you see that?' The client rejects this suggestion, saying in effect that he *doesn't* have that belief; rather, he just has a feeling. However, in the second extract the therapist speaks of 'really believing': 'If you really *believed* this, would you then feel fundamentally rotten?' And the client naturally acknowledges that in *that* sense of 'believe', which means something like 'see himself as rotten, take himself to be rotten, feel himself to be rotten', he *does* believe he is rotten. And of course he also finds it hard to resist the suggestion that if he didn't believe he was rotten (in that sense of 'really believe') he wouldn't *feel* rotten. That is right, but only because there is no significant difference between 'feels he is rotten' and 'believes he is rotten' in the sense of 'really believes'. It is *not* because his feeling is caused by his belief, and it follows that there is no reason to suppose that getting him to change his (intellectual) belief will result in a change in his feelings. As I mentioned in Chapter 3, there is indeed some research evidence against the hypothesis that therapeutic changes in CBT result from its cognitive interventions. See Jacobson et al. (1996) and McLeod (2009, p. 161).

Some cognitive therapists would say that cognitive therapy is not really a matter of therapists engaging in rational debates with clients. In a radio interview in 2003, Beck is on record as saying that teaching clients rationality in problem-solving is 'really an over-statement of what we really do.... Cognitive therapy is also an experiential type of treatment... in that experience itself will reshape their beliefs if they [clients] will only open up the channels for new learning' (Neenan & Dryden 2004, p. 46). This echoes the remark of Beck's student client that I quoted above, where after managing to give his talk to the class he says, 'I guess it's a matter of experience'. However, I am not at all clear how Beck sees this as fitting with the basic principle that it is beliefs that are primary in cognitive therapy, or the fact that cognitive therapists *do* engage in rational debate with clients:

> By treating maladaptive cognitions as hypotheses, patients are put into the role of observers – scientists or detectives... In order to challenge these thoughts, therapist and patient discuss the evidence for and against a particular assumption in a debate. (Hofmann 2012, p. 30)

Assuming that the client actually is helped by such interventions the crucial question, so far theory goes, is whether this happens because the client comes to change their beliefs, and whether this change in their beliefs results in changes in how they see and respond to their situation. The alternative view of how the interventions are effective is the one I mentioned earlier: that what the cognitive therapist is doing is exposing the client to the reality of things; according to that view the change process is not essentially different from those that occur in other kinds of 'exposure' therapy. The therapist could be seen not as debating with the client about the unreasonableness of their belief system, but as emphatically confronting the client with the 'hard reality' of their situation. Ellis (1973, p. 185) writes that the therapist

> quickly pins the client down to a few basic irrational ideas which motivate most of his disturbed behaviour; he challenges the client to validate these ideas; he shows them that they are extralogical premises which cannot be validated; he logically analyses these ideas and makes mincemeat of them.

This is hardly reasoned debate, and any effectiveness it has, I suspect, comes less from reason than from a kind of dramatic exposure to what the client already knows.

The problem for the cognitive approach remains that the person who is irrationally scared of spiders *doesn't have* a belief that spiders are dangerous; that is what makes their fear response an irrational one, and why they seek help. But if that is right, it is hard to see how the basic hypothesis of cognitive theory, that feelings are caused by beliefs, could be a helpful one, even if it were true. The *practices* of cognitive therapy can be helpful, but that helpfulness can't be understood in terms of cognitive theory.

The conflation of 'cognitive schemas' with beliefs

The development of cognitive therapy can be seen partly as an aspect of the general move in psychology away from behaviourism in the 1950s and 1960s. This thoroughgoing re-thinking of psychology has become known as the 'cognitive revolution', and has drawn on work in many different disciplines, including computer science, artificial intelligence, linguistics, anthropology and neuroscience. A survey of this development is provided in Howard Gardner, in his book *The Mind's New Science: A History of the Cognitive Revolution* (1987). Gardner suggests that what is central to the new cognitive science is the idea of 'mental representations' (p. 383). The failure of behaviourism is seen as being due to the fact that one can't account for human activities simply by considering externally observable 'stimuli' and 'responses'; one needs also to make reference to 'internal' factors, such as how the person or animal perceives or understands the situation. 'Internal' here doesn't mean *anatomically* internal. Cognitive science is not concerned with the neurophysiological level of explanation but with 'schemas' or 'mental models' that are hypothesized in order to make sense of behaviour. The analogy is often drawn with computers: in order to understand what a computer is doing, one doesn't go down to the level of electronic changes in the processing chips of the computer, but thinks at the level of the computer *program*. Talk of 'cognitive processes' is held to be analogous to programming talk, not electronics talk. Thus 'cognitive processes' are not 'internal' in the sense that brain processes are internal, but nor are they internal in the sense that the introspectionist psychologists were concerned with. For the introspectionists, the idea was that one could observe (introspect) one's inner mental processes. These processes were held to be there at the observational level, whereas the 'mental processes' of cognitive science have a hypothetical, explanatory role.

The notion of cognitive 'representations' can take the form of talk about schemas, scripts, frames, mental models and so on, but this whole way of thinking remains controversial. Gardner, who is generally sympathetic to the project of cognitive science, writes (ibid., p. 384): 'If representation is indeed the lynchpin of cognitive science, it must ultimately be stated as clearly, and accepted as widely, as quantum theory in physics or the genetic code of biological science. Such clarity and consensus seem a long way off.' One criticism of cognitive science has been that it places far too much emphasis on 'cognition', at the expense of other factors such as (p. 387) 'the role of the surrounding context, the affective aspects of experience, and the effects of cultural and historical factors on human behaviour and thought'. Gardner continues (pp. 387–388):

Scholars differ widely from one another in their intuitions about the extent to which these other factors may ultimately engulf cognitive factors. From the perspective of a philosopher like Hubert Dreyfus, a linguist like Roy Harris, a psychologist like Benny Shanon, or an anthropologist like Clifford Geertz, these factors are so important, so constitutive of human experience, that they, rather than cognitive factors, ought to be regarded as primary.

An important distinction needs to be made at this point. Cognitive therapy does not in fact draw much on cognitive science for its main ideas. Cognitive therapy and cognitive science developed at roughly the time in the 1970s, in a shared *zeitgeist* in which the emphasis was on 'cognition', but the two writers who are usually seen as the originators of cognitive therapy, Albert Ellis and Aaron Beck, did not come from cognitive science backgrounds. They came from psychoanalysis. Their approach, and their theories, arose in reaction to their earlier psychoanalytic views, and their central idea is that in understanding people and their difficulties we need to emphasize people's 'cognitions', that is, what they know, believe and think, how they 'see' things. However, *this kind of talk about 'cognitions' is not the same as cognitive science talk about 'representations' or 'cognitive schemas'*, since 'representations' and 'schemas' are theoretical notions, whereas 'beliefs' and 'thoughts' belong to the level of ordinary language. We may explain a person's behaviour in terms of their beliefs, but that is a different kind of explanation from one in which a cognitive psychologist gives a theoretical explanation in terms of a 'cognitive schema'. Sometimes cognitive therapists run together the notions of 'schemas' and '(core) beliefs' (De Rubeis et al. 2010, p. 280; Hofmann 2012, pp. 2–3, 21), but this can only lead to confusion.

It is important to see that there are two distinct accounts of psychological disturbance here. The first account holds that psychological disturbance originates in distorted thoughts and beliefs, and this account can be criticized, as I have done above, through an investigation of what we actually mean by 'thinking' and 'believing'. Such criticism need make no reference at all to the theoretical conceptions of cognitive science. The second account draws on the *theoretical* notion of cognitive schemas, and criticism needs to be directed at *that* notion. Such criticism is relevant to CBT insofar as in thinking about CBT a theorist *does* invoke the notion of cognitive schemas. The discussion here will also be relevant to the theory of process-experiential therapy (PET), which draws heavily on the notion of 'cognitive *schemes*'; these 'schemes', as we shall see in Chapter 7, have much in common with 'cognitive *schemas*', so that the discussion here will be relevant later in connection with PET.

The notion of a 'schema' was first used in psychology by Jean Piaget in his work on child psychology and by Frederic Bartlett (1932) in his work on memory. However, the notion has its roots further back, in the philosophy of Immanuel Kant (Nevid 2007). Kant's view was that human knowledge is not built up simply on the basis of sense experience, but nor does it arise entirely from reasoning. Rather, it arises through a 'filtering' of pre-conceptual experience through schemas of thought that determine what can count as a *possible* experience. Kant held that the world *in itself* – which he calls the 'noumenon' – has no determinate structure; the structure is imposed rather by the categories that are inherent in the mind. Social constructionist views of knowledge can be seen as a relativistic variant of this position, in which Kant's 'necessary categories' are replaced by the social categories of particular cultures. The important point for our purposes is the idea that in trying to understand human knowledge and behaviour we need to consider not just what comes to us through the senses, but also the schemas in terms of which we organize this sensory input.

Kant pictures the world as an undifferentiated noumenon about which nothing can be said. It is then given structure by the categories imposed by the human mind. Whether this picture really makes any sense has been the subject of intensive philosophical debate since Kant's time, with some thinkers arguing that the noumenon plays no real role in a Kantian view of things; it should therefore be rejected, leaving us simply with our culturally relative interpretations. There would then be *only* the interpretations, and no reality *of which* they are interpretations. A different suggestion is that the idea of reality as an undifferentiated substratum of things is a muddle, and that the perceived structures of our world are, as most people assume, really there. This debate between 'anti-realists' and 'realists' continues and lies in the background of some contemporary discussion of psychotherapy theory. Much of such theory rests on realist assumptions, but is increasingly challenged by anti-realist social constructionist arguments. But also there are views that return to something like the original Kantian position, in which there is a dialectical interaction between 'pre-conceptual experiencing' and 'concepts' or 'schemas'. Examples are the dialectical constructivist view of PET, to be discussed in Chapter 7, and Gendlin's 'process model'.

To some extent cognitive science has a Kantian orientation, since it employs the notion of schemas through which our experience is filtered, yet at heart it is a realist theory that thinks of the schemas ultimately as 'models in the brain'. The central difficulty here is that of what exactly a 'schema' is supposed to be. In Bartlett's (1932) original work, he gave the following example of a schema: Participants in an experiment were asked to read a folk-tale and to recall it at intervals, up to a year later. The recalled versions of the story increasingly departed from the original in ways that reflected the participants' cultural expectations. For example, information that seemed irrelevant was omitted, there was a shift in emphasis and focus according to what seemed important to the participant, details that did not make sense were rationalized so as to make them more comprehensible, and the content and style were modified so as to be more consistent with the cultural background of the participant. Bartlett's way of summarizing these findings was to say that participants imposed their cultural schemas on the story that they had originally read. That is a useful way of understanding why people's memories of the same event are often divergent, but it is another matter if we now picture a participant as having a schema in their mind (or brain) which has causal effects on 'incoming stimuli'. To explain that a person remembers the story in a particular way 'because of his particular cultural schema' is to draw attention to that person's cultural background and exhibit how it relates to those parts of the story that have been modified or transformed. That explanation does not require talk of internal models in the mind or brain.

The notion of internal models, programs, schemas or maps in the mind or brain seems to be fundamentally confused. Each of these terms suggests an analogy that might function as an explanation of behaviour, but none of the analogies are workable. In Chapter 3, I referred to the work of Tolman who experimented with rats finding their way through mazes, and to Tolman's conclusion that the results could not be explained by conditioning theory. Instead, he suggested, the rats must have formed a mental map of the maze, and this idea was one of the starting points for the cognitive revolution. But what does it mean to say that the rat has formed a mental map of the maze? One way of understanding the statement is as a metaphorical way of saying that the rat now knows how to find its way round the maze. *That* is what is has learned; it is not, as the behaviourists held, that its movements have been conditioned in a particular way. There is no problem about the statement, understood in *that* way – we might similarly say of someone who knows Hastings well, that they 'carry a map of Hastings in their head'. However, cognitive science understands talk about 'mental maps' in a different way. It understands 'mental map' as a theoretical term which refers to an 'inner structure'. Whether the structure is in the mind or in the brain is left indeterminate, perhaps because the drift of cognitive science is towards *identifying* 'mind' with 'brain'. The analogy with a map would suggest that the animal (or its brain?) makes use of the map in finding its way through the maze. But the analogy can't work because in following a real map one is *interpreting* the marks on the paper (Bennett & Hacker 2003, pp. 76–81, 387–388). A map is a conventional device that involves a background of agreed rules that establish what each mark is to mean. (Consider here the fact that what *projection* a map uses may be crucial in making use of it.) But the traces allegedly laid down in the brain can't be interpreted by the rat, and equally it makes no sense to suggest that they are interpreted by other parts of the rat's brain. People, and possibly rats, can interpret what they see (though rats can't interpret *maps*), but brain parts can't be said to interpret anything, and neither rats nor people can interpret what goes on in their own brains.

Understood like this, the notion of a 'map in the brain' clearly falls apart, but how else can it be understood? Perhaps in causal terms, so that what is being suggested now is that as a result of running around in the maze certain changes are brought about in the rat's brain, and these constitute the 'map'. Now it seems undoubtedly true that the rat's brain and nervous system will be causally altered through its running about in the maze, probably in very complex ways. Without there being such changes the rat would no doubt be unable to find its way through the maze, but what point is there in calling the changes a *map*? The point of the map analogy was to suggest that brain states might form a representation of the world, but mere causal consequences are not a representation. The varying thicknesses of tree rings are causal consequences of annual climatic factors, but they are not *representations* of climate factors. Representations require social agreement on the *rules* for representing things.

The same kind of objection can be brought against speaking of models, scripts or programs in the brain. The notion of programs in the brain has been especially influential since cognitive science grew up along with the development of computer technology. The notion of a program in the brain may seem a little more plausible than the notion of a map, since there does seem to be a clear sense in which 'information' is stored in a computer. When information is stored in the computer it is not just that there are changes in the digital circuits of the computer, and it is not those changes, considered simply as physical changes, that constitute the stored information. The level of analysis on which we speak of a stored program is not the physical level, but a functional level where we classify changed computer states in terms of what they do, or how they function, in the overall use of the computer. Hence, it might be said, it is the stored *program* in the computer that corresponds to a stored 'schema' in an animal or person. However, this analogy can't work, for the same general reason that the map analogy can't work. The notion of a computer program belongs in a context in which people write computer programs, in accordance with conventionally agreed computer languages, in order to carry out certain tasks. The program is stored in the computer in the sense that the computer is being used by people in a certain way, for certain human purposes. It is this whole context that is missing if we try to think about 'programs' in the brain. The relevant changes in the brain are not being used by people, in accordance with agreed rules, to store information; they are simply the physiological changes involved when people remember things.

These issues deserve more discussion than there is space for here, but they have been discussed at greater length by others. I would refer the interested reader to Dreyfus & Dreyfus (1986) *What Computers Still Can't Do*, David Hamlyn *In and Out of the Black Box* (1990), and Bennett & Hacker's *Philosophical Foundations of Neuroscience* (2003).

The theory and its dangers

In this section I will first draw attention to two specific ways in which cognitive theory can mislead us when we think about therapy. Then I will discuss briefly the wider implications of approaching therapy from a cognitive standpoint.

The mind-set of cognitive therapy seems to encourage some writers on CBT to say things that are simply not true. For example, in a recent book Stefan Hofmann (2012, p. 5) writes:

> The central notion of CBT is simple. It is the idea that our behavioral and emotional responses are strongly influenced by our cognitions (i.e. thoughts), which determine how we perceive things. That is, we are only anxious, angry or sad if we think we have reason to be anxious, angry or sad.

Yet, as we have seen, how we think (in the sense of what we believe) *doesn't* determine how we perceive things, and the typical kinds of emotional difficulties with which CBT is concerned are often precisely those where we are anxious, angry or sad, yet *don't* think we have reason to be so. If we adopt the position of the cognitive theorists then, like Ellis and Beck, we will continually be trying to manoeuvre clients into saying things that they (rightly) don't want to say. This will inevitably interfere with the process of therapy: how can a client find an adequate way of expressing what they feel, if the therapist for dubious *theoretical* reasons keeps challenging their way of putting things?

Another consequence of a cognitive therapy mind-set is that it can lead to the fabrication of thoughts and beliefs which the client simply doesn't have. This is especially clear in Ellis's ABC account, in which A is an 'activating event' such as the appearance of a spider, and C is the emotional 'consequence', such as fear. Ellis maintains that A-events don't cause C-events directly, but only via B-events, which are the person's beliefs, such as the belief that spiders are dangerous. However, 'B' may also stand for *blank* because in some cases it seems that the emotional reaction *does* follow directly from the activating event, without the person having any intervening thoughts or beliefs. Ellis's view is that in these cases the intervening thoughts are still there, in the 'blank', but they happen so quickly and automatically that the person is not aware of them (Hofmann 2012, p. 6). This seems a clear case of fabrication. The idea that the person *must* have had such thoughts comes not from the facts of the situation but from the misleading theoretical picture of it. (One source of confusion here involves the point I made above, that cognitive theory to some extent draws on cognitive psychology's *theoretical, explanatory* notion of a 'schema', but at the same time talks about *thoughts and beliefs* which are not theoretical explanatory notions. A *schema* is not the *sort* of thing of which a client could be consciously aware.) This use of the theory to 'correct' what the client actually experiences seems likely to impede rather than facilitate the therapeutic process.

These specific dangers of approaching therapy from the perspective of cognitive theory are perhaps of minor importance compared with the more general danger of placing a narrow notion of rational belief at the centre of what is involved in human troubles. The importance of rationality runs through much of Western philosophy, but within this tradition there has always been a balance between those such as Socrates, Descartes and Kant who emphasized the importance of definitions, clear and precise ideas, and rule-governed concepts, and those such as Aristotle, Pascal and Wittgenstein who emphasized that general principles require personal judgement if they are to be applied in practice, that 'the heart has its reasons of which reason knows nothing', and that much of what we know cannot and does not need to be rationally justified. Cognitive science clearly belongs on the first side of this divide, and the general approach to human troubles that is found in cognitive theory brings with it the general attitudes to life and to people that are characteristic of 'rationalism'. Thus I think an appreciation of the dangers of cognitive theory can't be separated from an appreciation of the more general dangers of modern rationalism. This is much too large a topic to be treated properly here, but I think that a little more needs to be said about it.

Hubert and Stuart Dreyfus (a philosopher and a computer scientist, respectively) suggest that the growth of 'rationalism' in modern culture has its roots in three significant developments in the last hundred years or so (Dreyfus & Dreyfus 1986, pp. 193–203). There are first the huge changes in the organization of society. In earlier times, when institutions and businesses were much smaller, a decision-maker could rely on their own sense of what needed to be done, and proceed to make that choice. In large modern institutions, decision-makers at a particular level are responsible to those at a higher level, and have to justify their decisions to their superior in explicit, rational terms. This means that when there is a conflict between what they sense to be best, and what can be justified in terms of explicit criteria, they will be strongly inclined to follow the criteria rather than their own judgement. The hierarchical nature of modern institutions militates against wisdom and judgement, and leads to the ever-increasing proliferation of explicit rules and targets. Further, the rules and targets themselves need to be formulated in impersonal ways that can be assessed by anyone familiar with the system; the element of personal judgement that depends on individual experience is increasingly marginalized.

The second element in the development of modern rationalism is the impact of science and technology. Science, and especially the physical sciences, is characterized by precise, quantifiable observation, and the concern for prediction of experimental outcomes. It is an objective, impersonal approach to things that is appropriate enough in the context of our concern to predict and control the events in our environment. But for one person to take up this attitude towards another person is to relate towards them as a *thing* rather than a *person*. In special contexts, such as that of surgery, it is of course justifiable to think of the patient simply as a physiological system, but such an attitude does *require* special justification in terms of what the patient's own wishes are. Modern science and technology bring with them a particular kind of *attitude* to things, which on occasion is justified, but only in those special contexts where such things as prediction and control are appropriate. It is this rationalistic attitude that constitutes a major danger in applying the principles of cognitive science to therapy.

The third element in modern rationalism is the development of computers. Prior to this, there were practical limits to the extent to which institutional practices such as education and medicine could be rationalized. The rationalization of such practices could at best be a dream, since the range of factors involved in making appropriate decisions was beyond the scope of the human intellect, and practitioners instead needed, in the end, to use their professional judgement. However, with the advent of computers the dream of complete rationality has come to be seen as not just a dream but as a feasible programme. All that is required is data collection on a massive scale, the specification of goals and requirements, and then sufficient computing power to analyse and process the data. Personal bias is eliminated and objective results will be obtained. However, as Dreyfus and Dreyfus (1986, p. 196) remark in their own discussion of this theme: 'All of this sounds enlightened and progressive until one realises that genuine know-how, wisdom and good judgement are sacrificed in the process.'

It seems undeniable that cognitive-behavioural therapy gains much of its current popularity from the way in which it fits with a contemporary understanding of 'rationality' that over-emphasizes explicit beliefs and reasons for action. The difficulty is that such an understanding is itself unreasonable, and is incompatible with good judgement and common sense.

Summary

Modern CBT is an amalgam of ideas and practices drawn from behaviour therapy and cognitive therapy. The procedures of CBT are oriented partly towards the modification of behaviour, as is done in behaviour therapy, and partly towards the modification of thoughts and beliefs. These procedures, like those of other forms of therapy, can often be effective, but their effectiveness can be adequately understood in common-sense terms. There is little by way of an *overall* theory to the approach, since early behaviourist theory is seldom invoked; however, there is a theory which holds that feelings and behaviour are determined by thoughts and beliefs, and this is sometimes mixed with a very different theory, derived from cognitive science, according to which the explanation of feelings and behaviour needs to be given in terms of internal 'cognitive schemas'. There is much conceptual confusion here that is not easy to disentangle, but which can lead to therapists confusing clients about the nature of their difficulties. Perhaps more importantly, the rationalistic framework of CBT, while fitting well with contemporary managerial 'tick-box' approaches to human difficulties, is ill-adapted to the needs of many psychotherapy clients. *Modern* CBT admittedly incorporates from other forms of therapy some emphasis on listening, empathy and the therapeutic relationship, but this revised emphasis seems to owe nothing to the theoretical principles behind the CBT approach.

CHAPTER 7

Process-Experiential/ Emotion-Focused Therapy

Process-experiential therapy (PET), now often referred to as 'emotion-focused therapy' (EFT), aims to synthesize an experiential approach with the view that therapy is essentially concerned with facilitating emotional change. The experiential elements of the approach derive mainly from person-centred and Gestalt therapy, while the PET view of emotions and emotional change makes use of concepts taken from cognitive psychology. The approach was first presented by Leslie Greenberg, Laura Rice and Robert Elliott in their book *Facilitating Emotional Change* (1993) and has since been developed in an extensive range of publications that relate the approach to such areas as couple therapy and narrative therapy. Probably the most accessible general account is to be found in Elliott et al.'s *Learning Emotion-Focused Therapy: The Process-Experiential Approach to Change* (2004).

PET draws heavily on the cognitive science notion of a 'schema':

> The basic contribution of the schema concept is that it recognises that humans internally represent objects or events by a configuration of features. Schemas include but go beyond purely propositional representations to encode regularities in categories that are both perceptual and conceptual. Schemas abstract in that they extract regularity to encode what is generally true, rather than concretely encoding what occurred in a particular instance. They encode what experiences have in common. Schemas are also thought of as being hierarchically organized, with higher-level schemata being overarching generalization structures and more specific schemas being applied in a more context-specific manner. Thus person may have a high-level schema for dating, or for applying for a job, and more specific ones for making a phone call in these different contexts. Schemas of this sort have more of the character of goals or intentions and sets of procedures for attaining them, rather than being purely a representation of an event.... In cognitive science, schemas are thus viewed as complex information networks or mental models that operate out of awareness to guide memory and experience. (Greenberg et al. 1993, pp. 46–47)

This places PET theory firmly within a cognitive science framework, but the theory goes on to modify the schema concept so that rather than being understood as a purely cognitive representation, it is construed as an 'embodied cognitive/affective/action structure' (p. 47). Such structures are then referred to as 'emotion schemes' rather than 'schemas'.

> We use the word 'scheme' instead of 'schema' because 'schema' implies a static, linguistically based mental representation, whereas 'scheme' refers to a plan of action.... Emotion schemes are not directly available to awareness, they can be accessed indirectly through the experiences they produce... Emotion schemes are involved in complex self-organizing processes and result in emotion-based self-organizations... each person has many emotion schemes that may be activated separately or simultaneously. The self-organizations based on emotion schemes are like 'voices' in the person... emotion scheme processes and resulting self-organizations can be viewed as consisting of component elements linked together in a network, with the activation of single elements spreading to other elements. (Elliott et al. 2004, p. 25)

Greenberg and colleagues' book *Facilitating Emotional Change* is divided into two main parts: the first is concerned with theory, and the second with practice. I will suggest below that if a therapist reads the part on practice they will find it easily comprehensible even if they skip the theoretical sections on 'underlying process difficulties'. In fact, it may well be that this is how most therapists have read the book; as Elliott and colleagues note in their sequel *Learning Emotion-Focussed Therapy* (2004, p. ix), the detailed presentation of the theory and tasks in the original work was not 'user-friendly'. They also throw some light on why PET was set within the framework of cognitive science. It seems to have been because, although they see PET as at heart a humanistic therapy, they are concerned that humanistic therapies

> have often been criticised for being vague or untestable. For these reasons neohumanistic principles require reformulation in contemporary terms, with emotion theory and dialectical constructivism (neo-Piagetian development theory). (ibid., p. 24)

They refer to their own approach as 'neo-humanism because it is an attempt to restore a theoretical tradition that largely fell out of favor in North America in the 1970s and 1980s, particularly among academic psychologists'. The 1970s–1980s was the period in which cognitive ideas were becoming dominant in psychology, so that the way that PET theory is presented may be understood partly as a political move that would help to make the approach academically more respectable.

My strategy in this chapter will be to set out first what is involved in PET practice and to suggest that such practice makes good sense without much reference to theories of any kind. Then I will return to the theory of emotion schemes and their formation.

The common-sense core: 'treatment tasks' in PET

The practice of PET centres around six different kinds of client difficulty.[1] For each of these difficulties a particular kind of therapeutic procedure is recommended, most of which, such as focusing and two-chair work, are drawn from other modes of therapy. 'Markers', or ways of spotting particular kinds of difficulty, are described, and then the procedure appropriate to each marker is put into practice.

The first kind of client difficulty is that in which a client finds themself reacting to a situation in an unreasonable or exaggerated way. Greenberg and colleagues remark (ibid., pp. 141–142) that the significance of such problematic emotional responses 'lies in the fact that the clients are aware of some discrepancy between their own actual reaction, and their view of an appropriate or self-consistent reaction, and are thus motivated to explore and understand it'. They suggest that in cases of this sort a helpful approach is to encourage the client to attend closely to the scene in which the problematic response arises, and also to the response itself. This procedure, known as 'evocative unfolding', was first developed by the person-centred therapist Laura Rice. It is designed to help the client appreciate how the distorted way in which they are construing the scene may be generating the problematic reaction, or to how their habitual response tendencies are distorting their view of the scene. Greenberg et al. (1993, p. 141) write: 'The evocative unfolding of such problematic reactions can lead to important self-discoveries. Their significance lies in the fact that the clients are aware of the discrepancy between their actual reaction, and their view of an appropriate or self-consistent reaction.' This seems to make good sense without any invoking any theory.

A second kind of trouble is that in which a person has a vague sense of something not being right in their life, but is unable to articulate what it is. This is the classical situation addressed in focusing-oriented therapy, and for Greenberg and colleagues the appropriate therapeutic response is along the lines recommended by Gendlin: the therapist encourages the client to attend to the murky 'felt sense' of the problem, and then open themself to ways of articulating this response. The details of the focusing procedure provide practical guidance on how to work with troubles of this kind. However, as I have suggested in Chapter 4, the focusing procedure seems to make good sense without the need for any particular theory. It is a matter of attending closely to one's response and then finding ways of articulating it.

The next two kinds of troubles involve variants of what Greenberg and colleagues call 'splits', that is, situations in which people incorporate 'societal standards, attitudes and ways of thinking and acting that are to differing degrees at odds with their more basic needs, goals or concerns... For a variety of different reasons, cultural and family influences overwhelm individual preferences or requirements' (p. 186). One kind of case is that where a client is split between what they spontaneously want and what they feel they ought to do. Slightly different is the case where the client actively interrupts or suppresses their spontaneous response (p. 218). This is the territory of Gestalt therapy and of Rogers' 'conditions of worth', although there is less emphasis in PET on the idea that individual preferences are 'good' and societal standards are 'bad'; it is rather that a balance is needed between the two. Greenberg and colleagues suggest that in these cases what is likely to be helpful is Gestalt 'chair work', in which the client role-plays their conflict through identifying with 'each side' in turn, while moving between two chairs. The hoped-for result of this dialogue is that one or both sides may soften their attitude, so that a working compromise may be reached.

What this amounts to is the idea, found in many approaches to therapy, that people often experience conflicts between what they want to do and what they feel they 'ought' to do, yet they may not be conscious of the conflict. It is the unconscious conflict that gives rise to the difficulties, so that the first step in therapy involves helping the client to be more aware of what the conflict is. Then through experiencing more fully the conflict in their responses they can begin to look for a compromise that gives something to each side.

The fifth kind of trouble is that which Gestalt therapy calls 'unfinished business' (Perls et al. 1951). It is the kind of case where a person has been involved in an emotional situation which has been left unresolved. Examples are a situation where a relationship has ended unhappily, or a person has been unable to come to terms with tragic loss, or has been abused but has had no opportunity to confront the abuser. People in such situations often ruminate on the issue, or continue to relive the experience. They may also misperceive or overreact to situations that are reminiscent of what has not been 'finished' in connection with another person (Greenberg et al. 1993, pp. 242–243).

In such cases Greenberg and colleagues recommend the use of the Gestalt 'empty-chair' procedure, in which the person involved is imagined by the client to be sitting in a chair opposite them, and the client is encouraged to 'talk to' this person. It may be helpful to summarize an example that Greenberg and colleagues give of this procedure. It is a moving account of a woman who doesn't feel accepted, especially by her mother. She can't escape from the sense of not being accepted, although she doesn't see why she should feel like this. The therapist works to evoke the client's feelings for her mother, which involves articulating many details of the situation she found herself in with her mother, for example that mother was persuaded by father to give up horse-riding (which she loved) because it was too risky now that she was a mother. This draws out the client's feeling that it was not *her* (the client's) fault that mother made this sacrifice. Another part of her childhood situation was that mother did little to look after her emotionally, didn't much care for her and indeed preferred the company of animals. Then later there was the situation in which mother takes to drink, no longer cares for herself and dies at a relatively early age. The client feels this as the ultimate abandonment.

The therapist encourages the client to sense what the situation was like for mother (imagined in the empty chair). Mother feels that she wasn't cut out to be a mother; that was not what she wanted in her life, she didn't want to live for her daughter, and in the end didn't want to live at all. The therapist encourages the client to ask 'mother' what she wants, and 'mother' replies:

> I want you to let me go . . . I did let you massage me [towards the end of her life]. I even asked you to do it . . . I let you into my wall . . . You got closer than anyone else . . . . You were right about the animals, but I wasn't scared of them . . . maybe it wasn't all the things that you needed it to be, but it was the best I could do.

Following this the client says to 'mother': 'You were a character. (smiling) You really were something else. Much as I was ready to bash your brains out, I really sort of like ya . . . . I don't disapprove of you. I did, but I don't anymore. I think that for whatever reasons, your life was really, really hard for you.'

My understanding of this session is the client is making a profound imaginative attempt to understand and come to terms with the whole situation involving herself and her mother. The therapist helps by encouraging her to articulate her own feelings, but also to imagine vividly how things were for her mother. What emerges is a much deeper and richer view of the whole situation, a view that fits with what she now feels. Her earlier responses have been modified in the process of the session: she no longer responds angrily to thoughts of mother, and feels now that mother had a really hard life. The Gestalt understanding of this sort of example, which PET theory draws on, is a little different, and I will discuss it below.

The sixth and final kind of trouble is that where a client feels so vulnerable that they can hardly begin to express what it is that troubles them. They may feel that what they have done is 'beyond forgiveness', or that if they begin to express their anger they will be 'overwhelmed', or that they are in some way 'irredeemably flawed'. The special difficulty here is that the client is too vulnerable for any approach that would help them to articulate their feelings, or for any approach that would help them to modify their responses. Instead, Greenberg and colleagues suggest, what is needed here is above all 'empathic affirmation' of the client. The difficulty for the client is essentially that they see their feelings as being beyond the bounds of what is normal or acceptable, and hence they may experience a deep sense of hopelessness. What is required is for the therapist to convey that, after all, such feelings are understandable human reactions, that other people have such feelings and that having such feelings need not isolate the person from others. The therapist needs to convey this not just in words but in their whole attitude towards the client; it is a matter of the therapist sharing with the client their humanity and lack of judgement of what the client feels. As with the other kinds of difficulty, Greenberg and colleagues include a section on 'the underlying process difficulty', but in the case of 'empathic affirmation at a marker of intense vulnerability' no mention is made of 'emotion schemes'. Instead, there is a more straightforward account in terms of feelings and emotions. Perhaps the authors sensed that here there *clearly* is no need for their theory.

The theory and its confusions

I turn now to PET theory itself. It comprises two main parts, first the theory of emotion schemes which, as we have seen, is a modified version of the cognitive science theory of 'schemas', and second, a theory of how these emotion schemes are constructed, which is drawn from the work of Juan Pascual-Leone, who was a student of Piaget. This latter theory is known as 'dialectical constructivism'.

I have outlined the difficulties with the notion of 'cognitive schemas' in Chapter 6, and much the same criticisms apply in the case of 'emotion schemes'. Greenberg (2000, pp. 67–68) writes:

> One of the increasingly common theoretical notions used to explain human functioning is that of an internal model or scheme... These are dynamic structures through which the world, and interactions with it, are coded and which operate by influencing one's current view.... Schemes of one's personal experience are laden with emotional memories, hopes, expectations, fears and learnings gleaned from lived experience... It is these highly idiosyncratic, personal schemes, or to emphasise their emotional basis, emotion schemes, that are highly influential in determining our experience and action. It is these that are seen as the basic psychological unit and as the targets of therapy. They need to be evoked in therapy so that they are 'up and running' determining experiencing in the session.

The crucial question, in connection with PET theory, is that of the status of the 'internal models' or 'dynamic structures'. They are explicitly stated not to exist in a person's awareness; rather they are explanatory theoretical concepts analogous to the 'schemas' of cognitive psychology. Given that, we might try to think of emotion schemes as being 'in the brain' either in a straightforward physiological sense or in a sense analogous to that in which a program is stored in a computer. However, neither of these options makes any sense, for the reasons explained in the previous chapter, in relation to cognitive schemas.

In the case of emotion schemes there is also the difficulty that they involve emotions (as well as perceptual, symbolic, motivational and bodily sensation elements (Elliott et al. 2004, pp. 26–27)). As discussed in Chapter 5, emotions are not inner things or structures; to see them that way is to remain caught in the Cartesian picture. To have an emotion, such as fear, is to be inclined to respond in certain ways (e.g. withdrawal, freezing, aggression) in a particular kind of situation, such as that of perceived danger. As the child develops their linguistic abilities they come to replace the behavioural response with utterances such as 'Ooogh!' or 'Scary!' or 'I'm scared'. The Cartesian picture construes utterances such as 'I'm scared' as reports on inner states, but that is a misconstrual; the idea of emotions as 'inner states' (physical or mental) is a myth generated by a misunderstanding of how language works here.

In the same way, I suggest, the notion of an 'emotion scheme' embodies a mythological way of talking about inner entities or processes. *What is conveyed* in this way often makes good sense, and that is why much of what is said about process-experiential *practice* is readily comprehensible. In a passage quoted earlier Greenberg and colleagues write:

> [A] person may have a high-level schema for dating, or for applying for a job, and more specific ones for making a phone call in these different contexts. Schemas of this sort have more of the character of goals or intentions and sets of procedures for attaining them, rather than being purely a representation of an event.

If we 'translate' this back into ordinary language it says little more than that a person may wish to have a date or to apply for a job, and realize that in order to achieve these aims they need to make a phone call. As the authors themselves note, what we are talking about here is, in effect, goals or intentions, and ways of attaining them, but it is misleading to picture intentions and beliefs about how to realize them as 'internal schemas'. Talk of intentions and beliefs is part of our *everyday* way of understanding what people do, whereas schemas belong within a psychological theory. There is nothing wrong in speaking about a scheme that someone has for getting a job, and we might say that this person has the scheme 'in his head', or 'in his mind'. However, these ways of speaking do not commit us to picturing the scheme as *there*, in the person's brain or in his Cartesian mind. That would be like insisting that when someone has a song in her heart there must be something *there*, in her heart.

The PET theory of emotion schemes is used to interpret the first five of the treatment tasks discussed above. I have already suggested that the effectiveness of each of the 'treatment tasks' can be understood without the theory, but it may be of interest to see in a bit more detail how the theory is supposed to apply in the case of each task.

In the case of 'evocative unfolding at a marker of a problematic reaction point', Greenberg and colleagues write, as quoted above:

> The evocative unfolding of such problematic reactions can lead to important self-discoveries. Their significance lies in the fact that the clients are aware of the discrepancy between their actual reaction, and their view of an appropriate or self-consistent reaction.

That seems to make good sense, but Greenberg and colleagues (p. 142) then say in more theoretical vein:

> Clients can become vividly and irrefutably aware of their own meaning construals concerning the impact of the stimulus situation and the connection between their construal and their own problematic reaction. Furthermore, exploration can lead to awareness of their broad dysfunctional emotion schemes that underlie their own construals.

Yet it is hard to see how this adds anything to the non-theoretical account; rather it seems simply to dress up that account in the language of cognitive psychology theory, as well as conflating 'stimulus' and 'situation' in the way the behaviourists did (see Chapter 3).

The second treatment task is 'experiential focusing for an unclear felt sense'. Greenberg and colleagues' (p. 165) theoretical comment is:

> [T]he central process in Focusing is the full articulation of emotion schemes, that is, cognitive/affective structures that integrate a variety of levels of processing including bodily sensory experiencing and verbal propositional representations.

However, this re-description achieves little unless (a) there is something wrong with the ordinary way of explaining Focusing and (b) the talk of cognitive/affective structures makes sense.

The two kinds of treatment task that involve 'splits' both make use of the Gestalt two-chair procedure in which conflicting 'wants' and 'oughts' are role-played. The first step involves helping the client to be more aware of what the conflict is, and further steps involve encouraging a zigzag between the 'wants' and the 'oughts' that can lead to a resolution of the conflict. Greenberg et al.'s theoretical account of 'the underlying processing difficulty' (p. 187) in this case is:

> The general schematic processing difficulty that needs to be changed.... is the simultaneous evocation of two opposing schematic structures involving incompatible behaviors, thoughts, feelings and desires, either or both of which may be out of awareness. Of special interest in this form of disturbed functioning are the two sets of conflicting schemes. One is based on emotion schemes representing biologically adaptive emotions and needs, and the other set involves negative evaluations and introjected standards based on social learnings that oppose the feelings and desires.... It is the conflict between schemes containing societal shoulds and those containing organismic feelings and needs that must be brought to awareness and changed.

This articulates the difficulty in PET terminology, but again it is hard to see how doing so leads to any increased understanding of what is going on. The talk of 'emotion schemes' here doesn't add anything to what can be said without it.

In connection with the fifth kind of difficulty – that of 'unfinished business' – PET theory draws on the idea that where strong emotions have been aroused but their natural expression blocked, the emotions remain within the person in a suppressed state. Then in an imaginative procedure such as the 'empty chair', they can run their full course for the first time, so that there is release from the tension and pain of holding back, and also the opportunity to see the whole situation in a fresh way that is not distorted by the suppressed feelings (Greenberg et al. 1993, pp. 245–246). This is the traditional notion of catharsis, in which a person fully feels and expresses their emotions for the first time. From a common-sense point of view it is likely to be therapeutic, since where emotions are not fully expressed the person remains in a divided state in which the things they say are not articulations of what they really feel. Typical examples are where the full expression of feelings is blocked by fear. However, in the case of 'unfinished business', the articulation of feeling is blocked not so much because of feared consequences but because of lack of a suitable opportunity; the person to whom the feelings would naturally be expressed is *not there*. Hence there is the need for the creation of an *imaginative* context in which the feelings can be expressed.

The context need not be as dramatic as that of the 'empty chair'; many therapists will recommend that a client write a letter to the 'missing' person, in which they can fully express their feelings. In doing this, as in the 'empty-chair' example discussed above, the client will naturally be drawn into imagining how that person might respond to what has been expressed, so that the procedure serves as a vivid way of exploring and understanding the whole situation with the 'missing' person. It seems to me that there is more to such procedures than simple catharsis. It is not that all the feelings that emerge during the procedure were already 'there', waiting to be released. Certainly there can be situations where the expression of anger is blocked by fear of the consequences, but where the person to whom the anger would naturally be expressed is missing, the 'block' seems to be of a different nature. What is blocked is not so much the anger as the whole development of the situation. The person can't 'work through' their feelings, or their beliefs, because their situation gives them no way of doing this. The 'zigzag' interaction that would naturally occur if the client could engage with the missing person is impossible in its normal form. However, an imaginative technique such as the 'empty chair' provides a way of activating the zigzag, which can lead to a reconciliation of response and view in which, typically, both are transformed. All kinds of feelings may emerge in this process, but it is misleading to picture these as having been 'dammed up' inside the client as an 'emotion scheme' that needs to run its course (Greenberg et al., p. 244). Rather, they are the feelings that are generated freshly *now*, as the client engages imaginatively with their situation.

Dialectical constructivism

One part of PET theory centres around the notion of emotion schemes, but there is another part, referred to as 'dialectical constructivism', that is concerned with how these schemes are constructed. Elliott et al. (2004) write:

> Basically, dialectical constructivism holds that in coming to know a thing, both the state of one's knowledge and the thing itself are changed: What one calls a 'fact' is actually a joint construction of the 'things themselves' and one's knowing process... This position differs from what might be called 'naïve' or 'radical' constructivism, the postmodern or relativist view that reality is irrelevant and only 'versions' or interpretations of the world are of interest. In contrast, dialectical constructivism argues that there are reality constraints (emotion processes being one) that limit our constructions... Thus dialectical constructivism is one of the contemporary philosophies of science that attempt to steer a middle course between relativism ('anything goes') and realism ('nothing but the facts').

This kind of position derives from Piaget and ultimately, as we saw in Chapter 6, from Kant. It is the idea that the interaction between 'the things themselves' and 'one's knowing process' results in what we experience. Greenberg et al. (1993, p. 55) write:

> The dialectic with which we are most concerned is that which constitutes consciousness – the dialectic between concept and experience, between reflexive explaining and direct being, between mediated and immediate experience... From a dialectical constructivist view, people are seen as continually engaged in a process of reflexively constructing reality from the dialectical synthesis of these two sources of experience.

Although I shall argue that the dialectical constructivist view is in the end incoherent, it may be helpful to elaborate a little on the picture of human consciousness as being constructed through an interaction between concepts (or language) and immediate experiencing. I myself have put it in the following way, in an earlier book (Purton 2007, pp. 84–85):

> There is the element of immediate sensation or feeling, and the element of meaning or concepts. Both elements are always present to some extent, but sometimes one is much more prominent than the other. For example, if we are blindfolded and given an object to touch we will be very aware of the sensations we have – that the object feels very soft at one end with a curious springy texture, otherwise smooth and rounded. In this experiencing the sensations are prominent, although some concepts are there too – the concepts of 'soft', 'hard' etc. But we don't have any understanding of what the object is, not even of what general category it falls under – for instance, is it an artefact or some naturally occurring thing? We are aware of *it*, through our sensations of it, through its feel, but we don't know *what* it is, what *kind* of thing it is. Experiences such as this draw our attention to the sensation element in our experiencing.

> The opposite kind of case is where we are so involved in making conceptual distinctions that we are hardly aware of the immediate sensations involved. For example think of someone who is identifying birds, using an illustrated guide book. They spot an oyster-catcher, then a little tern – and that one over there – it's another oyster-catcher. They don't pause to register anything of the 'feel' of the different birds, or any difference in feel between the two oyster-catchers. Their experiencing runs mainly along a conceptual track, although of course they have to have various sensations in order for the bird-concepts to have something to apply to. Another example would be that of the tourist who sees the architecture in a new country entirely through the concepts that are presented in the tourist guide. They are tuned into these general concepts rather than to the immediacy of their sensations.

> In all our experiencing the sensation-element and the concept-element are interwoven. If we could just have sensations we would have no idea what

the sensations were – they would have no meaning. And if we could just have general concepts they would be empty, abstract forms without application to our immediate feelings. As Kant (1781/1933, p. A51/B75) put it: 'Thoughts without content are empty; intuitions [i.e. sensations] without concepts are blind'. In our actual lived experiencing there are both elements: the particular, immediate awareness in the here-and-now, an awareness of *this*, and – at least to some extent – an awareness of *what* this is.

The interplay between concepts and sensation is something we can see in many therapy sessions – we have a concern which we can sense or feel, and which is formulated or conceptualised in a particular way. We then give our attention to what we sense, and now the formulation often changes. This process, which is especially emphasised in focusing-oriented therapy, would be impossible without *both* elements in our experiencing and the *interaction* between the two.

The appeal of this picture, running from Kant through Piaget to PET is considerable, yet I have come to think that there is something awry in it. We have already seen in Chapter 5 that the notion of 'immediate experience' or 'experiencing' is confused. The notion involves the Cartesian view that we don't perceive people and things, but our own experiences; we are each locked within a 'subjective bubble'. This is a philosophical fantasy which we don't accept for a moment in our practical dealings with people and the world, but it haunts us when we think philosophically. We are tempted to think of 'immediate experience' as essentially a matter of how things *seem* to us, and that how things seem to us is more basic than how things really are (the Cartesian picture pulls us strongly in that direction). Yet the reverse is actually the case. Children learn to say 'That's red' well before they learn the further move of saying 'That looks red to me'. Learning the language of colours couldn't possibly begin with how things *seem*. The language of 'seeming' or 'immediate experiencing' is a later development; in other words, talking about 'the experience of red' is a much more sophisticated activity than talking of red things.

We can't then ground our knowledge of things in how they *seem* to us; if we hadn't already mastered the concept of a red thing we wouldn't be able to have the concept of the experience of red. However, theories such as dialectical constructivism take us even further from the truth of the matter. The idea is not that we begin with our knowledge of how things seem ('this looks red') but with a pre-conceptual experiencing in which we don't even have the concept of red. This pre-conceptual experiencing is 'just there' (as Gendlin tries to convince us in the opening chapter of his book *Experiencing and the Creation of Meaning*), and nothing can be said about it *in itself*. It is in that way *different* from the notion of 'sensation' that I made use of in the passage above. For one can say all sorts of things about sensations such as an itch or a pain, or a soft touch: they have bodily locations, they may be acute or mild, lasting or fleeting and so on.

To criticize the dialectical constructivist notion of 'experiencing' is not to say that there is no such thing as experiencing, in the sense of how things seem to us, how they strike us or how we respond to them. Nor is it to deny that we experience a range of bodily sensations. The point is that one can't build our ordinary knowledge of the world out of an interaction between language and 'sensations' or 'how things seem'. Our ordinary knowledge of the world arises from our *living in* the world, from our interacting with things and people; and our language arises from our being drawn into a linguistic community. The world and our responses to it are more basic than either 'experiencing' or language, and so cannot be understood as being constructed out of *them*, as dialectical constructivism would have it.

According to PET theory, the construction of the human world is not limited to the case of interaction between language and 'immediate experience'. It also involves interactions between emotion schemes. For example, a person might have one emotion scheme that might be roughly articulated as 'vague disappointment' and another scheme that could be expressed as 'warm closeness' (Elliott et al. 2004, p. 36). These might then interact and become synthesized as something like 'reaching out for comfort'. 'Reflection on this set of vague feelings leads to a symbolised experience that is then articulated as, "I need a hug".' The question is whether this mythological account of the interaction of emotion schemes really helps us in understanding the person who exclaims 'I need a hug'. A more straightforward account would be that pre-linguistic children, when disappointed, literally reach out for comfort by extending their arms to a person to whom they are attached. Later the arm-stretching movement becomes more of a conventional signal, and then this is replaced by the linguistic forms 'Hug!' or 'I need a hug'. The sort of case that Elliott and colleagues have in mind is one where a person has suffered a disappointment (that describes a *situation*, not a Cartesian inner experience), and reaches out to another in a linguistically articulated way. But what the person says is not well explained in terms of the interaction of emotion schemes; it is better explained in terms of the person's situation, their response to it, and their having learned the particular language in which they articulate their response.

Summary

PET integrates practices drawn from humanistic therapies (especially person-centred and Gestalt) with ideas drawn from cognitive psychology. The effectiveness of the practices can all be understood in common-sense terms, but the theory of 'emotion schemes' is vulnerable to the same objections as those that can be raised against the 'schemas' of cognitive science. The attempted integration of pre-conceptual human 'experiencing' with conceptually structured 'emotion schemes' via the philosophy of 'dialectical constructivism' seems vulnerable to the kind of criticism that has been brought against similar ideas in the thought of Piaget and, much earlier, of Kant. However that may be, it does seem clear that in any case the practice of PET is quite independent of its philosophical background.

Note

1. In later versions of the approach (Elliott et al. 1998; Elliott & Greenberg 2002; Elliott et al. 2004) some additional kinds of client difficulty are included, but for reasons of space I will not discuss them here.

CHAPTER 8

Existential Therapy

Existential therapy is not grounded in a theory but in a philosophical understanding and appreciation of what it is to 'be in the world'. This philosophical understanding is drawn from the writings of philosophers in the tradition of phenomenology and existentialism, especially Edmund Husserl and his pupil Martin Heidegger, together with later thinkers such as Jean-Paul Sartre and Maurice Merleau-Ponty. However, it is not easy to set out briefly what the main features of existential and phenomenological philosophy are. There are a number of reasons for this: First, Husserl and Heidegger are generally agreed to be exceptionally difficult philosophers to understand. In the case of Heidegger, as the philosopher Michael Inwood (1997, p. 1) notes, one view is that '[he] was (with the possible exception of Wittgenstein) the greatest philosopher of the twentieth century', but there is the contrasting view that '[h]e was (with the possible exception of Hegel) the greatest charlatan ever to claim the title of "philosopher", a master of hollow verbiage masquerading as profundity'. Then there is the difficulty that both thinkers changed their views significantly during the course of their lives. Husserl's 'phenomenology' evolved through several stages, some of which have a more Cartesian emphasis than others. Heidegger was strongly influenced by Husserl, but increasingly distanced himself from his mentor's views. His thought, too, is not all of a piece, there being an 'early Heidegger' and a 'later Heidegger'. Then while 'existentialism' is probably best known through the writings of Sartre, who was in turn a pupil of Heidegger, Heidegger explicitly rejected Sartre's rendering of his thought.

There is also the difficulty that while Husserl was undoubtedly the originator of the phenomenological tradition in philosophy, what Husserl meant by 'phenomenology' is different from the way in which that term is used in contemporary psychology and social science (Jennings 1986; Jennings & Lucca 1989). Husserl's 'phenomenology' was rather similar to what in analytical philosophy is called 'conceptual analysis', that is, the exploration of the 'essences' of things (e.g. in the field of psychology, the exploration of what *feeling, intention, belief, memory*, essentially are). Analytical philosophy approaches 'essences' via consideration of the meanings of the relevant *words*, but neither approach involves empirical investigations such as those found in contemporary qualitative research projects. The notion of phenomenology as a branch of *empirical psychology* seems to derive not from Husserl but from another of his pupils, the psychiatrist and philosopher Karl Jaspers. (For a helpful discussion of Husserl and Jaspers in the context of psychotherapy, see Fulford, Thorton & Graham (2006), pp. 197–236.)

The philosophical background to existentialist therapy is thus highly complex, and full of controversy. That situation is not at all unusual in philosophy, but it does pose problems in connection with finding a grounding for therapy in existentialism. Given the diversity of the philosophical positions that have been held, it is not surprising that there is a wide divergence in how 'existential therapists' have embodied the philosophical ideas in their own work. Something of this variety is set out in Mick Cooper's book *Existential Therapies* (2003), in which he discusses Boss's 'Daseinsanalysis', Frankl's 'Logotherapy', the existential-humanist approach developed in the United States by writers such as May and Yalom, the approach of R D Laing in the United Kingdom and the more recent British school of existential analysis deriving from the work of Spinelli and van Deuzen.

One important difference among the various existential approaches is that Daseinsanalysis, developed by Ludwig Binswanger and Medard Boss, draws almost entirely on Heidegger's later ideas, and 'places a great deal of emphasis on clients opening up to their world' (Cooper 2003, p. 35). Psychological difficulties are seen as involving a chronic *closedness* to the world. Daseinsanalysis rejects all forms of therapy which understand a person as 'a world-less, isolated psyche', and with it such notions as 'intrapsychic parts' and 'intrapsychic dynamics' (Cooper 2003, p. 38). Heidegger himself held, as did Wittgenstein, that it is misleading to think in terms of 'mind' and 'body', or 'psyche' and 'soma'. He says, 'The term "psychosomatic medicine" endeavours to synthesize two things which simply do not exist' (Heidegger 2001, p. 199).

In contrast to Daseinsanalysis, which emphasizes the Heideggerian notion of 'being-in-the-world', the American existentialist-humanistic approach has more in common with the philosophy of Sartre, which emphasizes the importance of authenticity in the sense of a commitment to one's own projects (Cooper 2003, p. 27). Existential-humanist therapists 'have tended to take a more inward turn, focusing on the struggle of the individual to be true to her own subjective experience' (ibid., p. 63). They 'have tended to draw from the more individualistic elements of existential philosophy: those that emphasise the need for a human being to stand alone, and courageously face the anxiety of existence' (ibid., p. 64).

Three principles of existential therapy

Ernesto Spinelli (2007), conscious of the wide range of views and attitudes that exist in existential therapy, has set out 'three defining principles' of the approach as (a) relatedness (inter-relation), (b) existential uncertainty and (c) existential anxiety. 'Relatedness' is the principle that we cannot 'understand or make sense of human beings – our selves included – on their own or in isolation, but always in and *only* in and through their inter-relational context' (ibid., p. 12). Part of the importance of this principle in (Heideggerian) existential therapy is that it does not allow the therapist to focus their attention on their client in isolation, but on the client's relatedness to others (including the therapist) and to the world in general. This means that existential therapy, unlike some humanistic therapies, does not begin with 'subjective experience' or with 'the individual'; in short, it is not grounded in the usual Cartesian assumptions: 'This assumption of a foundational relatedness challenges the dominant Western tendency to divide and isolate and thereby generate a "split" between what are, as a consequence, viewed as distinct and separate "subject" and "object"' (ibid., p. 20).

Spinelli's second principle is that of 'existential uncertainty'. This is the principle that there are always uncertainties in our lives, in our values and in our worldview. It is not that there are *no* certainties; indeed, existential thinkers often discuss one 'absolute certainty' – that of death. However, 'each human being's *lived experience* of such certainties is open to multiple possibilities – and hence remains uncertain' (p. 21).

The third principle – that of 'existential anxiety' – follows on from the first two. 'The "given" of uncertainty provokes the experience of anxiety' (ibid., p. 28). Our worldview is threatened by our uncertainties, and this 'existential anxiety necessarily permeates *all* reflective experiences of relatedness' (p. 27). One implication is that in order to reduce our anxiety we develop and hold to meanings and truths that become fixed for us. 'What these rigid and inflexible stances reveal in general are symptoms of unease, commonly expressed in terms such as obsessive or compulsive behaviours, phobias and addictive disorders' (p. 28).

Spinelli goes on to discuss how our fundamental engagement in the world, which he calls our 'worlding', because it is faced with uncertainty and hence anxiety, creates a 'worldview' that imposes a meaningful structure on our worlding. However, this imposition of a particular structure inevitably creates dissonances and distortions, since no worldview is adequate to express the fullness of worlding. Psychological troubles are seen as dispositional stances that have become more or less rigid or 'sedimented' (p. 34), a notion that seems to derive from Heidegger's notion of Dasein ('human being') losing itself in 'everydayness' (see below). Then the task of therapy is to encourage de-sedimentation. Not all sedimentation can be de-sedimented, however, and indeed this would hardly be desirable:

> For each of us it becomes necessary to navigate some tolerable path between meaning and meaninglessness. The worldview is that path. Although the worldview is the structural reflection of worlding, because it *is* a structure, its reflection can only be incomplete, compromised. Equally, because it is a structure, the maintenance of the worldview *requires* some necessary degree of sedimentation and dissociation so that it can withstand the full impact of perpetual deconstructive challenges of worlding. (ibid., p. 39)

In other words, I think Spinelli's point is that there needs to be a balance between the conceptual views we develop in order to make our way in the world and our lived responses to the world. These lived responses always involve more than can be formulated in our worldview, and sometimes our worldview involves us in a significant distortion of our responses. That, in existential terms, is what is involved in 'inauthenticity': 'the problems presented by clients arise from, and are expressions of, the client's currently maintained worldview's derived distortions of, and inadequacies in reflecting, his or her lived experience of worlding' (p. 65). I think that what is being said here is close to what I have been suggesting in earlier chapters of this book: that psychotherapy is essentially concerned with helping clients to find a balance between 'response' and 'view', which in Spinelli's terminology becomes a balance between 'worlding' and 'worldview'.

From the perspective of the present book, the philosophical background to existential therapy is suspect so long as it retains a Cartesian flavour. Insofar as existentialism orients therapy towards 'the subjective experiences of the client', it is open to the kind of criticisms I have made in earlier chapters, especially those discussed in Chapter 5. However, a more Heideggerian emphasis on being-in-the-world, and an openness to the *world* rather than to 'our subjective experiencing', is not vulnerable to such objections. It is true that Heidegger, like Sartre, does emphasize the importance of individual choice and suggests that there is a kind of inauthenticity that is fundamental and pervasive in human life, namely our tendency to live within the familiar accepted patterns of our culture, rather than finding our own distinctive and creative path. In this connection he speaks of the 'they-self', that is, of what 'they' – 'anyone' – says or does. He sees much of human being, or 'Dasein', as lost in 'everydayness', but his solution is not to turn away from the public world towards one's own 'inner experiencing'. It is rather to reflect on one's embeddedness in a particular culture and to find creative ways in which the possibilities of that culture can be lived further. Guignon (1993) writes:

> [T]he 'they' as Heidegger describes it is Janus-faced. On the one hand, our participation in the 'they' is an enabling condition that first opens us onto a world and gives us the possibilities we need for being human. From the outset, Dasein draws its possibilities for self-understanding and action from the way things are interpreted by the 'they'. On the other hand, this involvement in public forms of life can have a pernicious effect. It threatens to level all decisions to the lowest common denominator of what is acceptable and well-adjusted; it restricts 'the possible options of choice to what lies within the range of the familiar, the attainable, the respectable – that which is fitting and proper'. (*Being and Time*, p. 167)

Heidegger, unlike popular Sartrean existentialism, does not see the individual as a lonely existential hero, set against society; he holds that human nature or 'Dasein' is inherently social, yet can lose itself in the *purely* social.

There is much of interest in this perspective, and it is intriguing that Heidegger himself thought that his philosophy could be of value for psychotherapy. He conducted long discussions with the philosopher and psychiatrist Karl Jaspers and spent a considerable amount of time towards the end of his life in explaining his philosophy to a circle of interested psychiatrists convened by Medard Boss. A record of these seminars, which took place between 1959 and 1969, is available in an English translation (Heidegger 2001).

The practice of existential therapy

I think that the doubts that one may reasonably have about using Heidegger's thought as a backdrop for therapy are essentially to do with whether the intricacies of Heidegger's philosophy really add much to what can be said without it. For instance, in regard to Heidegger's notion of authenticity, it could be argued that much of what needs to be said in the context of therapy can be said more simply in terms of our ordinary notion of self-deception. The situation here is perhaps similar to that discussed in connection with psychodynamic theory in Chapter 6. One *can* picture self-deception in the way Freud does, but the picture doesn't add anything useful to what can be said without it.

More generally, on looking through the characteristic features of existential therapy, it is not obvious that much is added *in practice* to what is done in other humanistic therapies. For example, Mick Cooper (2012) contributed an existential therapy chapter to a book edited by Pete Sanders, *The Tribes of the Person-centred Nation*. Cooper sees the similarities between the existential and person-centred approaches as involving an emphasis on the uniqueness of each client; an understanding of the client in terms of their subjective lived-experience; an understanding of psychological disturbance in terms of distortion or denial of experience; a preference for spontaneous human encounter over the use of techniques in therapy; and an emphasis on the importance of accepting and validating the client (Cooper 2012, p. 158).

On the other hand, regarding the differences, he sees the existential approach as involving

(a) more emphasis on conscious deliberation and choice and less emphasis on the client's inherent tendency to find the answers that are right for them (and hence a more directive role for the therapist). I am not sure whether there really is much difference regarding 'conscious deliberation and choice', but the point about directing the client towards 'the right answer' certainly marks a significant difference, if that is what existential therapists do. I will return to that theme below.

(b) rejection of the idea that all 'distortion and denial' arise from imposed conditions of worth, so that challenge and confrontation may be needed as well as unconditional positive regard. This points to the inadequacy in Rogers theory that I discussed in Chapter 4, but in later person-centred therapy 'challenge and confrontation' are often included as valuable therapeutic responses under

the rubric of 'therapist congruence', which can be seen as an attempt to expose the client to the reality of things, or at least to the therapist's perception of that reality. It is not in principle very different to the cognitive therapist's method of 'challenging irrational thinking', or even the behavioural method of exposure to the reality of the situation.

(c) the view that 'limitations, struggles and discomforting feelings are intrinsic to the human condition' (so that therapy may be more about helping clients to come to terms with their difficulties, rather than moving beyond them). This again seems to fall under the heading of helping the client to see how things really are.

(d) a specific view about what the 'real', underlying issues are for clients. This is undoubtedly true. However, it could be argued that person-centred therapy also has its view of what the underlying issue is for clients, namely, 'incongruence'. And more generally, I think, any approach to therapy must have some view of what counts as *therapeutic* issues, as distinct from legal issues, welfare issues, financial issues and so on.

(e) a less individual-centred view of human existence, together with more scepticism about whether human beings are inherently pro-social. This seems valid in connection with earlier person-centred therapy, but would hardly be true of later theorists such as Mearns and Thorne (2000). One important point does seem to be that existential therapists, unlike many humanist therapists, will not simply want to draw out how the client sees their situation, but also how, in the client's view, *other people* see the situation. That *is* a genuine difference.

On the whole, it seems to me that the *practice* of existential therapy does not involve significant differences from the practices that are characteristic of person-centred therapy. Spinelli (2007, pp. 106–103), for example, lists the following existential therapy practices: other-focused listening, respect for the worldview of the client, the suspension (or 'bracketing') of all expectations and assumptions regarding the client's statements, acceptance, curiosity, certain kinds of confrontation, the exploration of 'sedimented attitudes'. Some of the terminology, such as 'bracketing' and 'sedimentation', is distinctive of existential therapy, and that terminology may sometimes be valuable in drawing attention to novel possibilities in familiar practices. However, it is hard to find much here that is significantly different from person-centred practice, which itself is comprehensible largely in common-sense terms, as I discussed in Chapter 4.

The existential approach and its dangers

Perhaps the central concerns one may have about existential therapy relate to the fact that existential therapists claim to have a deep understanding of human life that is grounded in existential and phenomenological philosophy. There are two distinct elements of concern here. One is that of the validity of the existential-phenomenological philosophy (or some variant of it); the other is a more general concern about grounding therapy in *any* particular philosophical system, since this is likely to lead to a view of the therapist–client relationship according to which the therapist has a profound knowledge of the nature of the world that the client does not have, so that therapy will involve something like teaching. That would not of course constitute a difficulty for those who favour more directive forms of therapy, but at least some existential therapists, such as Spinelli (2007, p. 74), hold that 'attempts at directive change act to undermine and contradict the very enterprise of existential therapy'.

Regarding the first point, concerning the validity of existential philosophy, there is the worry raised above by Inwood – that some competent philosophers regard Heidegger's philosophy as 'hollow verbiage masquerading as philosophy'. Readers unfamiliar with philosophy should be aware that this is not an uncommon view of Heidegger, at least among 'analytical' philosophers.[1] Spinelli touches on the same kind of worry in connection with his own notion of 'worlding'. He discusses attempts to describe and communicate the existential principle of 'relatedness': Such attempts

> have generated, and continue to generate, all manner of confusion and have given rise to difficult, if highly rewarding descriptive narratives as well as to any number of half-baked 'deep and meaningless' guru-like statements and descriptors. Whether my preferred term of worlding (and its relation to the worldview) will turn out to be an instance of the former or the latter remains to be seen. (p. 22)

Then in addition to the issue surrounding 'hollow verbiage', there is that of whether an approach that is grounded in a particular philosophical scheme will tend to draw the therapist into a teaching, or even guru-like, role. It may be that today, as the philosopher Charles Guignon (1993, p. 217) argues, more clients than previously come to therapy with questions such as 'How I am going to live my life?' – problems which touch on the issue of what kind of life is worth living. Such client difficulties naturally tend to draw therapists into the role of a guide on how to live a meaningful life. Mick Cooper (2003, p. 149) notes that the existential therapist Emmy van Deuzen is inclined to see existential therapy 'as a tutorial in the art of living' and quotes another existentialist therapist's comment (on one of van Deuzen's case studies) that van Deuzen 'does seem surprisingly anxious to teach the client something' – the client herself remarking that she 'felt an ideology was being conveyed to me' (ibid., p. 117). In short, there seems to be in existential therapy a definite pressure on the therapist to become something of a 'guru' towards their clients.

Related to this is a point that Spinelli makes about different 'levels of change' in existential therapy (pp. 72–75). The concerns of existential therapy ultimately focus upon changes in which there are far-reaching 'transformational challenges to one's previously adopted way of being'. However, for many clients more ordinary changes are more than sufficient for their wants, expectations and ability to lead more fulfilling lives. This conclusion may be particularly difficult for existential psychotherapists to accept since such levels of change address only in a minimal, and likely distorted, fashion the central concerns of relatedness. (p. 75)

It would seem then that there is a danger in existential therapy of the therapist seeking to impose an agenda of deep, transformational change on clients whose difficulties require much less dramatic interventions. (Spinelli is aware of this and quotes the Buddhist sage Li Chi: 'If you live the sacred and despise the ordinary, you are still bobbing in the ocean of delusion.')

The general tenor of these objections to existential therapy centres around the danger of the therapist being related to as a 'guru', that is, as a person who has special knowledge, grounded in a profound existential-phenomenological understanding of human relations and of what Spinelli (p. 74) calls the 'ultimate aim' of minimizing the presence and impact of sedimentations. Existential therapists 'by virtue of the structured examination of their own lives which they have undertaken, may be experientially "closer" to this ultimate aim than their clients are likely to be' (ibid.). Spinelli continues with the qualification that the therapist's personal explorations at this level, which he calls 'Level 3',

> will have made them aware that *any direct attempts to provoke or induce Level 3 change are dangerously unpredictable in their consequences*. In addition...such attempts at directive change act to undermine and contradict the very enterprise of existential therapy. Instead, the therapist's inter-relational focus, stance and attitude within the therapeutic relationship seeks to express existential phenomenology's assumptions in a lived way.

Whether this qualification really meets the objection raised seems a moot point.

One final point, which I can't develop here, is that existential therapy is explicitly grounded in a philosophical system (just as, arguably, most of the other approaches are implicitly grounded in Cartesianism), while the Wittgensteinian approach to philosophy that informs this book does not involve a system. Heidegger wants to replace the contemporary view of the world that is articulated in terms of isolated 'things' with a view centred rather on 'process' and 'interaction'; this he sees as the way out of the difficulties in the contemporary worldview (similar moves are made in the 'process philosophy' of Whitehead (1978) and in Gendlin's 'process model' (1997)). However, Wittgenstein sees our present difficulties as rooted in misleading philosophical pictures, especially those that derive from Cartesianism. His aim is not to *replace* the Cartesian system with another philosophical system but simply to expose its incoherence, so that our ordinary ways of seeing things will no longer be distorted by it.

Summary

The *practice* of existential therapy seems to be very close to that of person-centred therapy, and hence can be understood in the common-sense kind of way that I have discussed in connection with the latter approach. It is the philosophy behind the existential approach that is distinctive, and this philosophy will undoubtedly appeal to some clients. However, existential philosophy is far from a unitary system and includes a wide range of ideas. Some of these have a Cartesian flavour that is likely to render them vulnerable to the critique of Cartesianism with which this book is concerned. Others, especially those drawn from Heidegger, are radically non-Cartesian, and could be of value to psychotherapy. On the other hand, Heidegger's philosophy is notoriously difficult to understand, and the philosophical community is divided over whether this is due to the depth and novelty of his ideas or whether it is a matter of 'hollow verbiage masquerading as profundity'. One danger of making such a philosophy central to our understanding of therapy seems then to be that it can encourage a culture of obscure language and 'deep insights' that turn out to be either nonsense or else just murky formulations of what can be said more clearly in common-sense language. Another danger is that the appearance of philosophical profundity may lure therapists into a guru-like role that is probably not appropriate in psychotherapy.

Note

1. There is also the delicate question of whether we should allow our assessment of Heidegger's thought to be influenced in any way by his association with the Nazi party in Germany (Farias 1989; Ott 1994), together with his failure ever to explain this association. Gendlin, whose work draws in an indirect way on Heidegger, has an interesting discussion of the latter question in a paper 'Heidegger and forty years of silence' (Gendlin 1986). My early philosophy of science tutor, Professor Heinz Post, once told me that he had been present in a small group when the question of Heidegger's Nazi associations had been raised, and that Heidegger had replied 'Great men make great mistakes.'

Chapter 9

Neuroscience

Over the past 20 years or so an approach to psychotherapy has developed which emphasizes the importance of 'affect regulation', or the regulation of emotional response, in effective therapy. The importance of affect regulation can be seen as running through all the major schools of therapy. Allan Schore, who has written extensively on this theme, remarks that 'all psychotherapies – psychodynamic, cognitive-behavioral, experiential, and interactional – show a similarity in promoting affect regulation' (Schore 2003, p. 37).

In psychodynamic therapy the procedure of free association encourages the expression of troubling emotions, but this is balanced by efforts to interpret and find adequate ways of articulating the emotions. As Cozolino (2002, p. 51) puts it in a book on the neuroscience of psychotherapy (see also Schore 2003, p. 202):

> Across psychodynamic forms of therapy, emotional expression is encouraged, thoughts are explored, and awareness expanded. Feelings, thoughts and behaviors are repeatedly juxtaposed, combined and recombined in the process of *working through*.... From the perspective of neuroscience, the techniques of psychodynamic therapy focus on releasing emotion via uncovering unconscious material in the context of a supportive relationship. The overall goal is combining emotion with conscious understanding.

In person-centred therapy, the provision of Rogers' conditions of acceptance, empathy and congruence in an atmosphere of quiet listening and reflection both encourages the expression of troubling emotions and provides a safe setting in which the emotions can be understood, re-organized and integrated with the rest of the client's attitudes and beliefs. In the context of neuroscience with which he is concerned, Cozolino (p. 53) writes:

> What might be going on in the brain of a client in Rogerian therapy? In the Rogerian interpersonal context, a client would most likely experience the widest range of emotions within the ego-scaffolding of an empathic other... Rogers' supportive rephrasing and clarification of what the client says may also optimize cortical executive functioning in the face of these emotions. The simultaneous activation of cognition and emotion, enhanced perspective, and the emotional regulation offered by the relationship may

provide an optimal environment for neural change. By being non-directive, Rogers' method creates the necessity of executive networks and the self-reflective functions of the client to become activated.

Behavioural approaches provide an especially clear example of how one might understand the effectiveness of therapy in terms of affect regulation. The procedure of systematic desensitization is designed so as to reduce responses such as fear responses to a manageable level, in a step-by-step way; it is a procedure of 'fear regulation'. Cozolino (2002, p. 55) writes:

> Exposure and response prevention means that the client faces the feared stimulus (e.g. germs or venturing outside) without being allowed to retreat back to the safety of the bathroom or home. Exposure is usually systematic, gradual, and paired with *relaxation training* used to aid the down-regulation of affective arousal.

As in the psychodynamic and person-centred cases, the regulation involves two things. First, the presence of a sensitive and supportive therapist who ensures that the client takes steps that are large enough to arouse the emotion, but small enough not to be overwhelming, and second, the client's intellectual understanding that the feared object, for example, is not really dangerous.

Cognitive approaches are often used in conjunction with behavioural procedures. The cognitive part of the therapy may involve, for example, educating anxious clients

> about the physiological symptoms of anxiety, such as a racing heart, shortness of breath, and sweaty palms. These patients are taught that feelings of dread are secondary to autonomic symptoms and should not be taken as seriously as they feel.... The boost of cortical processing from *psychoeducation* is combined with *exposure* and *response prevention*... This process combines increased cortical processing (thought) with the result of exposure (affect), allowing fear circuitry to integrate with cortical circuitry in order to permit inhibition, habituation, and increased conscious control. (Cozolino 2002, p. 55)

Over the last few decades a huge amount has been learned about the neurophysiological conditions for our abilities to perceive, reflect, remember and so on; and also much about what takes place in the nervous system when we experience sensations or emotional arousal. Most significantly, a body of knowledge is developing about what goes on in the nervous system during affect regulation. Very briefly, the picture seems to be that cortical processes, especially in the left hemisphere of the brain, are particularly active during rational thought, while emotional arousal involves limbic centres such as the amygdala. Thus in the regulation of emotional arousal there is a strong influence of left-cortical processes on the processes taking place in the limbic system. A further significant finding is that in infants the left hemisphere of the brain develops more slowly than the right, so that in the first year or two of life the infant has little capacity for modulation of its 'responses' by its 'view'. Such regulation has to be provided by the infant's mother or other carer. Gradually, through the mother's interaction with the infant (and through the interaction of the mother's left brain with the infant's right brain, together with slowly developing circuits in the infant's left brain), the infant becomes able to regulate their own level of emotional arousal; in Kohut's (1971) terminology, they become capable of self-soothing. How satisfactory this development is depends a lot on the quality of the mother–infant interactions, though infants are remarkably resilient and can cope with considerable 'defects' of maternal engagement. What is required, as Winnicot said, is a 'good enough' mother.

It seems likely that difficulties in attachment can lead to the child failing to develop an adequate capacity for the regulation of emotion, and this incapacity will presumably be grounded in abnormal circuits in the child's brain. However, it is an intriguing finding of recent neuroscience that brain circuitry has a significant degree of plasticity, so that there is in principle the possibility of 're-programming' the circuitry. Writers such as Schore (2003) have suggested that just as the early laying down of the circuits takes place in the reflective interaction with the mother, so the re-structuring of the circuits may be facilitated through therapy processes in which there is a sustained to-and-fro interaction between therapist and client, during which the client's emotional responses become more articulated and integrated more with the view of their situation that they have absorbed from society.

One thing that seems to me to be rather one-sided in this account of the neurophysiological background to therapy is that it centres largely around the modulation of the activity of the right brain by the left. This is understandable in that the left brain develops more slowly in the infant, and so it is the infant's right brain that needs extra regulatory input from the mother. However, as I will discuss in Chapter 11, psychological difficulties can arise as much from over-regulation of affect as from under-regulation. In cases of over-regulation the child loses touch with their own spontaneous responses and begins to live in a world of rules and, in Rogers' phrase, conditions of worth. It could be argued that it is *this* kind of imbalance that is more prevalent in contemporary culture, with its strong emphasis on rational thought, explicit goals and generally 'left-brain' attitudes. The psychiatrist and neuroscientist Iain McGilchrist (2009) has argued powerfully that the 'left-brain' dominance of our culture lies behind many of our contemporary difficulties, and while difficulties associated with under-regulation of affect are common enough in our culture, my impression is that therapists are consulted more often by clients who wish to 'find their feelings' than by clients who have problems in regulating their responses. A similar point is made by Mearns and Thorne (2000, p. 180).

Relating the person to their brain

The above brief sketch of current thinking on the neurophysiological underpinnings of the process of psychotherapy could be misleading. It could suggest that ultimately psychological troubles are a matter of brain dysfunction, and that psychotherapy is a matter of tinkering with brain circuitry. The issue here is that of the nature of the relationship between human troubles and brain processes, an issue that has been present from the start of psychotherapy. In 1895 Freud made an ambitious attempt 'to work out the direct links between the operations of the brain and the functions of the mind' (Schore 2003, p. 187). He was dissatisfied with this work, and it was not published until after his death, under the title 'Project for a Scientific Psychology' (Freud 1895). Freud's 'Project' mixes psychological and physiological concepts in a way that he later repudiated. In 1913 he wrote:

> We have found it necessary to hold aloof from biological considerations during our psycho-analytic work and to refrain from using them for heuristic purposes, so that we may not be misled in our impartial judgement of the psycho-analytic facts before us. But after we have completed our psycho-analytic work *we shall have to find a point of contact with biology*. (Quoted in Schore 2003, p. 191)

Schore raises the question of whether the time for a rapprochement between psychoanalysis and neuroscience has now arrived, and has suggested that the right brain is 'the neurological substratum of Freud's dynamic unconscious'. He writes (2003, p. 251):

> A common ground of both psychoanalysis and neuroscience lies in a more detailed charting of the unique structure-function relationships of the emotion-processing right brain, which Ornstein (1997) called 'the right mind'... I propose that Freud's affect theory describes a structural system, associated with unconscious primary-process affect-laden cognition and regulated by the pleasure-unpleasure principle, which is organised in the right brain.

However, there are difficulties with the idea that the left and right hemispheres of the brain are the 'neurological substratum' of the conscious and unconscious minds, respectively. These difficulties are not a matter of the details of the 'correlations of mental and physical processes' but fundamental conceptual difficulties in the project of correlating brain processes with 'mental processes'. As we have seen in Chapters 4 and 5, emotions, for example, can't satisfactorily be identified with 'mental processes'; whether someone is feeling pride is a matter not just of how they are responding but of the kind of situation they are in; it is not a purely 'internal' affair. Similar points can be made in connection with motives, intentions, beliefs, memories, sensations, perceptions and the many other things that are often included as examples of 'mental events (or states, or processes)'. We are tempted to think of all these 'things' as 'inner events', but thinking of them in that way conceals the huge differences in the way the words are used. Wittgenstein argues, as I discussed in Chapter 4, that saying 'I'm in pain!' is not a matter of reporting an inner event, but of articulating what could just have well been an inarticulate cry. And 'He is in pain!' normally has something of the nature of an expression of concern. Each of the words for the various 'mental events' has its own context of use, but none of them is used to refer to Cartesian 'inner processes'.

In their book *Philosophical Foundations of Neuroscience* (2003), the philosopher Peter Hacker and the neurophysiologist Max Bennett begin to get to grips with some of the detailed issues that are involved here. They consider methodically the ways in which the 'mental event' words are actually used and show in some detail the kinds of confusions that are generated by thinking of these words as the names of processes that go on in the mind. They are particularly concerned with the extra confusion involved in identifying the alleged mental processes with brain processes and draw attention to the misleading way in which some neuroscientists, such as Damasio, speak of the *brain* making decisions, or interpreting data. Their book is useful partly as a reference work in connection with how we actually use words such as 'emotion', 'intention', 'belief' and so on, but also in providing an overview of the kinds of confusions that can arise when neuroscientists ignore the established meanings of these words. Further details of the more specifically neuroscientific issues can be found in a sequel entitled *History of Cognitive Neuroscience* (Bennett & Hacker 2012).[1]

The picture we have inherited from Descartes, of 'the mind' as an 'inner realm', is fundamentally misleading, and the idea of the brain as 'the substratum of the mind' belongs with this misleading picture. However, having said all this, the question remains of what sort of relation *does* exist between, say, feeling proud (or remembering last night's events, wanting to have a holiday, intending to go to the shop, visualizing one's childhood home) and what goes on in the nervous system in these situations. I think the answer has to be that the neural processes in the brain are *physiologically necessary conditions* for our having our emotions, thoughts, desires, intentions, imagery and so on. What neurophysiological research tells us is what, as a matter of fact, has to be so in the brain if we are to live our normal lives. To *some* extent it is true that if specific regions of the brain are damaged then we will suffer from specific personal difficulties. If certain regions are damaged we will not be able to speak, and if other regions are damaged our memory will be impaired, though as I will discuss shortly this statement needs qualification. Damage to the frontal cortex of the brain tends to impair problem-solving abilities:

> Individuals with frontal damage will get stuck in a particular way of thinking or have difficulty in ways that are separate from the demands of their environment (concrete thinking). They have a hard time monitoring social interactions, such as keeping the listener in mind when talking and not referring to situations of which the listener is unaware. They will also have difficulty in remembering the outcome of past behaviors and repeatedly apply the same unsuccessful solutions to problems (perseveration). (Cozolino 2002, p. 144)

Cozolino goes on to say:

> Because these problems come from damage to the frontal areas, it is generally assumed that the lost abilities arise from the frontal areas. This, however,

is not necessarily the case. Although some specific functions – like temporal and sequential organization – may, in fact, be primarily be organised by the frontal areas, abilities like problem solving, creativity, and imagination emerge from the overall organization and integration of neural networks throughout the brain. Proper frontal functioning alone cannot account for the highest levels of human functioning. But if the frontal cortex only creates the conditions for processes such as imagination, empathy, and spirituality, how do these abilities and functions emerge? The answer is, we don't yet know.

Here Cozolino begins to ease us away from the picture that for each human ability there is an associated specific region in the brain that is its 'substrate'. That picture is like a modern version of phrenology and is not what neuroscience is teaching us. But Cozolino's last two sentences might suggest that it is only a matter of time before neuroscience will tell us what the 'substrate' is for such things as images, empathic feelings and – as Schore would have it – the unconscious mind. The picture of the 'substrate' suggests that whenever we imagine something, or are empathic with someone, a corresponding process takes place in the brain. However, what Cozolino is referring to is not imagining or empathizing, but the *capacities* for these things, and he is suggesting that such capacities may involve the proper functioning of the brain and nervous system as a whole. It is the *capacities* that are dependent on brain functioning: if Brocca's area in the brain is damaged by a stroke, one loses the capacity to speak, but it clearly doesn't follow that when that part of the brain is functioning normally then one is speaking. The proper functioning of this brain system is a *necessary* condition for speaking, but it is not a *sufficient* condition. Similarly, if the amygdala is damaged, one may not remember an emotional episode from last week, but it is not sufficient for *remembering* the episode that the amygdala is functioning normally; one also must have been present at the episode in question! Again, as I have argued earlier, it is not sufficient for feeling scared that one has certain sensations in one's body. There has to be in some way a *context of danger;* either the simple presence of danger or a more complex context such as that of running away from something that seems to be dangerous, or being upset by thoughts of danger, and so on. No 'inner sensation' *constitutes* fear, and equally no alleged physiological substratum of the 'inner sensation' can constitute fear. Nevertheless, feeling afraid, like everything else that is human, *takes place under conditions,* and these may include normal functioning of the amygdala; if the amygdala is damaged a person may not feel fear even in circumstances of danger.

Neuroscience can tell us interesting things about the physiological conditions involved in our normal functioning, and also something about what physiological conditions can interfere with that functioning. What it can't do is tell us anything about the nature of fear, or imagination or unconscious jealousy. Such concepts are not rooted in physiology; they are rooted in the everyday contexts of human life. Although Freud seems to have hankered for a physiological account of psychological disturbance and its treatment, he was perhaps wise to hold himself 'aloof from such considerations'. The current developments in neuroscience are bringing back to attention the questions from which Freud distanced himself. I am not suggesting that contemporary therapy should distance itself from neuroscience, but only from the misleading picture that sees neuroscience as further developing or even replacing our common-sense conceptions of human beings, their normal functioning and their troubles. Neuroscience can't do *that*, but it can help us to understand something of the neural conditions that can *interfere with* our normal functioning.

Such understanding may in some circumstances suggest, for example, pharmacological interventions that are therapeutic. Cozolino (2002, p. 316) writes:

> The neurotransmitters powering the frontal cortex (e.g., serotonin, dopamine and norepinephrine) are stimulated through positive experiences and social interactions. Patients suffering from anxiety disorders and depression limit or eliminate both of these activities, further downregulating their production. This downward spiral is often difficult to break with psychotherapy alone. The right medication can make more of these neurotransmitters available to decrease symptoms of anxiety and depression, thus decreasing focus on fears and negative thoughts. I encourage patients at this point to work on altering their lives in ways that stimulate the activities of these neural networks. In this way, if they choose to discontinue the medication, they have established behaviors and interpersonal relationships that may, in fact, have the same effects on brain functioning.

There are studies which suggest that the difference in function between the two brain hemispheres may be related to depressive symptoms (magnetic stimulation of the left hemisphere can relieve depression (ibid., p. 119)), and it is reported that 'orienting eye gaze to the left (stimulating the right hemisphere) results in increased optimism, while the opposite is true with right-ward eye gaze' (ibid., p. 118). It has been suggested that in obsessive compulsive disorder (OCD) a cortical-subcortical neural circuit that is involved in recognition of contamination and danger becomes locked into an activation loop. Brain scan studies suggest that improvement of OCD symptoms is correlated with decreased activation of some structures in the circuit, and that the changes in brain metabolism are the same whether patients are treated with psychotherapy or medication. More drastically, 'scan-guided psychosurgery for patients who do not respond to any other forms of treatment can disrupt runaway feedback by cutting neural links within the OCD circuit' (ibid., p. 309).

In these extracts I think we can detect a slide from quite reasonable suggestions to those that are much more questionable. It is quite reasonable to suggest that anxious or depressed patients might be encouraged to 'work on altering their lives' by giving more attention to positive experiences and engaging more with other people, with the result that their brain functioning may become more normal, and that this change in brain functioning could contribute to breaking 'the downward spiral'. However, the reference to brain functioning here is incidental and unnecessary.

When it comes to the question of medication and 'psychosurgery', things are different. As I will discuss in Chapter 10, it is misleading to think of medication as constituting a remedy for personal troubles in the way that insulin is a remedy for diabetes. In the latter case, the medication simply replaces something that was lacking, but there is little evidence that anxiety and depression are the simple effects of abnormal neurotransmitter levels. Even if the administration of the medication does to some extent alleviate the 'symptoms', this may not be a matter of replacing something that was missing. That would be like saying that since aspirin can relieve a headache, the cause of the headache must have been an aspirin deficiency in the body.

Similarly, in connection with Cozolinio's suggestion that 'psychosurgery' (a revealing term!) might be an appropriate treatment for alleged brain disorders in obsessive-compulsive clients, there is the difficulty that the evidence for the brain disorders is weak, but also there is little to be said for the idea that clients 'on the obsessive-compulsive disorder spectrum' must share neurophysiological characteristics (McNally 2011, pp. 177–178). I will discuss that point further in the next chapter. It remains possible that brain surgery, in the same way as medication, *could* play a role in the relief of some personal troubles, but the possibility seems somewhat remote. What makes it appear as something not at all remote is, I think, the Cartesian background picture that we still struggle with, in which emotions and thoughts, for example, are seen as 'mental states (events, processes)' with which certain brain states are correlated.

The talk of 'mental states' is, I have suggested, fundamentally confused, but to a lesser extent there are difficulties in talking about 'brain states', if by that is meant fixed localized areas of the brain that are dedicated to particular functions. One difficulty is that of the *neuroplasticity* of the brain. Although neuroscientists can say something about which areas of the brain are involved in, say, vision as contrasted with hearing, or emotion as contrasted with thought, this brain topography is not *fixed* (Doidge 2007). If one part of the brain is damaged its function may be taken over by another part. A second, related, difficulty is that talk of brain 'parts' is itself problematical. Anatomically there are of course a number of specific structures within the brain, such as prefrontal cortex, hippocampus, amygdala and so on, but much of the brain consists of intricate webs of neuronal connections that are physically much the same in whatever part of the brain they are found. There is some evidence (Rosen 1991; Pribram 1994, 2013) that the way the brain works is more like the way a hologram connects with a visual scene, than the way a photograph connects with it. In a photograph, distinct areas on the paper or slide connect with distinct things, but in a hologram *any* area connects with *every* thing. To the extent that this is so, the question of what part of the brain is involved in having particular thoughts or feelings will not be a happy question to raise.

Summary

Altogether, the suggestion that the origin of personal troubles can be traced to dysfunctional parts of the brain seems problematical. The picture of a human being as having processes going on in their mind that are correlated with processes going on in their brain is conceptually misleading on the 'mind side', and empirically uncertain on the 'brain side'. If we can let go of that picture, then while we will still be able to accept that in *some* way neurophysiological structures and functions underpin our capacities to think, feel and so on, we will no longer think that there *must* be simple correlations between our thoughts and feelings and what goes on in our brains.

Note

1. For criticisms of the Bennett-Hacker position by philosophers Daniel Dennett and John Searle, together with Bennett and Hacker's response, see Bennett et al. (2007).

PART II
STARTING AGAIN

Chapter 10

The Troubled Client

Why do people seek therapy? What sort of problems does a counsellor or psychotherapist work with? What is therapy *for*? One might think, and no doubt most members of the public do think, that some fairly straightforward answers can be given to these questions. There are, after all, professional organizations for counselling and psychotherapy, and there are courses through which people are trained to work as therapists, trained to help people who come to them with certain sorts of difficulty. But just what these 'difficulties' are is not so easy to say.

It might be suggested that there is no point in trying to pick out *any* identifiable class of troubles with which therapists deal. Could it not be said that people come to therapy simply because they are *troubled*, because they are in some kind of *predicament*? But that would hardly be a satisfactory response. It *is* true that clients may come to a counselling or psychotherapy service with almost any problem under the sun, but at the intake interview or first session, it will usually become clear whether this client's problem is an appropriate problem for a *therapy* service. For example, the client may have financial troubles, or be struggling with the practicalities of accommodation, or childcare issues, or be uncertain about the correct procedure for complaining about their line manager's behaviour. More generally, they may be seeking specialist advice on how to resolve their difficulties. Here the therapist will refer the client to the appropriate agency or individual specialist. But how does the therapist know when to do this? It seems to have something to do with whether the difficulty lies mainly in the client's circumstances or whether it lies mainly in how the client is responding to their circumstances. There is no very sharp dividing line here, but consider the following examples:

(1) A client is depressed because he can't find a job. Part of the difficulty here may lie in the simple fact that few jobs are currently available, and it may help the client to get some advice on how to market himself – how to draw up a CV, how to prepare for job interviews and so on. On the other hand, while being unemployed is usually distressing, not every unemployed person becomes seriously depressed, especially if they have not been unemployed for long. The therapist may sense that there is more to this client's depression than the fact that he is unemployed,

and they may say to the client that while they can't manufacture jobs, and are not an expert on how to sell oneself in the employment market, they may be able to help the client with how he is responding in his difficult situation.
(2) A client fairly close to retirement has to cope with changes in her office environment due to computerization of the office procedures. She feels she can't cope with the new technology, she doesn't like it, she has to go on relevant training courses in order to keep up with her responsibilities. Here there are matters on which she could well seek advice – for example, on the best way to think about the new systems, why they are being used; talking with colleagues who have had the same difficulties, but who have found a way through them; looking at the possibility of buying and becoming familiar with a similar computer system of her own, or looking at the possibilities of taking early retirement. The therapist may themself be able to help a bit with advice in connection with these possibilities, while feeling that in doing so they are not fully in their *therapy* role. But also, the therapist may sense that there are 'deeper' issues involved: the client is responding to the situation in a resentful, complaining way, rather than making the best of it or seeing it as a challenge. There is a 'client response factor' in the situation as well as a 'circumstances factor'.
(3) A young student, away from home for the first time, is lonely and finding it especially hard to relate to members of the opposite sex. The therapist may feel that such difficulties are a normal part of growing up, and also may be able to give a little helpful advice on thinking about ways of meeting people, of practicing making the first move in social situations and so on. But they might also sense that this student's difficulty goes beyond ordinary adolescent shyness; that the student is unable to make use of such advice; and that the student's level of social anxiety is truly paralysing for them.
(4) A mother has become depressed since the children have left home. She remarks that she has 'empty-nest syndrome'. As with the young student, the therapist may sense that her sadness is in part a natural response to the changed circumstances of her life, and that this aspect of her trouble requires some reflection on what her options now are, discussion with others in a similar situation, consideration of what she likes doing but hasn't done previously because of family responsibilities and so on. The therapist may have a useful role to play here, a role analogous to that of a friend or advisor. Such roles can't be sharply separated from a 'purely therapeutic' role, yet the therapist may be aware that this woman's depression is not quite the same as ordinary sadness. It is as if she is not just sad but *caught in* her sadness; 'depressed' seems a better word than 'sad'.

It seems important, then, to make some kind of distinction between 'client response factors' and 'circumstances factors', since what is really needed in some cases may be help in changing the client's circumstances, either in this specific situation or through activities of a social or political nature that will ensure that the damaging circumstances are less likely to arise in the future. Clearly, therapy can't be a substitute for such social or political activity. In other contexts, while the client's circumstances may be difficult, it may be that this is – at least for the moment – just how things are. Yet the client may still be helped through reflection on how they can best relate to their difficulty. In the examples above there seems to be an aspect of the therapist's role that is not entirely distinct from that of a friend or advisor.

I think it would be foolish to deny that therapists can sometimes usefully perform such roles, though they are not then, in a strict sense, acting as therapists. However, clients *themselves* often want something different. They may say such things as 'I know I just need to get out more, and meet more people', 'I know I don't need to get so upset about it', 'I know this is normal for people of my age', but in spite of what they *know* they still don't *feel* the way they would like to feel, or are not able to do what they 'should' be able to do. We reach a point where 'ordinary helping responses', the sort of thing that might be provided by a friend or advisor, are not sufficient, and of course it is at that point that friends and advisors may start to become impatient or irritated. It is also at that point that we may come to see that there must be something more to therapy than friendly discussion, sympathy and advice.

The question is what the 'something more' amounts to, both for the client and for how the therapist may effectively respond. It may help to look more closely at the kinds of troubles that clients bring to therapy, while bearing in mind that we are primarily concerned with aspects of these troubles that are not likely to be resolved through efforts at 'social intervention' or solely through 'ordinary helping responses'. The question is the fundamental one of what kinds of trouble therapy, in a strict sense, is concerned with.

Psychiatric classification: The *DSM*

One answer would be that just as medicine is concerned with the relief of mild or severe physical disorders, ranging from flu to cancer, psychotherapy is concerned with the relief of 'mental disorders', ranging from social shyness to schizophrenia. However, the notion of 'mental disorder' or 'mental illness' is a highly contested one. On the one hand, the notion of 'mental health' is strongly embedded in our society, for example in the context of 'mental health provisions', and in the Mental Health Acts that in many countries allow people to be forcibly detained in hospital if they are deemed to be sufficiently 'ill'. Associated with this acceptance of the notion of 'mental illness' is the (always changing) classification scheme for 'mental disorders' that is found in successive editions of the *Diagnostic and Statistical Manual* (DSM) of the American Psychiatric Association. On the other hand, there is a growing literature which in one way or another challenges the very idea of 'mental illness'. There is the anti-psychiatry movement, the work of Szasz (1961, 1978) on 'the myth of mental illness', together with more moderate critiques that see talk of 'mental illness' as essentially metaphorical (Cooper 2007).

One difficulty with the *DSM* is that it does not distinguish well between mental disorder and mental distress. In *DSM IV* many of the categories have a criterion such that symptoms count as a disorder only if they cause clinically significant distress or impairment in social, occupational or other important areas of functioning. Yet some quite extreme states of distress may be natural responses to extreme situations. For the category of major depression there is in *DSM IV* an exclusion clause in the case of recent bereavement,[1] but it is arguable (Horwitz & Wakefield 2007) that there should be similar clauses for other major losses such as divorce or unemployment. However, it is not just that only *some* cases of distress are cases of disorder, but also that only *some* cases of disorder are cases of distress. In bipolar disorder it seems not uncommon for people to enjoy the manic phase, and to hesitate about whether they should take medication that damps down their 'highs' as well as their 'lows' (Jamison 2011). Similarly, there are some people with schizophrenia who see their disorder as a good thing (Cooper 2007, p. 26). 'Disorder' needs to be distinguished from what people like or dislike, as is clear even in the case of physical disorders. For example, some tribes in South America have a skin disorder known as pinta, or dyschronic spirochaetosis. The disorder results in a pattern on the skin that they consider attractive, so that far from it being distressing for them to have this disorder, those who do *not* have it are not permitted to marry (Clare 1992, pp. 24–25).

Another difficulty is that, beginning with *DSM III*, the classification scheme has been purely descriptive in nature. The system of categories is not based on any *understanding* of the nature of mental disturbance but simply on features of human behaviour that are found together, and seen as 'dysfunctional', or at least are regarded by psychiatrists as 'going together' and 'dysfunctional'. When *DSM III* was first introduced, psychoanalysts objected (Spitzer et al. 1980) to this purely descriptive, and from their perspective, superficial, way of classifying mental disorders, since it did not reflect the underlying 'psychodynamic causes'. The objection was disregarded, since American psychiatry was becoming increasingly sceptical about psychoanalysis. More recently, rather similar objections to the *DSM* (McNally 2011, p. 176) have come from those who see 'mental disorder' as rooted in brain dysfunction: they argue that the *DSM* categories need to be reshaped by taking into consideration neurophysiological information. The philosopher Dominic Murphy (2006, p. 5) argues that an effective nosology (classification system) for mental disorders should be based on the underlying causal factors that are involved. Of course the difficulty is that we know so little about the 'underlying causal factors' or even whether there are such factors. McNally (2011, pp. 176–177) writes:

> [W]e seem to be at an impasse. We have had a series of relatively atheoretical descriptive systems since DSM-III that organise the domain of psychopathology in terms of surface similarities of signs and symptoms, not in terms of their causes. Yet few psychopathologists would claim that we

now possess sufficient knowledge about etiology and pathophysiology to establish our nosology on a causal foundation.

Further, it seems likely that a *DSM* category such as 'obsessive compulsive spectrum disorder' may involve radically different kinds of difficulty (pp. 177–178):

> According to this concept, several seemingly unrelated syndromes fall along a continuum anchored at one end by compulsive characteristics associated with avoidance of harm and behaviour designed to reduce anxiety, and by impulsive characteristics associated with pleasure-seeking at the other end. Risk aversion anchors one end of the spectrum and risk taking anchors the other. The compulsive end includes obsessive-compulsive disorder (OCD), body dysmorphic disorder, hypochondriasis, and tic disorders (for example, Tourette's syndrome). The impulsive end includes syndromes such as trichotillomania, exhibitionism, and pathological gambling. Other conditions that researchers include within the spectrum are eating disorders, autism, and compulsive shopping. What supposedly ties these incredibly diverse syndromes together is that each involves repetitive thoughts and behavior.

McNally goes on to point out that some neuroscientists have suggested that the 'disorder' arises from certain abnormalities in brain circuitry, and Cozolino (2002, p. 309) draws attention to suggestions that brain-scan guided neurosurgery could therefore be appropriate. However, the evidence for the brain abnormalities is weak (McNally p. 178). Further, the reason that the evidence is weak may well be that the various syndromes involved have little in common apart from the factor of repetition:

> Focusing on the mere *form* of the behaviour – its repetitive character – at the expense of its *function* – the motivation for performing it – misleadingly implies etiological commonalities when none exist. For example, postulating unconfirmed neurobiological abnormalities shared by obsessive-compulsive washers and heroin addicts merely because one group repetitively washes and the other repetitively injects drugs provides no basis for nosological refinement. The motive for compulsive washing is stress reduction, not pleasure. The motivation for heroin use, at least initially, is pleasure and only later acquires the additional motivation of avoidance of withdrawal symptoms.

McNally argues (pp. 178–179) that the obsessive-compulsive spectrum concept

> requires us to pluck repetitive behaviour out of its context and ignore its motivational basis...We cannot make sense of OCD by focusing on neurobiology alone. We must examine the cognitive and motivational bases driving the symptoms of the disorder.

The moral I would draw from this is that the purely descriptive approach of the *DSM* is likely to be misleading when it comes to any *understanding* of 'mental disorder', since given its 'surface similarities' approach it will inevitably lump together things that a proper understanding would keep separate, and will separate things that a proper understanding would keep together – the *DSM* is like a library that classifies books by their colour, height and number of pages. This is the point that has been made both by the psychoanalysts and by those who think that a proper understanding will come from neuroscience. In the absence of any general acceptance of psychoanalytic theory, and the lack of sufficient neurophysiological theory, it might then seem that there is at present no hope of developing *any* classification scheme for psychological troubles that goes beyond surface similarities.

A common-sense classification

Yet this is not entirely true. What is needed are categories informed by some understanding of human behaviour and its disturbances. Such understanding could be provided by a theory, but psychoanalytic theory is not widely accepted, and neuroscientific theory is not well developed. However, there is our ordinary common-sense understanding of human behaviour, which often involves relating the person's behaviour to what they want and to how they see their situation. In the passage quoted above, McNally pointed out that if we are to make sense of OCD we need to 'examine the cognitive and motivational bases driving the symptoms of the disorder', which is just another way of saying that we need to examine *how the client views their situation and what the client wants*. The heroin addict (initially) wants the pleasure that comes from taking heroin, and sees buying and injecting heroin as the means to that pleasure. That is not a *theory*; it is part of a framework of understanding that we could hardly abandon without abandoning our general understanding of people. Of course such a common-sense understanding doesn't account for why people come to want heroin more than they want anything else. Nor does it necessarily offer any suggestions for how the addicted person may free themselves from their addiction, although cognitive-behavioural procedures may be helpful in treating addiction, and as I suggested in Chapter 6, these procedures can be seen as grounded more in common sense than in behavioural or cognitive theory.

There is a large class of common-sense explanations of behaviour that have the general form of pointing out what the person wants, how they view their situation and what therefore they take to be an appropriate way of getting what they want. There are also plenty of common-sense explanations that account for why, in some circumstances, people *don't* do what they believe to be necessary for achieving their goals. For example, they may be *mistaken* about the nature of their situation (she did take the teacher's book home, but it was because she had mistaken it for her own), or about what the situation requires (she did depress the accelerator, because she thought it was the brake). Or what they did may be explained by saying that it was done *accidentally* (he did break the vase, but it was because he slipped on the wet floor), or *unintentionally* (he did break the vase, but he didn't mean to – he was just tapping it to see whether it was genuine Ming porcelain). Other common-sense explanations relate what the person did or felt to what people can normally be expected to do (he snapped at her because he was tired and worried), or feel (she felt sad because her cat just died). Common sense has large and subtle resources for explaining what people do and feel, although *sometimes* we may find ourselves at a loss. In those cases we may be inclined to look more closely at the details of the situation and reflect on whether there are parallels or analogies in, say, fiction or mythology that can make some sense of what the person did or felt.

I think that people usually come for therapy because their common-sense attempts to understand themselves or change their behaviour have failed. They realize that there is something wrong in their lives, but either it is hard to say quite what it is, or there is no reason for things being as they are, or they can't do things that they want to be able to do, or they find themselves doing or feeling things that they don't want to do or feel. It may help to list some examples of what I take to be typical 'psychotherapy/counselling issues'.

(1) 'I want to stop smoking (eating so much, getting angry with my partner,...) but I don't seem able to manage this.'
(2) 'I feel depressed (anxious, guilty,...) for no obvious reason. I don't know what this is all about.'
(3) 'I just don't relate well to people.'
(4) 'I feel weak (unacceptable, useless,...) though others see me as strong.'
(5) 'The voices in my head distract me.'
(6) 'I can't see any way forward in this dilemma (any way out of this situation,...).'
(7) 'I can't get the images of the accident out of my mind.'
(8) 'My partner says I am "pushy" but I can't understand why he feels that.'
(9) 'I've been cutting myself, and it scares me (I'm embarrassed about it, I want to stop,...).'
(10) 'I'm lonely, although there are plenty of people around that I can talk to.'
(11) 'I am confused about my sexual orientation.'
(12) 'I'm irrationally scared of spiders (heights, telephones,...).'
(13) 'I no longer seem to care about anything.'
(14) 'I often seem to get in with the wrong people - it just happens.'
(15) 'I have no belief in myself.'
(16) 'It's really frightening – the aliens are now trying to control my brain, but no-one believes me.'
(17) 'I keep on making the same mistakes, but I don't know why.'
(18) 'My life is empty.'
(19) 'I keep having to check everything.'
(20) 'I don't feel I have a place in the world; I don't feel "solid" like other people.'
(21) 'I keep putting things off.'
(22) 'I often seem to get people's backs up.'

Type A troubles

There are no doubt many possible ways of classifying these troubles, but I will suggest for a start that there are at least three broad kinds of difficulty involved. In the first group I would place the following:

(3) 'I just don't relate well to people.'
(10) 'I'm lonely, although there are plenty of people around that I can talk to.'
(13) 'I no longer seem to care about anything.'
(15) 'I have no belief in myself.'
(18) 'My life is empty.'
(20) 'I don't feel I have a place in the world; I don't feel "solid" like other people.'

Here the trouble seems to involve a broad sense of disconnection from people, or an alienation from life. Common sense would suggest that in such cases what is needed is some way of re-connecting with people or with life generally. It might also suggest that *many* forms of therapy (apart from those that are heavily task-oriented, or psychoanalytically detached) could be helpful here, simply because in taking part in therapy the client is already engaging with another person, and hence is doing something by way of relating to the world. This is connected with the common view that in therapy generally 'it is the relationship with the therapist that matters most', something that is one of the best-established findings in therapy outcome studies (e.g. Orlinsky et al. 1994, p. 308). I will refer to troubles of this general kind as Type A troubles. (The 'A' might be taken to suggest that there may be something of this kind of trouble in All psychological difficulties.)

Type B troubles

Consider now another selection of 'troubles' that seem to have something in common.

(1) 'I want to stop smoking (eating so much, getting angry with my partner,...) but I don't seem able to manage this.'
(7) 'I can't get the images of the accident out of my mind.'
(9) 'I've been cutting myself, and it scares me (I'm embarrassed about it, I want to stop,...).'
(12) 'I'm irrationally scared of spiders (heights, telephones,...).'
(19) 'I keep having to check everything.'
(21) 'I keep putting things off.'

Such 'troubles' seem fairly specific or clear-cut: the client is irrationally scared of heights or telephones, they want to stop smoking, or getting angry with their partner, or putting things off; they want to be 'cured' of their compulsions or flashbacks. In these cases the client has a clear sense of how they would like to be, or what they would like to be able to do, but 'something gets in the way'. They can't help feeling panicky as they climb higher, or contemplate answering the phone; they can't resist having a cigarette; they just find themselves putting things off, or getting angry with their partner without significant cause; the compulsive actions and flashbacks are beyond their control. In all these cases, how clients find themselves responding doesn't fit with their view of how things really are: they don't really think the stairs are dangerous, or that any terrible consequences are likely if they answer the phone, or that it is important to have the cigarette, or that their partner has significantly infringed their rights, or that they really need to continually wash their hands, or think about the accident. We could say that in such cases the problem is essentially that the client's behaviour, or their response to their situation, doesn't fit with their view or considered judgement about how things really are. It is this discrepancy that they want to overcome. I will refer to such troubles as Type B troubles. (The 'B' could be taken to connect especially with the point that the client's concern is primarily with their own Behaviour.)

Within this group of cases there are common-sense differences. For example, suffering from repeated flashbacks is something that *happens* to a person; it is not at all within that person's control. Compulsive hand-washing is different – the person may often be unable to resist the desire to wash, while at other times they may find a way of resisting. There is the *possibility* here of forms of therapy that look for ways of helping the client to resist. Ordinary cases of getting unreasonably angry with one's partner seem different again; here, in addition to considering ways of resisting the temptation to attack, one might be inclined to reflect on what exactly is making one so angry. Thus one might want to assimilate this case into another group of troubles (Type C, below) – those in which one is not *clear* just what one is feeling or wanting. Then there may be a worthwhile distinction to be made between compulsive hand-washing and compulsive cigarette-smoking, in that hand-washing often seems to be a way of avoiding anxiety, whereas cigarette-smoking is, on the face of it, driven by a desire for stimulation. But having made that common-sense distinction we might then wonder whether the cigarette-smoking is also a way of avoiding anxiety. Once we begin to make such distinctions they may lead us on to further questions, and to new possibilities in approaching the client's problem.

Type C troubles

Other troubles in our list seem less focussed on specific responses; I will refer to them as belonging to Type C, where the 'C' can be understood as suggesting Confusion, lack of Clarity and also lack of Congruence (in Rogers' sense):

(2) 'I feel depressed (anxious, guilty, ...) for no obvious reason. I don't know what this is all about.'
(4) 'I feel weak (unacceptable, useless, ...), though others see me as strong.'

(6) 'I can't see any way forward in this dilemma (any way out of this situation, ...).'
(8) 'My partner says I'm "pushy", but I can't understand why he feels that.'
(11) 'I'm confused about my sexual orientation.'
(14) 'I often seem to get in with the wrong people – it just happens.'
(17) 'I keep on making the same mistakes, but I don't know why.'

In some of these examples (2, 4, 8, 14, 17) the client is responding in an unhelpful way, but it is not clear why they are responding in that way; in others (6, 11) it is more that they are just not clear how they should respond, or how they really want to respond. There is no sharp distinction between these two kinds of case, since 'not knowing how to respond well' fades into 'responding in an unclear way', but the theme of lack of clarity runs through all these examples. Example (22) 'I often seem to get people's backs up...' seems to belong in this group if the statement continues with something like '...but I don't understand why this happens', but if it continues with something like '...by always pointing out exactly why they are wrong, but I can't seem to stop doing it', then probably it should be included in the previous, Type B, group.

Within this third group of troubles we can again begin to make some common-sense distinctions. A client who is unclear about what they want, or how to move forward in a difficult situation, may simply need to take some time in the midst of an over-busy life to reflect on what really appeals to them. A therapist, simply by listening and reflecting, may be able to help them do that. A rather different case is where the client's 'not being clear' is *motivated*. They say they don't know what they want, but the truth is that they do know, but they also know that if they were to make their desires explicit they would have to act on them, and that is terrifying. In such a case, which is in common-sense terms a case of self-deception, the therapist might need to do more than listen and reflect; they might need to draw the client's attention to features of their situation that the client is ignoring. There are of course many ways in which we can deceive ourselves, and consideration of such strategies would be another common-sense way of making useful distinctions within the general category of 'not being clear about one's own responses'.

Leaving aside the Type A group of troubles, which are to do with clients' general disconnection from life, I suggest that there is a rough, common-sense distinction between Type B troubles in which clients consider their *responses* to be in some way awry, and want to bring those responses into line with their considered view of their situation, and Type C troubles in which clients sense that their *view* of their situation is unclear or confused, and want achieve a view that clarifies how they are responding.

These two kinds of trouble are in a sense opposites, but they also have something in common. What is common is the theme of some discrepancy between how they are responding in a situation and how they view their response. These troubles are all troubles where clients experience a division within themselves: either they can't do effectively what they know is the thing to do or they can't get a clear view of what they are up to. The first kind of case is one where we might be inclined to speak of 'irrationality' (e.g. 'irrational fears'); the second kind of case is where we might be more inclined to speak of 'unclarity' or 'self-deception' (for instance, not knowing what one wants, or not knowing that one is jealous). I don't mean to suggest that this distinction is a completely sharp one. There is inevitably something of confusion in the phobic client's response to spiders: it is not *clear* to them why they respond in the way they do; they feel they should be able to approach the spider, but *somehow* they can't. Similarly, there may be something of felt irrationality in the case of the client who 'doesn't know who they are any more'; they may well say 'How *stupid* to feel like this! – other people don't.'

Unclarity and irrationality are not the same thing, but they both involve an unsatisfactory mode of engagement with one's situation. In the one case we are not clear what the situation really is, and if we are asked what sort of help we long for, we might say something like 'I need someone who is kind, intelligent and understanding to sit down with me and listen in a perceptive, caring kind of way so that I can begin to find myself in all this.' In the other case we find ourselves doing or feeling things that we don't want to be doing or feeling, and here we might wish for a rather different kind of help, perhaps something along the lines of 'There are aspects of how I respond to situations that I really want to change, and I need some help in making the changes. I don't seem able to do it by myself.' Yet there is the common factor that in both cases there is some kind of discrepancy, or lack of balance or integration in how we are living. We are not wholeheartedly responding to the situation in terms of how we view it (Type B cases), or we can't find a wholehearted way of expressing what our response is (Type C cases).

In the rest of this book I will be suggesting that what lies at the heart of therapy is the project of helping people to find ways of integrating, or balancing, their view of their situation with their response to it. In some cases, where the trouble is mainly one of unclarity, the most effective mode of therapy will tend to involve helping the client to clarify their responses; in other cases, where the trouble is mainly one of responding in an irrational way, the most effective mode will tend to involve helping the client to modify their responses. But we should not lose track of the fact that clarifying one's responses involves *modifying* those responses, and that modifying one's responses may bring clarity into how one views one's situation. The client who becomes clear that they feel hurt as much as angry about what their partner said is already responding differently to their partner, and the client who faces and overcomes their fear of dogs now views dogs differently. And whether we emphasize 'irrationality' or 'confusion' it seems clear that a further significant element in therapy will almost always involve the nature of the client's interaction with the therapist, and with the wider world.

Therapy, psychiatry and medication

There are two troubles in the list above that I have not yet fitted into any of my three broad categories. They are

(5) 'The voices in my head distract me.'
(16) 'It's really frightening – the aliens are now trying to control my brain, but no-one believes me.'

Psychiatrists thinking in terms of the *DSM* categories would probably suggest a diagnosis of 'psychosis', or more specifically 'schizophrenia', and consider treatment with a drug such as dopamine. Common sense, on the other hand, will say that people who say such things are 'out of touch with reality', that they seem to be 'living in a world of their own'. The common-sense suggestion would be that such clients need help in coming back into a fuller relation with the ordinary human world, and that troubles of this kind fall into the Type A group. That might seem naïve to the psychiatrists, but in fact there is good evidence that forms of treatment for schizophrenia that centre around making human contact with the client can be remarkably effective.

Examples are to be found in the work of Gary Prouty (Prouty 1990; Prouty et al. 2002), in which the activity of the therapist consists very largely in spending time with schizophrenic clients, listening to them and trying to engage with those who remain silent. Eugene Gendlin (1972, p. 336), who worked in a large schizophrenia project in the early days of person-centred therapy, says of schizophrenia:

> *It is not so much what is there as what is not there.* The interactive experiential process is lacking, stuck, deadened in old hurt stoppages and in disconnection from the world. It cannot be ongoing, except in and toward someone and in the world. If a toaster is unplugged, would you take it apart to find out what is wrong inside of it? The concrete reality of humans is the experiential process, and this is no purely internal thing, but a feeling-toward others in situations. If it is not ongoing, then it cannot be made ongoing, except as we respond empathically to make interaction happen, as well as reconnect the person at least to a promised and imagined outside situation in which he might be able to live.

More recent confirmation for this kind of view is found in work with schizophrenic patients in Finland (Seikkula & Trimble 2005; Seikkula 2011). The method involves, as part of standard mental care provision in Western Lapland, what are called Open Dialogue meetings, in which the patient and concerned family members take part in an unstructured dialogue with members of the mental health team. The dialogue involves ordinary language, engaged listening and reflection, acceptance of strong emotions, participants' comments on what others have said, the gradual finding of ways of speaking about terrible experiences and a growing sense of emotional connection between the participants. Meetings last about 90 minutes and take place at intervals of several months. The approach has had remarkable outcomes (Seikkula 2011, p. 185):

> At five-year follow-up 85% of patients did not have any remaining psychotic symptoms and 85% have returned to full employment. Only one third used antipsychotic medication. There is also some evidence that in Western Lapland the incidence of schizophrenia has declined during the 25 years of the open dialogue practice.

Seikkula comments that it can be hard to believe that such a simple, commonsense approach can be so effective:

> It is its very simplicity that seems to be the paradoxical difficulty. It is so simple that we cannot believe that the healing element of any practice is simply to be heard, to have response, and that when the response is given and received, our therapeutic work is fulfilled.

I do not mean to suggest that all there is to schizophrenia is a difficulty in relating to people, or that genetic and physiological factors are not involved. However, such factors may best be seen as *predisposing* people to the disorder, while the disorder itself *is* essentially a disorder of human relationship. A psychiatric perspective based on the *DSM* makes it difficult to see this, since the *DSM* first classifies personal difficulties in terms of clusters of 'symptoms', and that way of thinking naturally suggests that for each cluster of symptoms there is an underlying disorder-entity, in the form of a physiological abnormality. Then it is but a step to thinking that what is required in the case of schizophrenia (or, for example, bipolar disorder or ADHD) is suitable medication that will correct the abnormality. However, as discussed earlier, the *DSM* categories are purely descriptive and hence have no immediate implications for the existence of underlying disorder-entities. One can't produce a disorder-entity simply through the setting up of a definition by a *DSM* committee. Secondly, the existence of characteristic neurophysiological abnormalities which are the cause of alleged disorder-entities such as schizophrenia is highly controversial. For some time schizophrenia was held by many psychiatrists to be associated with abnormally high numbers of dopamine receptors in the brain, but the evidence for this now seems flimsy (Valenstein 1998, pp. 113–115; Moncrieff 2009, pp. 10–11). The use of neuroleptic drugs (which block dopamine activity) in the treatment of schizophrenia is thus thrown into question, and the doubts one may have are confirmed by the fact that there is very little hard evidence for the effectiveness of such medication. The same is true in connection with bipolar disorder and ADHD, for example (Valenstein 1998; Moncrieff 2009). The question arises here, and in connection with the use of many other kinds of medication in psychiatry, of how it is that the prescription of such medication continues in spite of lack of evidence for its effectiveness, and several writers (Horwitz & Wakefield 2007; McNally 2011, pp. 35–39) have suggested that what lies in the background is psychiatry's financial links with the pharmaceutical industry, and the intensive advertising and promotion that are carried out on the part of that industry. It is reported, for instance, that in the United States alone the amount of money spent each year on such advertising and promotion is over $12 billion (Wolff 1996).

It does not follow that antipsychotic medication is never of value. For example, the psychiatrist Kay Jamison (2011), who herself suffered from what the *DSM* would categorize as bipolar disorder, came to accept that she needed to continue with lithium medication if she was to avoid the extremes of emotion that were interfering with her work. However, she was not altogether happy with this solution, as the effect of the medication was a general dampening of emotional response. It has been suggested by the psychiatrist Joanna Moncrieff (2009) that it is mainly in this sort of way that antipsychotic medication 'works', insofar as it does work. It is misleading to picture the medication as a *cure* for an *illness*; a better analogy is that of *intoxication*. The medication produces an abnormal state of the brain in the way that alcohol does. Alcohol can be useful in reducing social anxiety, for example, since it 'substitutes the alcohol-induced brain state, with its characteristic weakening of inhibitions, for the normal anxious state' (Moncrieff 2009, p. 13). The question regarding the use of medication will then be, as with the parallel question regarding the use of alcohol, whether the sufferer prefers the consequences of the abnormal drug-induced state to those of their original troubled state.

The final section of this chapter has been necessary in order to counter the notion that a general common-sense approach to therapy must inevitably fail because some 'mental disorders' are grounded in neurological abnormalities about which common sense knows nothing. However, the doubts about neurological abnormalities that have arisen in the cases of schizophrenia, bipolar disorder and ADHD seem substantial and suggest that a common-sense approach is possible in connection with most client troubles. On the other hand, common sense itself may suggest that in *some* situations resort to medication may be entirely appropriate.

Summary

In this chapter I have considered what characterizes 'therapy troubles' as distinct from other kinds of trouble, and I have suggested that we can distinguish three broad classes of trouble. The first, which I have referred to as Type A, involves a general disconnection from people and an alienation from life, and includes a wide range of cases, from the client who says that they are unhappy because they just don't relate well to people, or the client who 'no longer cares about anything', to people whom psychiatrists might diagnose as schizophrenic. From a common-sense standpoint, what is needed in such cases is to help the client to overcome their alienation; to 'rejoin the human race'.

The second group, Type B, includes clients who suffer from fears or compulsions that they consider to be irrational. The general theme running through this group of troubles is that clients find themselves responding in ways that they don't want to respond, in ways that they feel are inappropriate. A gap has opened up, as it were, between their view of things, how they take things to be, and how they find themselves responding. They share the commonly accepted view of their situation, for example that spiders are not dangerous, but they can't bring their responses into line with that view. From a common-sense standpoint, the aim of therapy in such cases would be to help the client find ways of modifying their responses so that these responses become more appropriate to their view of the situation.

The third group, Type C, includes clients who find it difficult to articulate their feelings effectively. They feel confused, or uncertain, about important aspects of their lives. They may find themselves doing things that make no sense to them. Unlike the previous group, it is not that they know that what they feel or do is inappropriate and needs to be changed; it is that they don't really know what it is that they are feeling or doing. In these cases the common-sense standpoint would be that such clients need help in clarifying what they feel, or *what they are up to* in doing what they do.

Having considered the sorts of issues that are involved on the client's side of therapy, I will turn in the next chapter to the question of what therapists typically *do* in response to the troubles that clients bring. I will suggest that through looking at how we can usefully group therapeutic *procedures*, we will get some confirmation for the usefulness of the broad groupings of client troubles that I have presented in the present chapter.

Note

1. This exclusion clause has been removed in *DSM 5*.

Chapter 11

Psychotherapy Integration

The previous chapter set out a rough classification of the kinds of trouble for which clients seek *therapeutic* as contrasted with other kinds of help. In this chapter I will consider how we might classify the ways in which therapists respond to the troubles that clients bring. This chapter is concerned with what therapists *do*, and I will suggest that a natural classification of therapeutic responses can be drawn up that parallels my earlier classification of client troubles. This classification is not a purely descriptive one but is grounded in what the reasons are for responding in particular ways to particular troubles. However, consistently with my rejection of the traditional theories in the first part of this book, the reasons are of a common-sense nature. I will draw on my earlier accounts of the various therapeutic approaches, and then show how, when understood in a common-sense way, the procedures of these approaches can be brought together in an integrated account of therapeutic practice.

A common-sense account of what therapists do

We have seen in Chapter 1 that the main obstacle to psychotherapy integration is the incompatible nature of the theories that underlie the different approaches. These theories are rooted in different conceptions of the nature of human beings, so that it can seem that psychotherapy will always be theoretically divided, with it being in the end a matter of personal choice to which theory one should commit oneself. However, my discussion of the various theories in the first part of this book throws a different light on the situation. I have argued that although the various theories are radically different in some ways, most of them are permeated by the Cartesian picture in which a human being is a composite of 'mind' and 'body'. Introspectionist psychology emphasized the mind, and behaviourist psychology the body, but both of these early schools of psychology operated within the basic Cartesian framework. I have suggested that most of the subsequent approaches to psychotherapy have not freed themselves from this framework, and that as a consequence most psychotherapy theory suffers from the incoherence that is implicit in Descartes' picture of human beings.

The alternative to Cartesianism that I have suggested is that instead of beginning with the notions of 'mind' and 'body' that we have inherited from 17th-century metaphysics, we should start from our *ordinary* understanding of people, which is framed in terms of everyday notions such as 'wanting', 'believing', 'intending', 'feeling' and so on. These notions hang together in an intricate conceptual framework that is picked up by young children long before they encounter philosophical or psychological notions such as 'mind' and 'matter'. This everyday conceptual framework involves, as I discussed in Chapter 1, not only broad distinctions between, say, thinking and doing but also finer and subtler distinctions between, for example, doing something by mistake, by accident, unintentionally or inadvertently. We learn these distinctions along with learning the use of the words, although we do not normally learn how to *explain* the differences. Nevertheless, as Austin suggested, we can if we reflect sufficiently on our situations come to appreciate that in one case a mistake was made, whereas in another case what happened was an accident. I have suggested that bound up with this everyday conceptual framework is a framework of explanation or understanding. In describing what happened as a mistake, we are fitting it into a familiar pattern, a pattern that is distinct from the 'by accident' pattern. Once we have seen that a seemingly puzzling action was a *mistake,* we understand what was going on. Explanations of this kind don't involve theories, but that does not bar them from being genuine explanations.

In the course of this book I have drawn attention to a number of everyday kinds of explanation, such as explaining what a person does in terms of their aims and beliefs, explaining what someone says in terms of their being unaware of what they really feel and explaining a person's behaviour by pointing out that they were not fully attending to what they were doing. More specifically, I have been concerned with forms of explanation that seem to be characteristic of various schools of therapy, but which are not strictly dependent on the associated *theories* of those schools. The theories themselves cannot be integrated with one another, but what I hope to do now is to show how the practices, and *common-sense understandings*, of the various schools can be brought together in an integrative account of therapy.

(a) Behaviour therapy. In Chapter 3 we saw how behavioural techniques can be understood straightforwardly in terms of the client working to bring their responses into line with what they believe. Initially, their response is simply a reaction that is not modulated by what they believe, but gradually the client comes to respond less automatically and less intensely to the disturbing aspects of the situation. Do we need a theory in order to understand this? What would a world be like in which people *never got used to* events that they recognized to be harmless, never became familiar with new places or situations? Our ordinary way of putting the central theme of behaviour therapy is in terms of 'getting used to', 'feeling more familiar with' and so on. These ways of talking express familiar features of our lives and are part of the background of our

understanding of ourselves. The central theme of behaviour therapy is really grounded in that understanding.

To summarize, the practice of behavioural therapy suggests that it can be important in psychotherapy to help and support clients in their efforts to bring their responses into line with what they believe.

(b) Person-centred therapy. I suggested in Chapter 4 that there are two central themes in person-centred therapy, which to some extent are associated with the earlier and later versions of Rogers' thinking. In his early work, there is the emphasis on reflecting what the client says, partly in order to check the therapist's understanding, but also to help the client clarify what they are feeling. It is this clarification or articulation of feeling that is most emphasized in the focusing-oriented variant of person-centred therapy. One reason for reflecting what clients say is that clients often find it difficult to be clear about what they *really* want to say, because of social expectations about what they *should* say, or unthinking adherence to what is conventionally said. The person-centred context of a safe, accepting therapeutic relationship is thus important in allowing the client to express what they previously were afraid to express. I have argued that nothing in the way of theory is needed in order to understand what is happening in this variety of person-centred therapy. In therapy the client comes to be more 'congruent', but that just means that they are no longer confused or self-deceived about their feelings, and it is easily comprehensible in common-sense terms how this can come about, given that the therapist creates conditions in which feelings can be expressed safely.

In Rogers later work there is less emphasis on the specific procedure of reflecting and more on the principle of engaging with the client in an open, spontaneous, human way. In later person-centred therapy this is sometimes expressed in the idea that 'It's the relationship that matters.' But this idea again is hardly a matter of theory, although there are schools of therapy that don't place so much emphasis on it. It is hard to see how anyone could doubt that it must be of *some* importance whether a therapist relates to a client in the broad person-centred way. One doesn't have to use the term 'person-centred', but can we really imagine a world in which a therapist's (or teacher's or lawyer's) personal relation with a student, or client, was completely irrelevant to the success of the work being done? If someone nevertheless asks *why* this should be so, I think we reach something of an impasse. Such a question, like the question of why people become less anxious in more familiar situations, is difficult to respond to because it tries to raise doubts in areas where we have no doubts. There are, as it were, certain 'givens' in human life, but these 'givens' are not the sort of 'givens' that are familiar in traditional philosophy, such as 'immediate experiencing' or 'the laws of logic'. As Wittgenstein (1953/2009, p. 238e) puts it, 'What has to be accepted, the given, is – one might say – *forms of life.*'

To summarize, the practice of person-centred therapy suggests two things that are important in therapy (a) the creation of a real, empathic and accepting relationship between therapist and client, and (b) helping the client to clarify their feelings or articulate their responses.

(c) Psychodynamic therapy. Here the central theme is that of helping the client gain insight into their feelings and relationships, and this is achieved through encouraging the client to say whatever comes to mind, followed by close listening and interpretation. At the heart of psychoanalysis is the idea that people are often unconscious of what they really feel, or what they really are up to, and the point of the therapeutic process is to bring what is unconscious to consciousness. However, as I argued in Chapter 5, what this amounts to is that the therapeutic procedure is designed to help clients to see where they are deceiving themselves, and I suggested that the notion of self-deception is independent of the Freudian theory of 'the unconscious mind'. Other aspects of Freudian theory, such as the 'defence mechanisms', can equally be understood in common-sense terms, so that while psychoanalysis may have played a useful role in drawing our attention to the variety of ways in which we can deceive ourselves, the theoretical structure plays no essential role in understanding the different kinds of self-deception. My suggestion has been that although there is much of value in psychoanalysis, we do not need the theory. All that is needed is the realization that people can be self-deceived in many ways, and that an important way of helping clients to see through their self-deception is by providing an environment in which the therapist listens 'with evenly hovering attention' (as Freud put it), and then 'interprets' what the client says, that is, draws the client's attention to aspects of their situation that don't seem to fit with how things actually are.

To summarize, the practice of psychodynamic therapy, like that of person-centred therapy, indicates the therapeutic importance of helping the client to articulate their responses, or to bring what they say into line with what they really feel.

(d) Cognitive-behavioural therapy. I have argued that there are two distinct kinds of therapeutic procedure involved in CBT, which draw on ideas deriving from the cognitive and the behavioural traditions out of which CBT originated. The cognitive part of CBT helps the client to clarify what they really believe about their situation. The therapist helps the client to look more closely at their beliefs and then challenges these beliefs if they seem unreasonable. However, a purely intellectual change in what is believed is unlikely to be therapeutically effective; the client needs to be helped to bring their behaviour into line with what they have come to see is the real situation. I have discussed something of the conceptual complexity that is involved here in Chapter 6, but insofar as we can separate 'belief' from 'response', it could be said that CBT is effective through its dual practice of first working with beliefs, and then using behavioural procedures (often given as 'homework') to transform the client's behavioural responses.

In sum, CBT helps the client both to express what they really believe and to bring their responses into line with those beliefs.

(e) Process-experiential therapy. As in the cases of person-centred, psychodynamic and cognitive-behavioural therapies, I have argued that practice of PET can also be understood in common-sense terms. The six 'treatment tasks' of PET in one way or another draw on the same principles that I have already discussed. In the case of 'problematic reactions' the 'evocative unfolding' procedure is a way of drawing the client's attention to 'the discrepancy between their actual reaction, and their view of an appropriate or self-consistent reaction' (Greenberg et al. 1993, p. 14). The second treatment task uses focusing to clarify what the client really feels about their situation. The third and fourth treatment tasks work with 'splits', situations in which 'societal standards, attitudes and ways of thinking and acting...are to different degrees at odds with their more basic needs, goals or concerns' (p. 186). These tasks are often embodied in role-play, through which the conflicting concerns can more clearly be articulated and brought to awareness. The fifth treatment task is the use of imaginative techniques such as the 'empty chair' to help to elicit client responses and the further articulation of them. The sixth and final treatment task is simply that of 'empathic affirmation at a marker of intense vulnerability', in or in common-sense terms, empathizing with vulnerable clients.

To summarize, PET employs procedures that have two main functions. The first function is that of drawing out the client's real response to their situation, and the articulation of that response. The purest version of this is found in the second task – that of focusing. Then in Tasks 1, 3, 4 (and possibly 5) there is the second function of helping the client to modify their actual response in the light of what they see as an appropriate or reasonable response. In addition there is Task 6 which embodies the more general function of providing a safe human relationship without which the other tasks cannot be effectively approached.

(f) Existential therapy. In my summary of what is involved in the practice of the other forms of therapy, the emerging common themes were that therapy often involves (a) the establishment of a genuine, accepting, empathic human relationship with the client (b) ways of helping the client to express or articulate what they really feel, often in contrast with what they think they 'should' feel and (c) ways of helping the client to embody, or carry forward, what they really feel into their actions, into their actual living. These three common-sense features of therapy are all clearly present in the existential approach. Existential therapy strongly emphasizes the importance of the relationship between therapist and client, and it also emphasizes the importance of finding authentic responses that will undermine 'sedimented' views. Thirdly, such 'therapy is effective to the extent that it influences and mobilizes patients' wills. This means that an important aspect of the existential-humanistic approach is helping clients to recognize points at which they could – or can – make choices, and encouraging them to act in wilful, rather than compulsive ways' (Cooper 2003, p. 78). As we have seen earlier, it is difficult to say much *in general* about existential therapy, because of the wide variety of ideas involved, but in

Spinelli's account, at least, I think we can see the familiar theme of a good therapeutic relationship, together with a twin emphasis on both finding an authentic *view* of things and modifying compulsive *responses*.

Three therapeutic accounts

Three accounts of what is centrally important in therapy have emerged from the above discussion. *The first account* emphasizes the importance of a real, empathic and accepting relationship between therapist and client. This account is central in person-centred therapy, although today it is widely accepted as an important therapeutic element in most therapeutic approaches. *The second account* emphasizes the importance of helping clients to see themselves more clearly, often in the face of a tendency to misconstrue their behaviour, or deceive themselves; this account talks about the importance of 'congruence' (in person-centred terminology'), or 'making the unconscious conscious' (in psychodynamic terminology). Similarly, PET talks about eliminating the discrepancy between the client's actual response and their view of what an appropriate response would be and existential therapy focuses on the issue of client authenticity. There is a strong common theme here, which is that psychotherapy often involves helping the client to bring their views into line with their actual felt responses. *The third account* is also concerned with a discrepancy between 'client view' and 'client response', but here the theme is that while the client sees things pretty much as they are, they are unable to act in accordance with their view. This idea is central to behaviour therapy, which aims to help the client modify their behaviour so that it comes into line with what they actually believe. To some extent (in its more behavioural aspect) CBT invokes this kind of account; but CBT may also invoke something similar to the 'clarification' account, through challenging what clients believe.

The three accounts do not correspond in a simple one-to-one way with the schools of therapy, but we can see that the different schools tend to draw on these accounts to different degrees. Today most schools of therapy acknowledge (A) the importance of the therapeutic relationship. Behavioural therapy, as incorporated into CBT, emphasizes the importance of (B) working with changes in behaviour ('homework' in connection with such changes is important in CBT). Person-centred, psychodynamic and existential therapy all emphasize the importance of (C) clarification, self-awareness, congruence and authenticity. PET, as we have seen, incorporates an A-type account in its sixth therapeutic task, and something of both C- and B-type accounts in the other tasks. Existential therapy also involves variants of all three accounts.

Now these three accounts of what is involved in psychotherapy correspond rather closely to the three categories of client troubles that I discussed in Chapter 10. There I grouped client troubles as (A) those that involve a general disconnection with other people, an alienation from them and from life in general; (B) those that are more specific, and which involve the client being unable to do things that they would like to do, or responding in ways that they do not want to respond; (C) those where the client is confused, or unclear about their feelings, or can't understand why they should feel the way they do, can't understand why they do what they do. The three broad approaches to therapy that I have sketched fit fairly well with these three types of client trouble. Type A therapy, as found paradigmatically in later person-centred therapy, seems most appropriate for Type A troubles, where the central issue lies in the general difficulties the client has in relating to others. Type B therapy, as found paradigmatically in behaviour therapy, seems most appropriate for Type B troubles, where the central issue is that the client wants to change how they are responding. Type C therapy, as found paradigmatically within early person-centred, focusing-oriented and psychodynamic therapy, seems most appropriate for Type C troubles, where the central issue is that the client finds it difficult to express or articulate what they are really (authentically) feeling.

The different kinds of therapy procedure fit the different kinds of trouble, and it is not hard to understand *why* the procedures are likely to be effective for their corresponding troubles. It does not require much in the way of theory to understand how a person troubled by a traumatic animal phobia might be helped by a desensitization procedure, or how a withdrawn 'schizoid' client could be helped though an increasingly in-depth relationship with a therapist. The use of the procedures thus makes sense in a very commonsensical kind of way.

Integrating the accounts

From a pluralist or eclectic point of view, it might be said that this is the end of the matter: we simply select the kind of procedure that best fits the kind of trouble that the client brings.

However, that would leave us without an integrated account of what therapy involves. As we saw in Chapter 1, it is important to have such an account, partly in order to assess whether a proposed approach counts as a genuine form of therapy, and partly to distinguish therapy from projects that in some ways border on it, such as advising, education, medical care, social welfare and so on. *Within* a particular school of therapy we can specify easily enough what the therapy project involves: for Freud, it is a matter of making the unconscious conscious; for Rogers, it is a matter of helping the client to become more congruent; for Skinner, it is a matter of undoing the effects of faulty conditioning; for Beck, it is a matter of changing the client's core beliefs. None of these projects has much in common with what lies beyond the borders of therapy, and their practitioners can confidently feel that they are engaged in the distinctive professional practice of therapy.

The question is whether we can give an account of how the groups of troubles and procedures that I have identified 'hang together' as distinctive of *therapy* troubles, and *therapy* procedures, once we have eliminated the theories. Here my fundamental 'common-sense' suggestion is that counselling troubles are rooted in what could broadly be called 'human relationship difficulties'. There is the Type A kind of case where the client does not participate much in the back-and-forth interaction that is such an important aspect of human living. Such clients do not move easily between their own responses and the responses of others; they do not engage easily in dialogue. But then there are two different ways in which this difficulty in dialogue can manifest itself. One way, Type B, is that in which the client's individual responses dominate, so they do not sufficiently 'take on board' the way others see things. For instance, they may intellectually agree that a situation is not dangerous, but they don't take this in and make it *their* response. The other way, Type C, is that in which the responses of others (individuals or society) dominate, so that the client does not sufficiently 'hold on to' their own response. They are clear about what 'should' be done, but they are less clear about what their own feelings and attitudes are. They may indeed misidentify their sense of what should be done as being also their own response; but it isn't, and they are self-deceived.

I think that there is a common-sense view here which sees interaction and relationship as central to human life. A human child is born into a community, and while it has its own innate responses to situations from the start, these responses are continually shaped and developed through interactions with others, especially those with whom it forms its early attachments. Infants for whom this early pattern of intensive personal relationship is not available do not develop normally, as can be seen in tragic examples, such as those of infants in Romanian orphanages under the Ceauşescu regime, and in the rare cases of feral children. Everything we know about early child development confirms that, while infants are resilient and adaptable to unfavourable circumstances, a significant degree of personal attachment and interaction is essential for normal development. Recent neurophysiological studies suggest that not only the functioning but also some of the structure of the infant's brain is determined through interactions with caregivers (Schore 2003).

To some extent deficiencies in early interactions may be remedied by intensive later interactions, and again there is evidence of consequent changes in neural functioning. This has been seen as one reason why sensitive and sustained personal interaction with clients who find relating difficult may have significant therapeutic effects. Examples are the work of Prouty and the results of the Finnish schizophrenia studies that I discussed in Chapter 10.

That human life and human difficulties are deeply rooted in human relationships seems undeniable, and this realization is reflected in the view of many counsellors that 'it is the relationship that matters'. But in addition to this general point there is the further one that even where there is a significant degree of personal interaction between infant and carer that interaction may in a sense be unbalanced. In his book *The Interpersonal World of the Infant*, Daniel Stern (2000, p. 221) draws attention to a phenomenon that has been termed 'social referencing'. A familiar example is that of a young child falling down and beginning to cry. 'If the mother quickly moves into a fun-surprise mode "Oh, what an interesting and funny thing just happened to you", the infant is likely to switch gears into a gleeful state.' A group of researchers has studied this phenomenon in more detail (Stern 2000, p. 132):

> The year-old infants are placed in a situation bound to create uncertainty, usually ambivalence between approach and withdrawal. The infant may be lured with an attractive toy to crawl across a 'visual cliff' (an apparent drop-off, which is mildly frightening at one year of age or so) or may be approached by an unusual but highly stimulating objects such as a bleeping, flashing robot like R2D2 from *Star Wars*. When the infants encounter these situations and give evidence of uncertainty, they look towards mother to read her face for its affective content, essentially to see what they should feel, to get a second appraisal to help resolve their uncertainty. If the mother has been instructed to show facial pleasure by smiling, the infant crosses the visual cliff. If the mother has been instructed to show facial fear, the infant turns back from the 'cliff', retreats, and perhaps becomes upset. Similarly, if the mother smiles at the robot, the infant will too. If she shows fear the infant will become more wary.

Stern suggests that such social referencing (making reference to another's response before finding one's own response) can contribute to an infant's confidence (as in the case of the infant who responds with glee to falling over), but can also lead to less happy outcomes, as in the following mother's responses to her child (Stern 2000, p. 222):

> Whenever her son did something maladroit, as is expectable in a one-year-old, so that something got knocked over or a toy was disarranged, the mother would let out a multimodal depressive signal. This consisted of long expirations, falling intonations, slightly collapsing postures, furrowing the brows, tilting and drooping the head, and 'Oh, Johnnys' that could be interpreted as 'Look what you've done to your mother again', if not 'What a tragedy that your clumsiness with that toy train has caused the death of another dozen people'.

> Gradually, Johnny's exuberant exploratory freedom became more circumspect. His mother...had brought an alien affective experience into an otherwise neutral or positive activity. She may also have succeeded in making it part of the infant's own affective experience during that activity, which then became a quite different lived experience.

What such examples suggest is that from a very early age human beings develop responses to their situations that are determined partly by individual (and in the beginning largely innate) dispositions and partly through attunement to the responses of others. In some circumstances (e.g. if the infant's own emotion is strong), the 'individual response' will override the 'social response'; in other circumstances, especially where there is no very marked individual response, the social response will dominate. To take an example from later in life, when the child is beginning to learn words for colours, there is no initial individual preference for calling or not calling grass 'green' and snow 'white', so that here the child naturally learns a response that is 'our' response. This applies, of course, to a vast range of human learning, all the way from learning what shoes are to learning what is a plausible interpretation of the tracks in a cloud chamber photograph. It is only in a social context that the child learns what shoes are; it is not something a child could conceivably learn on their own. Similarly, learning about plausible interpretations of the photograph involves a long training in physics, and an initiation into the concepts and practices that are shared by the community of physicists.

Human learning is a complex phenomenon that involves spontaneous individual responses, but also the responses of other people. It is not a matter of 'conditioning' but of coming to appreciate what is so and what is not. As David Hamlyn (1978) has argued, such an appreciation can't possibly be acquired by the child on their own, because what the child is learning is what, in our culture, is regarded as the *correct* way of seeing things, and it learns what is correct through being *corrected*, through being initiated into the way *we* see things. Thus relationships with other people are essential to learning what and how things are, but it is not simply a matter of the child coming to conform with what their carer wants and says. There has to be, to *some* extent, the possibility of the carer being *wrong*, as distinct from simply being in conflict with the child. This possibility is presumably brought to the child's awareness through their experience of *disagreement* among the adults, and also through a growing awareness that the adults *distinguish* between what they themselves want and what is a good thing, or between what they believe and what is true. Whatever the details of this may involve, it seems clear that from the start, the way the child sees things is utterly bound up with the nature of their relationships with others.

This social dimension of human experience hardly needs emphasizing today, but equally there are limits to what can be said to be 'socially constructed'. It is not a social construction that we become hungry if we have not eaten for some time, that we can't run a mile in three minutes or that we will drown if we are submersed in water for too long. It is also true that, to a significant extent, the relation between facial expressions and emotions is not socially constructed. Smiling and human responses to smiling do not derive entirely from culture, although they may be modified by it. There are spontaneous patterns of response here without which culture could not get off the ground. Further, within the patterns that are laid down in human cultures, there is always room for deviant responses. While if we are human at all we will to a very large extent respond to situations in ways that are characteristic of our culture, if not of human societies generally, there will be times when our own individual responses override what is culturally laid down. This applies again all the way from cases such as a child denying that this ball is red to cases such as a physicist challenging the principle that nothing can travel faster than light. And while such disagreements normally end with the individual becoming reconciled to the standard cultural response, in exceptional cases it is the cultural response that becomes modified in order to cope with the individual's response. For example, the parent may concede that this ball really is orange when they view it, as the child has done, in better lighting conditions, or the physics community may have to accept certain experimental results even if they go against 'what we physicists all know'.

The interaction between individual responses and acceptable social responses is central to human life. If we simply followed our individual responses we would learn almost nothing about the world; but if we *always* followed the accepted social responses we would lose something of ourselves, and society would lose our individual contribution to *its* response.

The difficulties that can arise either way can be seen even at the beginning of human life, as the phenomenon of social referencing shows. The child with the depressed mother tends to lose his vitality and spontaneity through taking on his mother's way of responding; but also, an infant that didn't take on the mother's light-hearted response to falling over would lose the chance of being light and spontaneous. Human responses to situations involve an attunement to the responses of others, beginning with parents and later extending to wider groups to which we belong. This is, however, a double-edged sword: if we don't allow ourselves to attune to the ways of the group, to be 'initiated' into the group, then we will lose much of what we are capable of. To fulfil our potential it is often the case that we need to 'apprentice ourselves' to someone who is a 'master' in the field we wish to enter; it would be absurd for an apprentice blacksmith to be always challenging the master craftsman, or for the beginning violinist to be always asking the maestro why they need to do it this way rather than that. To such questions the only appropriate answer might be 'Just accept it for the moment – you don't yet know enough for these questions to make sense!' (cf. Wittgenstein 1969, p. 310). On the other hand, if we *always* attune ourselves to the group, or its representatives, we will miss the chance of discovering things that the group does not know, and this will in turn be an impoverishment for the group.

Attachment patterns

The balance between attunement to the responses of others and the following of one's own individual responses is so fundamental to human life that if anything goes wrong with the balance there are likely to be serious consequences both for the individual and the group.

Attachment theory draws attention to some basic patterns in this connection (e.g. Howe 2011). In the 'avoidance pattern' children learn to contain their feelings and mask their distress. They tend to be good readers of other people's emotional states. 'It makes sense to gauge the other person's expectations of you if you are anxious about being rejected if you get things wrong, but accepted if you get things right' (ibid., p. 102). They don't find it easy to explore their own emotional makeup. Thoughts are trusted; feelings are not (p. 105). It is 'best to trust only what you are told, rely on what you know, ignore what you feel' (p.119). In general, their affect, or emotional response, is over-regulated (p. 44). This pattern, in which the person attends anxiously to the feelings of others, but finds it hard to access their own feelings, seems to be associated with what I have called 'Type C' troubles.

By contrast, in the 'ambivalent pattern' expressions of need and distress are exaggerated (p. 46); feelings are acted out rather than managed or contained (p.137); and the person is caught up, enmeshed in, preoccupied with their own anxious feelings. 'Feelings and thoughts can rapidly spin out of control' (p. 148). In general, their affect is *under*-regulated. This pattern seems to be associated with my Type B troubles.

In attachment theory both the avoidant and ambivalent forms of attachment are said to be 'organized'. They are the child's way of adapting in an organized way to the specific deficiencies of the care-giving environment. In their different ways the strategies 'increase and maintain proximity to the attachment figure at times of need, danger and threat' (p. 45). They are in that sense successful strategies, though they succeed at a cost. By contrast, 'disorganized attachments' are those where no form of attachment strategy is effective. The relationship with the parents is more fundamentally disturbed than in the first two kinds of case. 'Some parents appear to "abdicate" their caregiving at the very moment their children seek protection, comfort and regulation' (p. 153), so that the child does not experience the safety of a containing relationship. This overall *absence* of relationship, rather than the presence of an under- or over-regulated relationship, seems to embody the extreme form of Type A troubles.

'Balancing' and the 'zigzags'

These links with attachment theory are rather schematic, but I think they can be useful in providing a context for my conclusion that running through the variety of approaches to therapy there are two contrasting, yet related, themes, together with the more general background theme of 'relationship'. One is the theme of clients who don't have a clear sense of what they really feel and want. Their feelings and desires may be more apparent to others than to them, so that in psychodynamic terms there is much in their behaviour that is 'unconscious', while in person-centred terms they are significantly 'incongruent'. They are concerned more with the feelings of others than with their own feelings; it is as though their 'radar' is primarily turned outwards in order to pick up signals from others. The second theme is that of clients who are unable to feel or act upon what they genuinely know to be the case. Their attention is very attuned to their own emotions, especially their fears, and while they are able to appreciate to some extent that their responses are inappropriate to their situation, the situation itself does not strongly engage their attention; it is as if their 'radar' is primarily turned inwards in order to register their own responses. What I suggest in the present chapter is that these two themes have their roots in very basic features of the human situation, especially the fact that our understanding of the world grows not just out of our own responses but also out of the responses of others with whom we are closely involved, and that in various ways the balance of these two 'inputs' can be upset. If we think about psychological troubles in this way, as a disturbance in the balance between individual and social response, then it will be natural to think of therapy as involving a restoration of the balance. For some clients this will involve helping them to give more attention to their own responses, as is typical of psychodynamic and person-centred therapy, while for others it will involve helping them to give more attention to how 'we' see the situation, to 'how the situation really is', which is in effect what behavioural and cognitive forms of therapy do.

The way in which the 'balancing' is done involves what I have called the 'zigzags' between response and view. The client who needs to discover what they 'really feel' will need to give attention to their responses, and to the details of their situation, and then try to find words to express or articulate their response to the situation. When they have some words, they *weigh up* whether these words really do articulate their response. They ask, 'Is this really what I want to say *here*?' They are trying to find an authentic expression of their response by moving back and forth between their response-in-the-situation and their changing articulation of it. In time they may find a way of saying exactly what it is that they feel, and thus reach a clear view of things. There is then no longer any incongruity or imbalance between their response and their view.

On the other hand, the client who wants to be able to respond in a way that embodies their considered view of things will need to give attention to what their view really is and then try to find ways of bringing their response into line with it. Their view may encourage them to weigh up what might be an achievable instance of what they would like to do: 'I just can't do *that*,.... Hmm... but I'm pretty sure I could do *this*.' Then they try this response, and either it is too difficult for them (and they return to weighing up what would be an achievable step) or they succeed with the step they have chosen, and find that now a slightly harder step feels possible. It is a process in which the client goes back and forth between their response ('That's really scary') and their belief ('But I could do *this*'), and then from doing *this* to feeling that now it isn't so scary, so that it might be possible to take another step. In time they may find a way of getting to respond in a way that fits exactly with what they believe, so that, as with the first zigzag, there is no longer any imbalance between their response and their view.

A third kind of situation is that in which a zigzag between 'how I feel' and 'how things are/how things "ought" to be' leads not to victory for one side or the other but to a resolution in which 'view' is modified by 'felt response', but also 'felt response' is modified by 'view'. We saw in Chapter 7 how such a zigzag operates in the two-chair work that PET takes from Gestalt therapy. I suspect that in psychotherapy practice it is often this *mutual* modification of 'response' and 'view' that leads to the resolution of clients' difficulties. For example, a client may talk about how depressed they are, and about how they have no reason for feeling as they do. Later in the session they talk about how their current life situation is really quite good, but they can't *feel* that it is. If they 'stay with' their depressed feelings and talk around them, it may emerge that in fact there are things in their present life, or in their past – perhaps things involving significant loss – that begin to make sense of their depression. Their feelings begin to be articulated, as characteristically takes place in Type C therapies. Then later, as they begin to confront the reality of how their life is actually satisfactory in some respects, they may begin to be able to *feel* this, perhaps by choosing to make some small change in their life that is clearly incompatible with a belief that things are completely hopeless. This process involves a version of exposure to reality that is in principle little different from what takes place in Type B therapies.

Finally, there is what we might call the fundamental (Type A) zigzag, which is that between the client and the therapist. For either of the first two zigzags to work effectively, the client needs to be in communication with the therapist, to consider what the therapist says and does, but also to find their own words and their own way of doing things. They need to be able to weigh up what their own responses and beliefs are, in the light of how the therapist responds to them. The client needs to be open to the therapist, but also needs to sense that the therapist is open to *them*. In short 'the relationship' is crucial. Neither ignoring the therapist nor simply going along with the therapist's way of doing things is likely to lead to therapeutic change. Yet clearly the onus is on the therapist to try to find ways of making the relationship 'work'. If it is not working then neither of the other zigzags is likely to work, whereas if it is working then that may be all that is needed. Not all client troubles fall into the categories of 'not finding feelings' (Type C) or of 'not making appropriate responses' (Type B); some are more a matter of 'not finding a human connection' (Type A).

To summarize, my suggestion is that in the familiar facts of human relationship we can locate the kinds of trouble that bring people to therapy, and also the main ways of responding helpfully to those troubles. There is the broad trouble of finding human relationships difficult, and the corresponding therapeutic response of creating a human relationship with the client that will do something to remedy what the client missed in their early years. This is the response especially of (later) person-centred therapy, but something of it will be there in almost all forms of therapy. Then there are two contrasting forms of trouble: one is that in which the client is over-involved in their own responses, and cannot find a way of bringing those responses into line with what they know through social learning to be the case. This trouble requires the therapist to help clients, little by little, to expose themselves to the reality of their situations, a reality that they already recognize, but cannot yet feel. It is a kind of help that is characteristic especially of behavioural and some cognitive forms of therapy. The other form of trouble is that in which the client is over-involved in conventional ways of seeing things (in Heidegger's '*they*') and cannot easily feel their own response as distinct from what they 'should' feel. In commonsense terms, their pre-occupation with what is socially accepted leads them into self-deception. This kind of trouble requires the therapist to help the client temporarily to put aside how they 'should' feel, so that they can begin to sense what their own authentic responses are. This kind of help is especially characteristic of psychodynamic, focusing-oriented and (early) person-centred therapy.[1]

Nothing in all this seems to require much in the way of theory, if by 'theory' we mean considering client troubles and therapeutic procedures in terms of theoretical concepts such as 'the unconscious', 'organismic experiencing', 'stimuli' and 'conditioning', 'cognitions as causes of feelings'. Such concepts, we have seen, are best rejected. However, the framework of thought I am suggesting, involving a balancing of 'response' and 'view', could itself be regarded as a theory in the sense that it pulls together the common-sense cores of all the major approaches. It is also a framework that can to some extent be integrated with earlier views of psychological disturbance, as I will discuss in the next section.

A traditional background for the common-sense rationale

I think it is worth noting that there is a long tradition of thought that broadly conceptualizes health and illness in terms of 'balance' and 'imbalance'. Something of this tradition is found in our common ways of speaking: someone who is troubled is said to be *upset*, or in more extreme cases *unbalanced*, and sometimes coroners record that a person committed suicide when the *balance of their mind* was disturbed.

At the beginning of Western medicine 'the cardinal concept in the Hippocratic Corpus was that health was equilibrium and illness was upset' (Porter 1997, p. 56). Further, Hippocratic medicine saw illness as a disorder of the whole person, rather than as just faulty physical functioning. 'Hippocratic healing was patient-centred and focussed on "dis-ease" rather than disease understood as an ontological category' (p. 60). In Plato, a distinction is made between 'body' and 'soul', but in both cases illness, or dis-ease, is seen as a matter of imbalance. In Greek, and later mediaeval thought, what we would call 'physical illness' was understood to involve an imbalance of the four 'humours', that is blood, phlegm, black bile and yellow bile. Each of these was associated with one of the four elements out of which the physical world was formed: blood was associated with air, phlegm with water, black bile with earth and yellow bile with fire. But the humours were not understood in a purely material way; they involved what we would call 'psychological' characteristics. In particular, a predominance, or imbalance, of one humour in a person would involve that person having a particular kind of *temperament*. An imbalance of air was associated with a sanguine temperament, of phlegm with a phlegmatic temperament, of black bile with melancholia and of yellow bile with a choleric disposition. Rather similar systems of thought are found in Indian Ayurvedic medicine and related forms of Chinese and Tibetan medicine and psychiatry (Clifford 1990; Maciocia 2005).

The details of these systems don't concern us here, but at their heart is the view of illness as imbalance. If we emphasize the 'physical' side of Greek thought, we will be concerned with an imbalance of the elements, and that perhaps is not so far from modern ideas of bodily self-regulation, and the disturbance of that regulation in physical illness, resulting in such things as fever, but also such things as the dis-regulation of cell growth in cancer. Although modern medicine is much concerned with the physiological *mechanisms* of health and illness, the mechanisms are not the whole story. There is also what the mechanisms are mechanisms *of*, which is the overall functioning of the organism.

The same is true of modern biology, which while concerned with the mechanisms of life can't wholly lose sight of the fact that it is concerned with *living things*, that is, organisms whose organs and processes need to be understood in terms of their function as well as in terms of causal mechanisms. A good illustration of that point is found in the development of ethology, the biological study of animal behaviour. Ethologists classify stereotyped behaviour patterns in terms of their biological function, rather than in terms of their causal mechanisms, just as anatomists often classify organs in a functional way. One can only understand the notion of an eye, for example, in terms of the contribution it makes to the organism's ability to see. The form and structure of the eye of a fly is very different from the eye of a mammal, but they are both eyes. Similarly, in ethology a threat display differs from an appeasement display in terms of its *function*, not its form or underlying causal mechanisms (Purton 1978). Health and illness belong within this functional way of seeing things; medicine *is* concerned with the mechanisms of illness, but this concern operates within the perspective of whether the functional balance of the body has been upset.

If we turn to the other side of Greek thinking, we find a similar view of disturbances of 'the soul'. In the *Phaedrus* Plato pictures the soul as a chariot pulled by two winged horses, one white and one black. Plato scholars have not always agreed on the details of how the imagery is to be understood,[2] but Eva Buccioni (2002) argues that the white horse stands for 'civilisation' (p. 340), 'the values held by society' (p. 341), 'the psychical force that drives the individual to seek social integration' (p. 343) and 'the opinion others have of one' (p. 344). The black horse stands for treating 'other people as one pleases' (p. 345); it is 'asocial' and 'anarchic' (p. 346). One might say that in allowing the white horse to determine the direction of one's life one can find harmony with the views of one's society, but can lose something of one's individuality; while in allowing one's direction to be determined by the black horse, one can find one's own feelings, but can lose one's grounding in society.

Something like this account of the balancing of the soul seems to be quite closely followed by a number of psychological writers. There is Freud's notion of the dynamic tension between superego and id, which needs to be balanced by the ego; Berne's transactional analysis scheme of the Adult mediating between the Parent and the Child; and Rogers' distinction between self-concept and organismic valuing. Mearns and Thorne (2000, p. 180) write: 'Perhaps it is the *balance* in the person's life which is important – that they are achieving a balance between the drive of the actualizing tendency and the restraint of social mediation.' Therapy, from this perspective, is largely a matter of helping clients to find ways of achieving balance, both within themselves and in relation to others. It is not that the therapist balances the client, but rather that their task is to help the client in the client's *self-balancing*. As Bohart and Tallman (1999) suggest, much of what happens in successful psychotherapy can be understood in terms of clients' *self-righting* capacities.

I have suggested that the therapist can be seen as helping clients to find balance in their lives, partly the fundamental balance between themselves and others that is implicit in *relating* to others, including the therapist, and partly the balance between their own spontaneous responses and what they consider to be the reality of their situation. The balancing here is not a balance within the body, such as medicine seeks, but a balance within what has traditionally been called the soul. 'Soul' is not a comfortable word in much modern thinking, perhaps because of its religious associations, but it is hard to find an adequate replacement. We might say that the balance that is sought in therapy is a balance of the *person* rather than of the body. When Plato speaks of the soul, he does in effect mean the person: the soul or person needs to balance their impulsive and rational social sides. Certainly, 'soul' here is being used in a very different way from 'mind', which in common usage is usually a way of talking about the intellectual capacities of the person.

Reference to 'the soul' connects with the point that while counselling and psychotherapy are recent developments in human history, personal troubles have always been with us, and so also, I imagine, has some kind of distinction between distress and *disorder* of the person. Szasz (1978) and Frank (1991), among others, have suggested that the role that therapists play in modern society is similar to that played in earlier societies by priests and shamans; these are practitioners who in one way or another work with disorders of the *soul*. Of course, there are differences between the older and the modern practitioners; but then there are differences between the older practitioners themselves. A 14th-century English priest is certainly different from a 14th-century Siberian shaman, but equally there is a significant difference between the work of a modern counsellor in a GP surgery and that of a Kleinian psychoanalyst. Yet between all these practitioners I think we can recognize a family resemblance.

In his study of healing systems in India, the psychoanalyst Sudhir Kakar (1982, p. 275) writes that western 'notions of mental health are pervaded by the humanistic ideals of moderation and responsibility, of balance, in short – a balance between inner needs and the demands of outer reality. Balance, as we saw earlier, also characterizes the ideals of many Indian approaches.' But in addition to facilitating *that* kind of balance, which in my terms is characteristic of Type B and Type C therapies, he remarks that there is a second kind of balancing involved in the Indian systems:

> What makes the majority of Indian approaches to mental health different from the dominant western view on the subject, however, is their emphasis on the *relational*. In the Indian prescriptive lists (for example in Ayurveda)

one is struck by the number of ideals of mental health that prescribe the person's behaviour in relation to others, especially family and community. A restoration of lost harmony between the person and his group, we saw earlier, was one of the primary aims of the healing endeavours in the local and folk traditions.

A version of this second kind of 'balancing' is to be found in any kind of therapy that primarily involves the relationship between client and therapist and is especially prominent in what I have called Type A therapies.

Thinking of therapy as the seeking of balance allows us to acknowledge that there is *some* analogy between medicine and what is called psychotherapy. They are both concerned with 'balance', but while medicine is concerned with bodily balance, psychotherapy is concerned with personal balance. Psychotherapy, as its etymology suggests, should be understood as concerned with balance not of the mind but of what the Greeks called the psyche or soul. For this reason, while the troubles of therapy clients can in a way be seen as 'disorders', such troubles are not well characterized as *mental* disorders; rather they are disorders of the soul, the psyche or the person. This way of thinking about the matter allows us to retain something of the distinction between 'mental disorder' and 'mental distress' that I discussed in Chapter 10. 'Mental disorder', or what I think would better be called 'personal imbalance', will often be distressing, but not necessarily so. As I suggested, it is perfectly possible for a person not to be distressed by a disorder that they have; they may even be delighted with it. Similarly, personal distress need not involve personal disorder. There is also the advantage that we can retain something of the appropriateness of the term 'therapy' in referring to the aim of helping those who come for therapeutic help. 'Therapy' can hardly be a good term if what we are dealing with is simply distress, but it does fit with 'disorder'.

This overall view of client troubles is itself a theory in the broad sense that it draws together a variety of phenomena in a coherent way, but it is the sort of theory that is an extension of common sense, rather than a replacement for it. It does not invoke concepts of 'underlying' entities or processes, but it does provide a broad framework for thinking about client troubles and ways to respond to them.

Summary

We have seen that the practice of psychotherapy does not depend much on the theories on which it is supposed to be based. We have also seen that the theories themselves are significantly incoherent. My criticisms in earlier chapters have usually been directed at the original versions of the theories. The justification for this, apart from the matter of available space, is that in each case there are fundamental confusions in the most basic concepts of the theories, confusions that can't be sorted out through any tinkering with the details. In the earlier versions of the theories it is often easier to see just what the difficulties really are; in later versions it tends to become less clear. For example,

Freud's theory has been developed in many different ways since his early work, but as McNally (2003, p. 171) remarks, 'psychoanalysis became increasingly incoherent as it evolved'. As early as 1936 the distinguished social psychologist William McDougall, in the course of attempting to make sense of Freud's later writings, described them as 'a great tangle in which Freud lashes about like a great whale caught in a net of his own contriving' (McDougall 1936, p. 60). To some extent this increasing incoherence is true also of CBT. The early writings of Beck and Ellis presented a brisk, focused account of a new way of thinking about psychological troubles, according to which what is needed in therapy is changes in cognition that will result in changes in feelings and behaviour. However, 'modern CBT' (Needham & Dryden 2004; Hofmann 2012) also emphasizes empathy, the client–therapist relationship and a focus on feelings. In the form of so-called 'third wave CBT' it has expanded to include 'mindfulness-based cognitive therapy' (Segal et al. 2002), 'dialectical behaviour therapy' (Linehan 1993) and 'acceptance and commitment therapy (ACT)' (Hayes et al. 2003). There is much that is clinically helpful in these developments, but they do mean that it is increasingly difficult either to defend or criticize 'CBT'; it is no longer clear what CBT *is*, let alone what justifies it theoretically.

Similarly, one could, in the earlier days of the person-centred/client-centred approach, say that Rogers' (1959) theory centred around the idea that psychological troubles were due to clients having introjected conditions of worth, and that effective therapy involves neutralizing these conditions through the therapist embodying the core attitudes of empathy, acceptance and congruence. Today it is very different; the person-centred approach is now a 'nation' encompassing several different 'tribes' (Sanders 2012), including classical client-centred therapy, focusing-oriented therapy, experiential therapy, emotion-focussed therapy and even some forms of existential and integrative therapy. There is no longer anything that could be called '*the* theory of person-centred therapy'. Even within the widely influential 'standard version' of person-centred therapy (Purton 2004, pp. 17–20), deriving largely from the work of Mearns and Thorne, there have been significant changes, as can be seen by comparing the first (1988) and third (2007) editions of their classic work *Person-Centred Counselling in Action*.

In any field there will of course be changes and developments in the course of time, but what makes assessment of the field of therapy difficult is that there has not been a gradual expansion of what can be taken to be the accepted theoretical basis of the field, nor even a growing agreement about the theoretical basis *within* the major schools of therapy. On the contrary, what we find is a continuing fragmentation, with today something like 400 different kinds of therapy available and, as I have said, a wide range of views obtaining even within the main schools. Yet in each school there is still, in the background, a set of theoretical concepts, which are taught on the training courses that associate themselves with the main traditions. In such training courses the basics of the original theories are still taught and are seen as still informing the general theoretical approach of the training. Freud and Rogers, Ellis and Beck, are still read, even if Hull and Skinner are not. If the writings of these theorists, or modern versions of their writings, were no longer read *at all*, it would be hard to see how there could be *any* justification for still distinguishing between, for example, psychodynamic, person-centred and cognitive-behavioural forms of therapy. Thus in focusing mainly on the original forms of the theories, I think I have done all that reasonably can be done.

I have also suggested that there is a kind of incoherence that most of the theories *share*, which is that their ways of putting things don't cohere with our everyday language or our common-sense ways of understanding things. Instead, they are rooted in the 17th-century metaphysical picture of the world that was crystallized by Descartes, or in its later development in Kant's philosophy. They take us away from common sense, rather than refining it or elaborating on it. And because they don't cohere with common sense, their elaboration does not lead to a gradually increasing body of accepted knowledge, but to increasing fragmentation, as different factions within each approach emphasize different aspects of something that simply does not hang together as a coherent whole.

I hope also to have shown that fundamental criticism of the theories is important not just because it is intellectually worthwhile to expose an incoherent theory as incoherent, but also because so long as the theories are seen as coherent, and therefore as *possible* ways of thinking about human troubles, they will remain as temptations to *practice* therapy in ways that can be harmful to clients.

The question then arises of how now we are to think about the theories. The simple answer is that they need to be abandoned, in the way that Hull's behaviourist theory, as expounded in his *Principles of Behavior* (1943), has been abandoned. One can acknowledge that Hull's theory is an extraordinary intellectual creation, but at best it can be seen now as a glittering 'castle in the air', or at worst, in the words of the philosopher and educationalist Richard Peters (1958, p. 2), as 'an enormity'.

I think that the other theories also need to be abandoned, but I have suggested that each of them involves at least *something* of the (largely commonsensical) explanatory framework that I have proposed. Thus something of the traditional approaches can be retained, and I see no reason why my proposed framework should not be 'dressed up' in a variety of ways. Some therapists, as Wampold (2001, p. 224) reports, have developed a version of cognitive therapy that uses Christian arguments and imagery in getting the principles of the therapy across to religious clients. In the same way, I suspect, something of the distinctive thought-pictures of the traditional theories may be retained, and consciously employed, in a way adapted to the preferences of clients. For example, there is no reason why a therapist shouldn't adopt the fairly down-to-earth, 'scientific' style that is characteristic of behaviour therapy; or something of the more 'rational' style of the cognitive approach. There can still be references to unconscious feelings for clients who find psychodynamic ideas appealing and are intrigued by the subtleties and contradictions in human motives; a more person-centred style may be most attractive to those who are primarily concerned with 'relationship'; Focusing talk of bodily located feelings will appeal to some clients; and existential ways of putting things will appeal to those who prefer an approach that conveys something of dramatic philosophical depth. To this limited extent, I agree with Cooper and McLeod (2011, p. 157) that one can make use of different 'worldviews' so long as they are 'held lightly'. However, this 'light holding of worldviews' can only be, in my view, a matter of the *style* in which the fundamental common-sense framework of therapy is presented. Therapists need to hold *firmly*, not lightly, to common sense itself, although it can be valuable to have different ways of presenting the common-sense framework to clients, depending on client preferences.

Notes

1. It perhaps should be added that such putting aside of conventional 'shoulds' is not a matter putting aside what one genuinely believes one should do. In ethical reflection one may be concerned about the fact that one *feels* that that a certain group of people are stupid or uncouth, whereas one doesn't actually *believe* this. This kind of case actually belongs with what I have called the Type B cases: being unable to *feel* that this group of people are normally intelligent and civilized, even though one *believes* that they are, is parallel to being unable to *feel* that the bridge is safe, although one recognizes it to be safe. Cases of this sort are more appropriately discussed in contexts of ethics than of psychotherapy, since working with them presupposes agreement on what one should (not 'should') feel. For an example of such a case, see Iris Murdoch (1970, pp. 25, 27–29), and my discussion of it in relation to therapy (Purton 2014).
2. One complication is that in the *Republic* Plato gives a rather different account of the soul, in which its three elements are something like Reason, Appetite and Spiritedness. However, Buccioni (2002) argues that the account in the *Phaedrus* should not be forced into the scheme of the *Republic*. In the *Republic* account it is natural to associate the two horses with two elements of the soul, Appetite and Spiritedness, while the charioteer is associated with a third element, that is, Reason. However, in the *Phaedrus* account the horses seem to stand for societal inclinations and spontaneous impulse. I think that the charioteer in the *Phaedrus* is best understood not as a third element *in* the soul, but rather as the *person* who tries to achieve a balance between two kinds of impulse. In the picture the charioteer is, after all, a person, whereas the other two elements are represented by 'animal instincts' (one social, one individual).

Chapter 12

Implications for Practice and Training

Summary of the suggested principles of therapy

What I have tried to do in this book is to provide an account of psychotherapy that is not tied to any of the current theories, yet does not simply present a list of helpful procedures. It is an integrative account based on a consideration of the broad nature of the troubles that bring clients to therapy. The troubles of therapy clients seem to be essentially connected with what I have called a lack of 'personal balance' that is manifested in troubled relationships, but also in a lack of balance between felt response and considered view. Although 'mental illness' is not a good term for such troubles, I think it is helpful to think of them as involving something of the nature of *disorder* rather than simply *distress*. Distress is often a response to difficult circumstances, and the appropriate way to deal with it is either to change the circumstances if that is possible or to accept them, if they can't be changed. Distress is not in itself a reason for seeking *therapeutic* help. Where therapeutic help *is* appropriate is in cases where the distress is in some way inappropriate in the circumstances, and the sufferer realizes that this is so. To feel 'down' because one has lost one's job is a case of distress, but if a person feels down for no reason, then we sense that there is something astray or out of order. To feel anxious about having to give a public talk is normal, and acceptable for most people, but to feel petrified by the prospect might make one consider therapy, as might feeling even moderately scared of spiders. The common factor in these cases is a discrepancy between what one believes about the situation and one's felt response to it, but there are two ways in which the discrepancy can arise. One is where one's response has not been sufficiently modulated by the rest of one's beliefs and experience; for example, the fear remains in spite of one's awareness that there is no danger. The other is where what one thinks and says is not a genuine expression of one's response; for example, one thinks and says that one is not afraid, when one *is* afraid.

I have suggested that the potential for discrepancies, or imbalances, between our responses and our considered view of things is deeply rooted in the human situation, since what we spontaneously feel may conflict with what we understand to be best. This is what is pictured by Plato in his myth of the charioteer trying to balance the impulses of the black horse and the white horse. In much of our lives there is an ongoing interaction between 'response' and 'view', but at times one side or other becomes suppressed, either through the influence of intense fears or of intense desires. The person then becomes *unbalanced*, either going with their spontaneous response in a way that ignores their considered view or holding to their view of things in a way that ignores their real response. Either kind of imbalance is closely linked with the person's relationship with others. The prototype of the first kind of case is where the young child, unable to regulate its own emotions, is not adequately soothed by their carer; there is insufficient 'affect regulation'. The prototype of the second kind of case is where the young child's spontaneous responses are *over*-regulated by the carer, so that the child loses touch with their own feelings. In therapy, I suggest, these imbalances, which are rooted in relational difficulties, can be corrected through a balanced relationship with the therapist. Simply being in a human relationship in which the therapist is neither overwhelmed by the client's feelings nor tries to change them will contribute to a balancing within the client. But also, the therapist may actively help the client to regulate their emotions through such procedures as calming and supporting them during a gradual exposure to the reality of things, or may encourage them to recover an awareness of feelings that have been suppressed.

Implications for practice

This sketch of what is involved in personal imbalance suggests that the therapist has two primary tasks.

(1) The first is to engage initially with the client in as balanced a way as possible. The tenor of the early sessions needs to be one in which the client is encouraged to talk about their trouble in any way they wish, except that the therapist also has *their* place in the interaction. The therapist needs to *respond to* the client, rather than simply listening. But the therapist also needs to give plenty of space for the *client's* responding. The ideal could be said to be maximum engagement with minimum direction. There needs at the start to be a dialogue rather than a monologue, but the dialogue is of a special kind. This is not an ordinary conversation, although such ordinary conversations outside the therapy room could also be helpful, as when a troubled person simply wants to 'have a chat'. In the therapy context the session is centred almost entirely on the client, so that while the therapist needs to be an equal partner in the dialogue, it would be inappropriate for them to bring in much of their own feelings and views. The method developed by Rogers of reflecting what the client says is admirably suited to this situation. Careful reflection helps the client to appreciate that they have been understood, but also, as Gendlin has emphasized, it helps them to check whether what they said expresses adequately what they meant to express. Reflection, or 'active listening', allows an interaction between client and therapist which in an important way simulates the kind of early interaction between infant and mother through which the

infant begins to get a sense of themselves as an independent being, while being safely 'held'. The inevitable ruptures in this early relationship, which can give rise to personal imbalance, may well be repeated in the therapy context, but here they can be repaired if the therapist is sufficiently concerned and aware.

(2) The second task is that of responding in a way that helps the client to correct the specific kind of imbalance which is the source of their trouble. This will involve exploring with the client whether they are primarily seeking to change their ways of responding, or whether the trouble is more a matter of not knowing what they feel or want. However, it may not initially be clear what the client is seeking, or which form of imbalance is primary for them, or whether both kinds are involved. For example, an unassertive client may find it hard to say 'No' to unreasonable requests. They may see their problem in terms of how to modify their behaviour so that it comes into line with how they would like to be. If that is the client's aim, then the therapist might suggest a role-play of assertive behaviour in the session, or participation in an assertiveness workshop. Another client might see such procedures as superficial and likely to deflect attention from what is really involved. They might sense that their way of responding to people is not a straightforward *inability* to assert themself but is *motivated* in a way that they don't understand. They want help in finding out what their unassertive behaviour *is all about*, or what it is that they are *really up to* in not asserting themself. If that is the client's aim, then the therapist might work with the client in a way that helps the client to articulate further what they are feeling, as might be done (in rather different ways) in client-centred, focusing-oriented or psychodynamic therapy. Such a procedure might then lead to the client realizing that they have a deep fear of dominating or harming other people, and that their 'lack of assertion' is better articulated as 'taking excessive care not to harm or dominate'.

Another example: a client with a spider phobia may be clear that spiders in Britain are harmless, yet they are terrified of them. Their aim in therapy is to reduce or eliminate their emotional response to spiders. Here the therapist might naturally suggest some variety of desensitization programme to gradually reduce their fear. But another client might sense that there is more to their phobia than a straightforward fear of spiders. The therapist might then encourage them to say more about what they are sensing, or to say more about what exactly it is about spiders that is so distressing. Then it might emerge that it is something about the 'spideriness', the curious tickly sensation that is not a real touch. Perhaps it brings back childhood memories of an emotionally unresolved situation involving a rather deranged old aunt, who had to be placated, in spite of her scary way of running her fingers through the client's hair in a spidery way. The fear of spiders now becomes articulated as a revulsion for certain people's invasive 'spideriness', and there comes the realization that something of this sort is going on in the client's current life, which needs to be addressed.

What I suggest here is similar to Cooper and McLeod's (2011) suggestion that we should place the client's goals at the centre of therapy, but I think that a *therapeutic* relationship needs to be concerned primarily with *therapeutic* goals. A client's goals may involve getting the therapist to do things that are therapeutically inappropriate, such as the forming of a friendship, help in settling a score with a rival, working together on a college assignment or discussing political matters. It is only *certain* client goals that a *therapist* can appropriately engage with, and these can only be specified in terms of what we take therapy to involve. My suggestion has been that therapy essentially involves helping clients to achieve and maintain a personal balance between 'response' and 'view', and that it is helpful to think about client goals within that framework.

In Chapter 10 I suggested that within the broad scheme of what I have called troubles of Types A, B and C we can make increasingly fine distinctions. The *broad* distinctions are between troubles that seem to call mainly for real and spontaneous human relating, those that call for help in ways of modifying behaviour and those that call for help in articulating feelings and attitudes. In practice, what this means is that therapists need to be familiar with procedures that are appropriate to each of these general kinds of trouble. Therapists trained in the later person-centred tradition may be especially competent in working with Type A troubles, but much less competent with Type B. Psychodynamically trained therapists, and focusing-oriented therapists, may be especially competent with Type C troubles and behaviourally trained therapists with Type B. Hence one implication of what I have suggested would be that therapists initially trained in one of the traditional schools will need to become more familiar with some of the procedures of the other schools. But this should not be seen as simply adding to one's repertoire of skills; it is more a matter of appreciating that while client troubles all involve personal imbalance, there are different aspects to such imbalance that require different emphases in therapeutic approach.

Finer distinctions between client troubles can no doubt be made in *many* different ways, and here the differing expertise of therapists from different schools may be invaluable. For example, psychodynamic therapy draws on the psychoanalytic distinctions between various 'defence mechanisms', such as projection, displacement and introjection. While in my view it is misleading to speak of *mental mechanisms*, there is no doubt that in connection with Type C troubles there are some worthwhile distinctions to be made between the different ways in which we can deceive ourselves about what we feel, and what we are up to.

How the procedures of an approach can be related to my classification of client troubles can be shown by looking again at process-experiential therapy. As we saw in Chapter 7, the first 'treatment task' in PET, that of 'systematic evocative unfolding', is appropriate to troubles where 'clients are aware of some discrepancy between their own actual reaction, and their view of an appropriate or self-consistent reaction, and are thus motivated to explore and understand it' (Greenberg et al. 1993, pp. 141–142). In my terms this would be seen as a Type C situation, in which the client is trying to find a way of articulating their response – 'I need to see what on earth I am doing here!' – or as a Type B situation in which the client wishes to change their way of responding. Either way, the problem is essentially one of integrating 'view' and 'response'. Greenberg and his colleagues suggest that in cases of this sort a helpful approach is to encourage the client to attend closely to the scene in which the problematic response arises, and also to their emotional response. In my terminology, there needs to be a 'zigzag' between these two. This can lead to the client appreciating how the distorted way in which they are construing the scene may be generating the problematic reaction, or how their habitual response tendencies are distorting their view of the scene.

PET's second kind of trouble is that in which a person has a vague sense of something not being right in their life but is unable to articulate what it is. This is the classical situation addressed in focusing-oriented therapy, and for Greenberg and colleagues the appropriate therapeutic response is along the lines recommended by Gendlin: the therapist encourages the client to attend to the murky 'felt sense' of the problem – to, as I would say, their felt response – and then open themself to ways of articulating this response. The aim is, again, to help the client integrate their response with what they really want to say, and the details of the focusing procedure provide practical guidance on how to work with troubles of this kind.

The next two kinds of trouble in PET involve variants of what Greenberg and colleagues call 'splits', that is, situations in which 'societal standards, attitudes and ways of thinking and acting... are to differing degrees at odds with their more basic needs, goals or concerns... For a variety of different reasons, cultural and family influences overwhelm individual preferences or requirements' (p. 186). This is also the territory of Gestalt therapy and of Rogers' 'conditions of worth', although there is less emphasis in PET on the idea that individual preferences are 'good' and societal standards are 'bad'; it is rather that a balance is needed between the two. As we have seen, the PET suggestion is that what is likely to helpful here is Gestalt 'chair work' involving dialogue between the two 'sides', in the hope that a compromise may be reached. This is another example of the zigzag between 'response' and 'view', but filled out with much in the way of detailed suggestions for practice.

The fifth PET trouble, which Gestalt therapy calls 'unfinished business', is that where the natural development of an emotional situation has been blocked, due to one of the relevant participants being absent. In such cases the client finds it difficult to engage in what would be the normal 'zigzag' between response and view. They cannot 'work through' their feelings or their beliefs, because the situation provides them with no opportunity for this. The 'empty chair' procedure provides an *imaginative* way of engaging in the necessary zigzag process that can lead to a reconciliation of response and view, in which, typically, both are changed.

The final kind of PET trouble is that where the client is too vulnerable for any approach that would help them to articulate their feelings, or for any approach that would help them to modify their responses. Instead, Greenberg and colleagues suggest, what is needed here is above all 'empathic affirmation' of the client, in which the therapist shares with the client their humanity and lack of judgement of what the client feels. In terms of my scheme this sort of case is of the Type A variety; it is a case where what is needed above all is simple, compassionate human relating. Later, it may be possible to begin to work with the client's troubles in ways that are more characteristic of Type B or C approaches.

All the 'treatment tasks' of PET fit with the account of therapy that I am recommending and the detailed PET account of how to engage with these tasks is the sort of thing that can help to fill out the schematic outline I have given of the three different types of approach to clients' troubles. However, as I argued in Chapter 7, this filling-out can be done without invoking the questionable theory of dialectical constructionism that is set out in the earlier part of Greenberg and colleagues' book. The second part of their book, the detailed discussion of *practice,* can stand on its own feet without any reference to the theory. It is true that the various 'treatment tasks' need to be pulled together into a coherent framework, but I suggest that we have such a framework in the account I have given of the different kinds of personal imbalance.

My general account of what is important in the practice of psychotherapy could be summarized by saying that a therapist needs to be able to do three things. First, they need to be able to connect with their client in a real and human way, rather than as an expert who is engaged in applying a psychological theory to the client. As Gendlin (1990, p. 205) put it in a passage I quoted earlier:

> The essence of working with another person is to be present as a living being...What matters is to be a human being with another human being, to recognise the other person as another being in there. Even if it is a cat or bird, if you are trying to help a wounded bird, the first thing you have to know is that there is somebody in there, and that you have to wait for that 'person', that being in there, to be in contact with you.

Without that connection between therapist and client, anything else that the therapist does is likely to be ineffective.

However, given that something of that connection is present, the two other main things that a therapist needs are (1) to be familiar with ways of helping clients to express or articulate what they are really feeling or thinking and (2) to be familiar with ways of helping clients to find ways of making changes in their behaviour, changes in their *lives.* Just how a therapist becomes familiar with these two things probably doesn't matter much. In the case of helping clients to find what they really feel, the approach might be through the person-centred way of reflective listening, or Gendlin's Focusing procedure, or it could be through learning about free association and tentative interpretation. Similarly, in the case of helping clients to make changes in their lives, the approach might be through learning some of the extensive range of CBT techniques that are available today, or through learning existential ways of confronting clients with their need to make choices.

Just how my account of therapy will be useful to practicing therapists will thus depend on how the therapist currently practices. A therapist who has been trained in, and largely practices, in a behaviourally oriented way may be encouraged by my account to consider the possibility that not all client troubles are of Type B; some are better conceptualized as of Types A and C. A therapist who sees that this is plausible might then consider ways of working that are typical of Type A and Type C approaches. It would be a matter of adding such ways of working to their repertoire, but not simply as 'extra techniques that are worth knowing'. The incorporation of the new ways of working would be based on a better understanding of the nature of client troubles, and of what is needed in different contexts. Contemporary behaviourally-oriented therapists already tend to include ideas drawn from other approaches to therapy, and for such therapists my account need not lead to significant changes in practice. Rather, it provides them with a needed *rationale* for such an approach and prevents it from becoming purely pragmatic and eclectic.

Similarly, a therapist who has trained in the psychodynamic tradition may be encouraged by my account to consider the possibility that not all client troubles are of Type C; some are better conceptualized as of Types A and B. As we have seen, contemporary psychodynamic approaches already tend to incorporate something of the Type A approach that is especially associated with person-centred therapy, but my suggestion is that an increased awareness of Type B approaches could also be helpful in working with some clients. Again, this would not be a matter of simply 'bolting on' some CBT techniques to psychodynamic practice; it is, rather, a matter of appreciating better the different forms that clients' troubles can take and of understanding better what approaches are likely to be helpful with *this* client.

I have suggested that the most important procedures in psychotherapy are those that I have characterized as of Types A, B and C. I do not mean to imply that other procedures can't ever help. It could be, for example, that the EMDR technique is effective for some clients although, if it is, we do not at present know *why* it is. However, many of the less obvious forms of therapy probably 'work', not because of anything inherently therapeutic in *them*, but because of the 'common factors' I discussed in Chapter 1, especially the 'placebo' effect of the *expectation* of therapeutic change, along with the 'Type A' factor of a good therapeutic relationship. The A, B and C factors I have discussed are not the *only* effective factors in therapy; as Frank and Wampold have convincingly argued, the fact that therapist and client *share a belief in* the efficacy of therapy is also important. My concern in this book has been to outline what therapists can reasonably believe in, *in addition to* belief in the importance of belief.

Implications for training

Cooper and McLeod (2011, p. 140) write:

> In recent years, there has emerged a broad consensus around the shape of therapist training. It is widely agreed that training programmes need to encompass theory, research, professional issues, work on self, development of therapeutic skills and supervised practice.

Theory. The view of therapy I propose would be largely compatible with this consensus. The theoretical background to therapeutic training would involve the themes I discussed above, that is, an outline of the main kinds of client difficulties, together with the various ways in which therapeutic responses and procedures can be appropriate. This background understanding of therapy is not highly theoretical but involves largely the bringing together of the 'common-sense cores' that I suggested are present in most of the main approaches to therapy. Such a 'bringing together' might well be centred in the ideas of attachment theory, as I indicated in Chapter 10.

The theoretical part of the training would also encourage some scepticism about the Cartesian theories that inform many contemporary schools of therapy. Nevertheless, although I have been critical of these schools, I think that some knowledge of their theories is still needed in any contemporary training. There are several reasons for this. First, trainee therapists need to have a general understanding of what the historical background to the profession is, so that they can appreciate what it is that they are taking forward into the future. Second, although I have argued that most therapeutic procedures can be understood in common-sense terms, the discussion of these procedures in the literature is often entwined with a range of theoretical concepts, and this literature would not be easily comprehensible without some grasp of what the various theoretical frameworks involve. Third, knowledge of a flawed theory is valuable as an 'inoculation' against the dangers of developing a harmful mode of practice that is 'infected' by theory. Fourth, it is not just that there are specific theories that can generate harmful modes of practice but that there are broad ways of seeing people and therapy that are likely to be harmful in working with clients. These ways of seeing people as, for example, *systems* to be repaired, *animals* to be trained, *subjective minds* that need to follow their inner feelings, *beings with dark depths* that need to be illuminated or *cognitive processors* that need to be re-programmed are perennial possibilities in our thinking about people. Quite apart from theories of therapy, we are never invulnerable to the temptations to think of a person as a thing, an animal, an unreachable private consciousness, as a being whose behaviour is determined by unconscious forces or as a rational calculator. These are not good ways to think about people, but *future* theories of therapy could easily fall into any of these ways of thinking, so that for the sake of theories yet to come it is as well to be aware of the kinds of danger that await us.

Trainee therapists need to have some understanding of the main theories that inform current practice, but the thrust of this book is that they also need to be aware of the extent to which the theories are infected by the Cartesian picture of a human being as composed of 'a mind' and 'a body'. This picture needs to be brought out into the open, and its misleading features discussed. For example, discussion might take place around such popular myths as 'we can never really know what other people feel', 'to say that one is in pain is to report a private experience', 'we can never know whether our memories are reliable', 'we know what we are feeling through looking at our inner experiencing' or 'our feelings are determined by our thoughts'. It is not easy to convey in *general* terms what is wrong with these ideas, and it may be best to draw attention to the difficulties inherent in them in the context of particular issues as they arise. Some people, clearly, are more intrigued by such philosophical issues than others, but I think that there are questions here that many trainees will have pondered over at some time, without realizing that they have important implications for psychotherapy theory.

Skills. Consistently with the overall view of therapy presented, the 'skills' element of the training course might draw attention both to the different kinds of therapy 'troubles' and to the most appropriate ways of responding to them. In connection with Type A troubles, and indeed in connection with *all* psychotherapy troubles, there would be an emphasis on the importance of relating to the client in a broadly person-centred way and on developing the 'core therapist attitudes' of acceptance, empathy and genuineness. In connection with Type B troubles there would be an emphasis on trainees becoming familiar with procedures that are currently most typical of the CBT approach. In connection with Type C troubles, there would be an emphasis on acquiring skills of reflection, on helping clients to Focus (in Gendlin's sense) or on learning skills of sensitive and facilitative interpretation. It would also be important for trainees to be helped to reflect on which of these skills come most naturally to them, and on how they use these skills in their *own* common-sense ways of approaching personal difficulties.

Personal development. What Cooper and McLeod call 'work on self' needs to be a central feature of any effective training. Trainees need to achieve some insight into their own troubles and into the impact that their difficulties may have on others, especially on their clients. They also need to have personal experience of being on 'the client side of the fence'. Such work could naturally be thought of in connection with the three types of approach as applied to the trainees' own lives. The Type A approach would involve a general emphasis on self-acceptance, or what the person-centred approach would call 'unconditional positive *self*-regard'. In short, trainees need to learn to take the caring, non-judgemental attitude of the Type A approach towards *themselves.* Then they would be encouraged to make use of whatever cognitive and behavioural procedures appeal to them in working with aspects of their behaviour that they would like to modify. Finally, Gendlin's focusing procedure, used either individually or with a focusing partner, could provide an excellent way of appreciating the benefits of Type C approaches.

Dave Mearns once suggested that a viable training course could centre entirely around discussion of particular cases. Each case would raise both clinical and theoretical issues, which would be taken up in the context of that case. Then it would be discussed to what extent the conclusions might be generalized. Theoretical concepts would be approached via trainees' own thoughts concerning how a particular client issue could be understood. Tutors would then draw attention to how such a line of thought has been developed in the therapy literature, and how it can be criticized. One advantage of such an approach would be that trainees would begin with their *own* common-sense ideas about how a client might be helped. In theory-oriented courses there is a tendency for trainees to think they must leave their common-sense responses behind and adopt the 'correct' approach that derives from a theory. But in that way they can lose their own personal grounding, their natural ways of connecting with people and much common-sense understanding of how people can be helped. The approach that I am recommending avoids this problem, since it grounds therapy in procedures that have a strong common-sense rationale. It in some ways extends and refines common sense, but it at least *grows out of it*.

As Cooper and McLeod (2011, p. 139) note, trainees need to have confidence in what they are trying to do and why they are doing it. My suggestion is that this confidence can best be grounded in an approach to training that begins with trainees' own common-sense responses. In the kind of course that I envisage, the training would build partly on trainees' common-sense responses to client situations, and then it could be shown how many of these common-sense responses do in fact constitute the core of much therapeutic practice. At the same time, it would sometimes become clear, from disagreements among the trainees, that what appears to be *common* sense may not always be so common after all. The *differences* in trainees' responses would be welcomed and would provide a basis for discussion of what these differences are grounded in. Typical differences, related to the types of approach that I have discussed, might take something like the following forms: One trainee says, 'Above all I need to *understand*, and find the meaning of things. I can't act until I understand. Therapy is about a search for meaning.' It could be helpful for such a trainee to realize that there are whole schools of therapy, especially the psychodynamic and existential, but also some varieties of the person-centred approach, that share this view of the centrality of the 'search for meaning' in therapy. But it would also be valuable for the trainee to realize that not everyone feels that way, or sees therapy in those terms. Another trainee might say, 'I need to get things sorted. If a method works for me I don't need to know why it works, and I don't see why the client needs to know. The point is that this procedure works in this situation.' Such a trainee may find increased confidence in learning that there are eclectic traditions of therapy that tend to share that pragmatic kind of view. The trainee's natural approach doesn't have to be abandoned, but at the same time it will be important to learn that an eclectic approach has its difficulties. A third trainee says, 'I need to be clear about things, to specify what my goals are and then think hard about the best ways of achieving them. If there is something puzzling, I want to investigate it and track down exactly what the problem is.' Such a trainee may find it helpful to explore cognitive approaches to therapy, to appreciate that there is something to be said for this approach, but also to see its limitations. A fourth trainee says, 'I need, above all, to relate well to people. Therapy is about relationship. I may not be able to fix things, and I may not be able to understand what is going on, but that doesn't matter so much. It may sound sentimental, but I really do think that "all you need is love".' Such a trainee may well be encouraged to learn that there are therapists such as Brian Thorne (1998, 2002) who

Implications for Practice and Training

share precisely this kind of view. It is a view that doesn't have to be seen as sentimental, though again *not everyone* feels like this, and the trainee may well encounter clients whose approach to life, and expectations of therapy, might be better expressed by 'love is not enough'. They may say that what they want is not to be loved but to be understood, or to be given practical support in facing their problems. The trainee might still say that those, too, are ways of loving, but that is just the sort of refinement of view that the course should encourage. Out of the variety of common-sense positions that emerge, it should be possible to identify the broad similarities and differences in approach with which this book has been concerned, and for trainees to appreciate how the theme of personal balance and imbalance runs through them all.

Within the broad framework of finding ways of restoring personal balance there will be many possibilities for a therapeutic response, and trainees will benefit from learning, and being able to work with, a variety of such responses. It is interesting that research suggests that experienced therapists often make use of a whole range of approaches when they *themselves* are seeking therapeutic help, although they restrict themselves to practicing a single approach with their clients (Norcross & Aboyoun, 1994). Perhaps in this we can see a broad common-sense understanding prevailing over an attachment to the theories. My suggestion is that it will be best for trainees to *begin* with common sense, and for experienced therapists to return to it. Yet starting with common sense need not lead to the adoption of an eclectic range of procedures. It can lead, as I have suggested in Chapter 10, to a better sense of what *kinds* of trouble psychotherapy is concerned with, that is, troubles of relationship, and of achieving a balance between 'response' and 'view'.

On the sort of course I propose, there would be no assumption that any particular trainee response is wrong because it fails to accord with some theory. Inevitably there will be disagreements; as we saw in Chapter 2, common sense is not entirely unitary, and is always liable to change in the light of new discoveries or new social developments. It is, however, where we must *start*, although finding an acceptable starting point within a therapy training course may itself take some time. Nevertheless, given time and good will it should be possible to arrive at a broadly acceptable starting point, for there is much that we all share. We are all human and are liable to a common range of human troubles; we all participate in the human form of life, and by comparing and reflecting on our responses we will, in many cases, be able to find a broad consensus about how best to respond to our clients. There will no doubt be cases where there are fundamental disagreements, but that kind of situation is an especially valuable one in therapist training. It opens the way to examining just why there is such disagreement – does it, for example, arise from differing beliefs about the facts, or differing interpretations of events, or differing values, or differing philosophical views, or from prejudice, or lack of attention to relevant aspects of the situation? Given sufficient time for reflection and discussion there will often be a movement in the direction of a common view, a *common sense* of what the situation requires. Given our common humanity, there is always the possibility of reaching agreement in the end, and if there is no agreement, then it is not the end.

Summary and conclusion

It could be said that this book proposes a new theory of therapy, in the sense in which 'theory of psychotherapy' refers to a broad framework of thought that helps to draw together, and provide some understanding of, a variety of client troubles and therapeutic practices. However, the framework of thought that is involved does not invoke ideas that go much beyond those that are found in our common-sense understandings of personal difficulties. It pulls together such ideas through making the notion of a 'balance between response and view' central. It to some extent develops and refines the notions of 'response' and 'view', but it does not introduce anything that fundamentally conflicts with common sense. Part of my argument has been that the traditional theories of therapy *do* introduce ways of thinking that conflict with common sense, and that this is so because they involve, in one way or another, misleading philosophical pictures, and especially the Cartesian picture of 'mind/body' or 'inner/outer'. My objection has not been to psychotherapy theory in general but to theories that essentially involve such misleading pictures. I have myself drawn on what is called 'attachment theory' in suggesting how imbalances between response and view can originate, but the point is that attachment theory need not involve any misleading philosophical pictures.

One way of thinking about the current situation in psychotherapy is that the *practice* of therapy has outstripped our *understanding* of what therapy involves. From the research work of the last 30 years or so we now have a fairly good knowledge of what is effective in psychotherapy, and this has naturally led many therapists to employ a range of procedures, without taking too seriously the theories which are associated with the procedures. It might be said that in *practice* there is no serious problem here, but the point is that we are then left without any overall framework that can orient the profession in a such way that clients, therapists and service providers would be able to agree on what psychotherapy is, and on a rationale, or justification, for psychotherapy practice. Such lack of a rationale is not only intellectually and professionally disturbing but, according to both common sense and the research findings, is likely to have deleterious effects on clinical practice. Both therapists and clients need to have good *reasons* for confidence about what is being done in therapy, and such reasoned confidence requires an overall framework of understanding.

The purpose of this book is to try to provide such a framework, but not so much in the spirit of adding a new approach to therapy that might perhaps be called 'integrative balance therapy'. Rather, I suggest that the sort of approach to therapy that I recommend is already practiced quite widely, but that it hasn't yet been well articulated, because the traditional theories have stood in the way. The fact that the *theories* can't be integrated has prevented us from seeing how there can be an integrative understanding of practice that draws largely on common-sense understanding and everyday language. Once we see that the traditional theories are at best unnecessary, and at worst harmful, the block to an integrative view of practice is removed.

References

Angus, L. & McLeod, J. (Eds.). (2004). *The Handbook of Narrative and Psychotherapy: Practice, Theory and Research*. London: Sage.

Austin, J. L. (1970). A plea for excuses. In J. O. Urmson & G. J. Warnock (Eds.), *Philosophical Papers* (pp. 175–204). Oxford: Oxford University Press.

Austrian Health Institute (ÖBIG) (2003). Regulation of the professions of psychotherapist, clinical psychologist, health psychologist in the member states of the EEA and the Swiss Confederation. www.pceeee-europe.org/file/Infos/Publ-EEA-Regulations.pdf. Downloaded 5 April 2014.

Ayllon, T. & Azrin, N. H. (1968). Reinforcer sampling: a technique for increasing the behavior of mental patients. *Journal of Applied Behavioral Analysis*, 1, 13–20.

Baldwin, M. (1987). Interview with Carl Rogers on the use of the self in therapy. In M. Baldwin & V. Satir (Eds.), *The Use of Self in Therapy* (pp. 45–52). New York: Howarth Press.

Barkun, M. (2003). *A Culture of Conspiracy: Apocalyptic Visions in Contemporary America*. Berkeley: University of California Press.

Barrett-Lennard, G. T. (1998). *Carl Rogers' Helping System: Journey and Substance*. London: Sage.

Bartlett, F. C. (1932/1995). *Remembering: A Study in Experimental and Social Psychology*. Cambridge: Cambridge University Press.

Bechara, A., Tranel, D., Damasio, H., Adolphs, R., Rockland, C. & Damasio, A. R. (1995). Double dissociation of conditioning and declarative knowledge relative to the amygdala and hippocampus in humans. *Science*, 269, 1115–1118.

Beck, A. T. (1976). *Cognitive Therapy and the Emotional Disorders*. New York: International Universities Press.

Beck, A. T., Rush, A. J., Shaw, B. F. & Emery, G. (1979). *Cognitive Therapy of Depression*. New York: Guilford Press.

Beck, J. S. (1995). *Cognitive Therapy: Basics and Beyond*. New York: Guilford Press.

Bennett, M. R. & Hacker, P. (2003). *Philosophical Foundations of Neuroscience*. Oxford: Blackwell.

Bennett, M. R. & Hacker, P. (2012). *History of Cognitive Neuroscience*. Chichester: Wiley-Blackwell.

Bennett, M. R., Dennett, D., Hacker, P. & Searle, J. (2007). *Neuroscience and Philosophy: Brain, Mind, and Language*. New York: Columbia University Press.

Bohart, A. C. & Tallman, K. (1999). *How Clients Make Therapy Work: The Process of Self-Healing*. Washington, DC: American Psychological Association.

Bouveresse, J. (1995). *Wittgenstein Reads Freud: The Myth of the Unconscious*. Princeton: Princeton University Press.

Bozarth, J. (1998). *Person-Centred Therapy: A Revolutionary Paradigm*. Ross-on-Wye: PCCS Books.

Brandon, S., Boakes, J., Glaser, D., Green, R., MacKeith, J. & Whewell, P. (1997). Reported recovered memories of child sexual abuse: Recommendations for good practice and implications for training, continuing professional development and research. *Psychiatric Bulletin*, 21(10), 663–665.

Buccioni, E. (2002). The psychical forces in Plato's Phaedrus. *British Journal for the History of Philosophy*, 10(3), 331–357.

Bugter, S. E. W. (1987). Sensus communis in the works of M. Tullius Cicero. In F. L. van Holthoon & D. R. Olson (Eds.), *Common Sense: The Foundations for Social Science* (pp. 83–97). New York: University Press of America.

Clare, A. W. (1992). *Psychiatry in Dissent: Controversial Issues in Thought and Practice* (2nd ed.). Cambridge: Routledge.

Clifford, T. (1990). *Tibetan Buddhist Medicine and Psychiatry: The Diamond Healing*. York Beach, ME: Samuel Weiser.

Cooper, D. E. (2002). *The Measure of Things: Humanism, Humility and Mystery*. Oxford: Clarendon Press.

Cooper, M. (2003). *Existential Therapies*. London: Sage.

Cooper, M. (2008). *Experiential Research Findings in Counselling and Psychotherapy: The Facts are Friendly*. London: Sage.

Cooper, M. (2012). Existentially-informed person-centred therapy. In P. Sanders (Ed.), *The Tribes of the Person-Centred Nation* (2nd ed) (pp. 131–160). Ross-on-Wye: PCCS Books.

Cooper, M. & McLeod, J. (2011). *Pluralistic Counselling and Psychotherapy*. London: Sage.

Cooper, R. (2007). *Psychiatry and Philosophy of Science*. Stocksfield: Acumen.

Cozolino, L. (2002). *The Neuroscience of Psychotherapy: Building and Rebuilding the Human Brain*. New York: W.W. Norton.

da Silva, P. (1984). Buddhism and behaviour modification. *Behaviour Research and Therapy*, 22(6), 661–678.

De Rubeis, R. J., Webb, C. A., Tang, T. Z. & Beck, A. T. (2010). Cognitive therapy. In K. S. Dobson (Ed.), *Handbook of Cognitive-Behavioral Therapies* (3rd ed.) (pp. 277–316). New York: Guilford Press.

Derrida, J. (1974). *Of Grammatology* (G. C. Spivak, Trans.). Baltimore, MD: Johns Hopkins University Press.

Doidge, N. (2007). *The Brain That Changes Itself*. London: Penguin.

Dreyfus, H. L. & Dreyfus, S. E. (1986). *Mind Over Machine: The Power of Human Intuition and Expertise in the Era of the Computer*. New York: Free Press.

Dwivedi, K. N. (Ed.). (1997). *The Therapeutic Use of Stories*. London: Routledge.

Ellingham, I. (2001). Carl Rogers' 'congruence' as an organismic, not a Freudian, concept. In G. Wyatt (Ed.), *Congruence. Volume 1 of Rogers' Therapeutic Conditions: Evolution, Theory and Practice* (pp. 96–115). Ross-on-Wye: PCCS Books.

Elliott, R., Davis, K. & Slatick, E. (1998). Process-experiential therapy for post-traumatic stress difficulties. In L. Greenberg, G. Lietaer & J. Watson (Eds.), *Handbook of Experiential Psychotherapy* (pp. 249–271). New York: Guilford Press.

Elliott, R. & Greenberg, L.S. (2002). Process-experiential psychotherapy. In D. Cain & J. Seeman (Eds.), *Humanistic Psychotherapies: Handbook of Research and Practice* (pp. 279–306). Washington, DC: American Psychological Association.

Elliott, R., Watson, J. C., Goldman, R. N. & Greenberg, L. (2004). *Learning Emotion-Focussed Therapy: The Process-Experiential Approach to Change*. Washington, DC: American Psychological Association.

Ellis, A. (1973). Rational-emotive therapy. In R. Corsini (Ed.), *Current Psychotherapies*. Itasca, IL: Peacock.

Ellis, A. (1994). *Reason and Emotion in Psychotherapy*. Secaucus, NJ: Lyle Stuart.

Eysenck, H. J. (1985). *Decline and Fall of the Freudian Empire*. Harmondsworth: Viking.

Fancher, R. E. (1979). *Pioneers of Psychology*. New York: W. W. Norton.
Farias, V. (1989). *Heidegger and Nazism*. Philadelphia: Temple University Press.
Fenichel, O. (1946). *The Psychoanalytical Theory of Neurosis*. London: Routledge and Kegan Paul.
Feyerabend, P. (1975). *Against Method*. London: Verso.
Fingarette, H. (1969). *Self-Deception*. London: Routledge.
Fingarette, H. (1998). Self-deception needs no explaining. *Philosophical Quarterly*, 48, 289–301.
Fogelin, R. (1987). *Wittgenstein* (2nd ed.). London: Routledge.
Frank, J. D. & Frank, J. B. (1991). *Persuasion and Healing: A Comparative Study of Psychotherapy* (3rd ed.). Baltimore: Johns Hopkins University Press.
Freud, S. (1895). Project for a scientific psychology. *New Introductory Lectures in Psychoanalysis: Standard Edition*, 22, 3–182.
Freud, S. (1915). The unconscious. *Collected Papers* (Vol. 4). New York: Basic Books.
Freud, S. (1916–1917). *Introductory Lectures on Psychoanalysis*. London: Penguin.
Freud, S. (1917). Introductory Lectures on Psychoanalysis. *The Standard Edition of the Complete Psychological Works of Sigmund Freud*, XVI, 241–463.
Frigg, R. & Hartmann, S. (2012) Models in Science. The Stanford Encyclopedia of Philosophy (Fall 2012 ed.). http://plato.stanford.edu/archives/fall2012/entries/models-science.
Frosh, S. (2012). *A Brief Introduction to Psychoanalytic Theory*. Basingstoke: Palgrave Macmillan.
Fulford, K. W. M., Thornton, T. & Graham, G. (2006). *Oxford Textbook of Philosophy and Psychiatry*. Oxford: Oxford University Press.
Gardner, H. (1987). *The Mind's New Science: A History of the Cognitive Revolution*. New York: BasicBooks.
Gellner, E. (1985). *The Psychoanalytic Movement or the Coming of Unreason*. London: Paladin.
Gendlin, E. T. (1959). The concept of congruence reformulated in terms of experiencing. *University of Chicago Counselling Center Discussion Papers*, 5(12), Available at www.focusing.org/gendlin/docs/gol_2077.html.
Gendlin, E. T. (1962/1997). *Experiencing and the Creation of Meaning: A Philosophical and Psychological Approach to the Subjective*. Evanston: Northwestern University Press.
Gendlin, E. T. (1968). The experiential response. In E. F. Hammer (Ed.), *Use of Interpretation in Treatment: Technique and Art* (pp. 208–227). New York: Grune & Stratton.
Gendlin, E. T. (1969). Focusing. *Psychotherapy; Theory, Research and Practice*, 6(1), 4–15.
Gendlin, E. T. (1970). A short summary and some long predictions. In J. T. Hart & T. M. Tomlinson (Eds.), *New Directions in Client-Centered Therapy* (pp. 544–562). Boston: Houghton Mifflin.
Gendlin, E. T. (1972). Therapeutic procedures with schizophrenic patients. In M. Hammer (Ed.), *The Theory and Practice of Psychotherapy with Specific Disorders*. Springfield, IL: Charles C. Thomas.
Gendlin, E. T. (1973/1964). A theory of personality change. In A. R. Mahrer & L. Pearson (Eds.), *Creative Developments in Psychotherapy* (pp. 439–489). New York: Jacob Aronson. Originally published in Worchel, P & Byrne, D. (Eds.). (1964). *Personality Change*. New York: John Wiley & Sons.

Gendlin, E. T. (1986). Heidegger and forty years of silence. In M. Frings (Ed.), *20th Annual Heidegger Conference*. Chicago: DePaul University. www.focusing.org/gendlin/docs/gol_2018.html.

Gendlin, E. T. (1990). The small steps of the therapy process: how they come and how to help them come. In G. Lietaer, J. Rombbauts & R. Van Balen (Eds.), *Client-Centered and Experiential Psychotherapy in the Nineties* (pp. 204–224). Leuven: Leuven University Press.

Gendlin, E. T. (1996). *Focusing-Oriented Psychotherapy*. New York: Guilford.

Gendlin, E. T. (1997). *A Process Model*. New York: Focusing Institute.

Greenberg, L. S. (2000). Emotion, experiencing and empathy. In J. Marques-Teixeira & S. Antunes (Eds.), *Client-Centered and Experiential Psychotherapy* (pp. 65–87). Linda a Velha: Vale & Vale.

Greenberg, L. S., Rice, L. N. & Elliott, R. (1993). *Facilitating Emotional Change: The Moment-by-Moment Process*. New York: Guilford Press.

Grencavage, L. M. & Norcross, J. C. (1990). Where are the commonalities among the therapeutic common factors? *Professional Psychology: Research and Practice*, 21, 372–378.

Grünbaum, A. (1984). *The Foundations of Psychoanalysis*. Berkeley: University of California Press.

Guignon, C. (1993). Authenticity, moral values and psychotherapy. In C. Guignon (Ed.), *The Cambridge Companion to Heidegger*. Cambridge: Cambridge University Press.

Hacker, P. (2007). *Human Nature: The Categorial Framework*. Chichester: Wiley-Blackwell.

Hacking, I. (1983) *Representing and Intervening*. Cambridge: Cambridge University Press.

Hacking, I. (1999). *The Social Construction of What?* London: Harvard University Press.

Hamlyn, D.W. (1953). Behaviour. *Philosophy*, 28, 132–145. Also in Chappell, V. (Ed.). (1962). *Philosophy of Mind* (pp. 60–73). Englewood Cliffs: Prentice-Hall.

Hamlyn, D. W. (1970). Conditioning and behaviour. In R. Borger & F. Cioffi (Eds.) *Explanation in the Behavioural Sciences* (pp. 139–166). Cambridge: Cambridge University Press.

Hamlyn, D. W. (1978). *Experience and the Growth of Understanding*. London: Routledge & Kegan Paul.

Hamlyn, D. W. (1990). *In and Out of the Black Box: On the Philosophy of Cognition*. Oxford: Basil Blackwell.

Haugh, S. (2001). A historical review of the development of the concept of congruence in person-centred therapy. In G. Wyatt (Ed.), *Rogers' Therapeutic Conditions: Congruence* (pp. 1–17). Ross-on-Wye: PCCS Books.

Hayes, S. C., Strosahl, K. D. & Wilson, K. G. (2003). *Acceptance and Commitment Therapy: An Experiential Approach to Behavior Change*. New York: Guilford Press.

Heidegger, M. (2001). *Zollikon Seminars: Protocols – Conversations – Letters*. Evanston: Northwestern University Press.

Hesse, M. (1963). *Models and Analogies in Science*. London: Sheed & Ward.

Hofmann, S. G. (2012). *An Introduction to Modern CBT: Psychological Solutions to Mental Health Problems*. Chichester: Wiley-Blackwell.

Holdstock, T. L. (1993). Can we afford not to revision the person-centred concept of the self? In D. Brazier (Ed.), *Beyond Carl Rogers* (pp. 29–52). London: Constable.

Holdstock, T. L. (1996a). Anger and congruence considered from the perspective of an interdependent orientation to the self. In R. Hutterer, G. Pawlowski, P. Schmid & R. Stipsits (Eds.), *Client-Centered and Experiential Therapy: A Paradigm in Motion* (pp. 47–52). Frankfurt am Main: Peter Lang.

Holdstock, T. L. (1996b). Discrepancy between person-centred theories of self and therapy. In R. Hutterer, G. Pawlowski, P. Schmid & R. Stipsits (Eds.), *Client-Centered and Experiential Therapy: A Paradigm in Motion* (pp. 395–403). Frankfurt am Main: Peter Lang.

Hollanders, H. (1999). Eclecticism and integration in counselling: Implications for training. *British Journal of Guidance and Counselling*, 27(4), 483–500.

Horwitz, A. V. & Wakefield, J. C. (2007). *The Loss of Sadness: How Psychiatry Transformed Normal Sorrow into Depressive Disorder*. Oxford: Oxford University Press.

Howe, D. (2011). *Attachment Across the Lifecourse: A Brief Introduction*. Basingstoke: Palgrave Macmillan.

Hubble, M., Duncan, B. L. & Miller, S. D. (199). *The Heart and Soul of Change: What Works in Therapy*. Washington, DC: American Psychological Association.

Hull, C. L. (1943) *The Principles of Behavior*. New York: Appleton-Century-Crofts.

Inwood, M. (1997). *Heidegger: A Very Short Introduction*. Oxford: Oxford University Press.

Jacobs, M. (1988). *Psychodynamic Counselling in Action*. London: Sage.

Jacobs, M. (2003). *Sigmund Freud* (2nd ed.). London: Sage.

Jacobson, N. N., Dobson, K.S., Truax, P.A., Addis, M.E., Koerner, K., Gollan, J.K., Gortner, E. & Price, S.E. (1996). A component analysis of cognitive-behavioral treatment for depression. *Journal of Consulting and Clinical Psychology*, 64, 295–304.

Jamison, K. R. (2011). *The Unquiet Mind: A Memoir of Moods and Madness*. London: Picador.

Jennings, J. (1986). Husserl revisited: The forgotten distinction between psychology and phenomenology. *American Psychologist*, 41, 1231–1240.

Jennings, J. & Lucca, C. A. (1989). Is the 'forgotten distinction' between psychology and phenomenology still forgotten? *American Psychologist*, 44(12), 1551–1553.

Kakar, S. (1982). *Shamans, Mystics and Doctors: A Psychological Inquiry into India and Its Healing Traditions*. New York: Alfred Knopf.

Kazdin, A. E. (1978). *History of Behaviour Modification – Experimental Foundations of Contemporary Research*. Baltimore: University Park Press.

Kirsch, I. (2009) *The Emperor's New Drugs: Exploding the Antidepressant Myth*. London: Bodley Head.

Kirschenbaum, H. (1979). *On Becoming Carl Rogers*. New York: Delacorte.

Kohut. (1971). *The Analysis of the Self: A Systematic Approach to the Psychoanalytic Treatment of Narcissistic Personality Disorders*. New York: International Universities Press.

Kuhn, T. S. (1970). *The Structure of Scientific Revolutions* (2nd ed.). Chicago: University of Chicago.

Laungani, P. (1999). Client-centred or culture-centred counselling? In S. Palmer & P. Laungani (Eds.), *Counselling in a Multicultural Society* (pp. 133–152). London: Sage.

Linehan, M. M. (1993). *Cognitive–Behavioral Treatment of Borderline Personality Disorder*. New York: Guilford Press.

MacIntyre, A. (2004). *The Unconscious: A Conceptual Analysis* (Rev. ed.). London & New York: Routledge.
Maciocia, G. (2005). *Foundations of Chinese Medicine*. London: Elsevier.
Mack, J. (1994). *Abduction: Human Encounters With Aliens (rev. ed.)*. New York: Ballantine.
Macmillan, M. (1997). *Freud Evaluated: The Completed Arc*. Cambridge, MA: MIT Press.
Malcolm, N. (1977). *Thought and Knowledge*. Ithaca: Cornell University Press.
Mandler, J. M. and Mandler, G. (1964). *Thinking: From Free Association to Gestalt*. New York: John Wiley.
Masson, J. (1992). *Final Analysis: The Making and Unmaking of a Psychoanalyst*. London: Fontana.
McDougall, W. (1936). *Psychoanalysis and Social Psychology*. London: Methuen.
McEachrane, M. (2009). Capturing emotional thoughts: The philosophy of cognitive-behavioral therapy. In Y. Gustafsson, C. Kronqvist & M. McEachrane (Eds.), *Emotions and Understanding: Wittgensteinian Perspectives* (pp. 81–101). Basingstoke: Palgrave Macmillan.
McGilchrist, I. (2009). *The Master and His Emissary: The Divided Brain and the Making of the Western World*. New Haven: Yale University Press.
McLeod, J. (1997). *Narrative and Psychotherapy*. London: Sage.
McLeod, J. (2009). *An Introduction to Counselling* (4th ed.). Maidenhead: Open University Press.
McNally, R. (2003). *Remembering Trauma*. Cambridge, MA: Harvard University press.
McNally, R. (2011). *What Is Mental Illness?* Cambridge, MA: Harvard University Press.
Mearns, D. (1997). *Person-Centred Counselling Training*. London: Sage.
Mearns, D. & Cooper, M. (2005). *Working in Relational Depth in Counselling and Psychotherapy*. London: Sage.
Mearns, D. & Thorne, B. (1988/2007). *Person-Centred Counselling in Action* (1st/3rd eds.). London: Sage.
Mearns, D. & Thorne, B. (2000). *Person-Centred Therapy Today: New Frontiers in Theory and Practice*. London: Sage.
Melden, A. I. (1961). *Free Action*. London: Routledge & Kegan Paul.
Merry, T. (2000). *Person-Centred Practice: The BAPCA Reader*. Ross-on-Wye: PCCS Books.
Moncrieff, J. (2009). *A Straight-Talking Introduction to Psychiatric Drugs*. Ross-on-Wye: PCCS Books.
Moyal-Sharrock, D. (2000). 'Words as deeds': Wittgenstein's 'spontaneous utterances' and the dissolution of the explanatory gap. *Philosophical Psychology*, 13(3), 355–375.
Murdoch, I. (1970). *The Sovereignty of Good*. London: Routledge & Kegan Paul.
Murphy, D. (2006). *Psychiatry in the Scientific Image*. Cambridge, MA: MIT Press.
Neenan, M. & Dryden, W. (2004). *Cognitive Therapy: 100 Key Points and Techniques*. Hove: Brunner-Routledge.
Nevid, J. S. (2007). Kant, cognitive psychotherapy, and the hardening of the categories. *Psychology and Psychotherapy: Theory, Research and Practice*, 80, 605–615.
Norcross, J. C. (2005). A primer on psychotherapy integration. In J. C. Norcross & M. R. Goldfried (Eds.), *Handbook of Psychotherapy Integration* (2nd ed., pp. 3–23). Oxford: Oxford University Press.

Norcross, J. C. & Aboyoun, D. C. (1994). Self-change experiences of psychotherapists. In T. M. Brinthaupt & R. P. Lipka (Eds.), *Changing the Self* (pp. 253–278). Albany: SUNY Press.

Nuttall, A.D. (1974). *Common Sky: Philosophy and the Literary Imagination.* London: Chatto & Windus.

Orlinsky, D. E., Grawe, K. & Parks, B. K. (1994). Process and outcome in psychotherapy – noch einmal. In A. E. Bergin & S. L. Garfield (Eds.), *Handbook of Psychotherapy and Behavior Change* (4th ed.) (pp. 270–376). New York: Wiley.

Ornstein, R. (1997). *The Right Mind: Making Sense of the Hemispheres.* New York: Harcourt Brace.

Ost, J., Costall, A. & Bull, R. (2002). A perfect symmetry? A study of retractors' experiences of making and then repudiating claims of early sexual abuse. *Psychology, Crime and Law,* 8, 155–181.

Ott, H. (1994). *Martin Heidegger: A Political Life.* London: Fontana Press.

Perls, F., Hefferline, R. & Goodman, P. (1951). *Gestalt Therapy.* New York: Dell.

Peters, R. S. (1958). *The Concept of Motivation.* London: Routledge & Kegan Paul.

Polanyi, M. (1958). *Personal Knowledge: Towards a Post-Critical Philosophy.* Chicago: University of Chicago Press.

Polanyi, M. (1966). *The Tacit Dimension.* London: Routledge.

Popper, K. (1959). *The Logic of Scientific Discovery.* London: Hutchinson.

Porter, R. (1997). *A Medical History of Humanity from Antiquity to the Present.* London: HarperCollins.

Pribram, K. H. (1994). *Shadows of the Mind: A Search for the Missing Science of Consciousness.* Oxford: Oxford University Press.

Pribram, K. H. (2013). *The Form Within: My Point of View.* New York: Prospecta Press.

Prochaska, J. O. (1984). *Systems of Psychotherapy: A Transtheoretical Analysis* (2nd ed.). Homewood, IL: Dorsey.

Prochaska, J. O., Norcross, J. C. & DiClemente, C. C. (1994). *Changing for Good.* New York: Morrow.

Prouty, G. (1990). Pre-therapy: A theoretical evolution in the person-centered/experiential psychotherapy of schizophrenia and retardation. In G. Lietaer, J. Rombbauts & R. Van Balen (Eds.), *Client-Centered and Experiential Psychotherapy in the Nineties* (pp. 645–669). Leuven: Leuven University Press.

Prouty, G., Van Werde, D. & Portner, M. (2002). *Pre-Therapy: Reaching Contact-Impaired Clients.* Ross-on-Wye: PCCS Books.

Purton, C. (1978) Ethological categories of behaviour and some consequences of their conflation. *Animal Behaviour,* 26, 653–670.

Purton, C. (1991). Selection and assessment in counselling training courses. In W. Dryden & B. Thorne (Eds.), *Training and Supervision for Counselling in Action* (pp. 33–48). London: Sage.

Purton, C. (2002). Person-centred therapy without the core conditions. *Counselling and Psychotherapy Journal,* 3(2), 6–9.

Purton, C. (2004). *Person-Centred Counselling: The Focusing-Oriented Approach.* Basingstoke: Palgrave Macmillan.

Purton, C. (2007). *The Focusing-Oriented Counselling Primer.* Ross-on-Wye: PCCS Books.

Purton, C. (2012). Focusing-oriented therapy. In P. Sanders (Ed.), *The Tribes of the Person-Centred Nation* (2nd ed.) (pp. 47–69). Ross-on-Wye: PCCS Books.

Purton, C. (2013a). The myth of the bodily felt sense. In G. Madison (Ed.), *The Theory and Practice of Focusing-Oriented Psychotherapy* (pp. 221–233). London: Jessica Kingsley.

Purton, C. (2013b). Incongruence and 'inner experience'. *Person-Centered and Experiential Psychotherapies,* 12(3), 187–199.

Purton, C. (2014). Wittgenstein and the expression of feelings in psychotherapy. *Philosophical Investigations,* 37(2), 152–166.

Read, R. (2012). *Wittgenstein Among the Sciences.* Farnham: Ashgate.

Rice, L. N. (1974). The evocative function of the therapist. In D. A. Wexler & L. N. Rice (Eds.), *Innovations in Client-Centered Therapy* (pp. 289–311). New York: Wiley.

Rogers, C. R. (1942). *Counselling and Psychotherapy: Newer Concepts in Practice.* Boston: Houghton Mifflin.

Rogers, C. R. (1951). *Client-Centered Therapy.* London: Constable.

Rogers, C. R. (1959). A theory of therapy, personality and interpersonal relationships, as developed in the client-centred framework. In S. Koch (Ed.), *Psychology: A Study of a Science, Vol. 3: Formulations of the Person and the Social Context.* (pp. 184–256). New York: McGraw-Hill.

Rogers, C. R. (1961). *On Becoming a Person.* London: Constable.

Rogers, C. R. (1964). Towards a science of the person. In T. W. Wann (Ed.), *Behaviorism and Phenomenology: Contrasting Bases for Modern Psychology* (pp. 109–133). Chicago: University of Chicago Press.

Rogers, C. R. (1980). *A Way of Being.* Boston: Houghton Mifflin.

Rogers, C. R. (1986a). Reflection of feelings. *Person-Centered Review,* 1(4), 375–377.

Rogers, C. R. (1986b). Client-Centered therapy. In I. L. Kutash & A. Wolf (Eds.), *Psychotherapist's Casebook* (pp. 197–208). San Francisco: Jossey-Bass.

Rogers, C. R. (1987). Comment on Shlien's article 'A counter-theory of transference'. *Person-Centered Review,* 2(2), 182–188.

Rogers, C. R. (1990) *The Carl Rogers Reader* (ed. H. Kirshenbaum & V. Henderson). London: Constable.

Rosen, R. (1991). *Life Itself: A Comprehensive Inquiry into the Nature, Origin, and Fabrication of Life.* New York: Columbia University Press.

Rosenzweig, S. (1936). Some implicit common factors in diverse methods of psychotherapy: 'At last the Dodo said "Everybody has won and all must have prizes."' *American Journal of Orthopsychiatry,* 6, 412–415.

Sanders, P. (Ed.). (2012). *The Tribes of the Person-Centred Nation* (2nd ed.). Ross-on-Wye: PCCS Books.

Schore, A. (2003). *Affect Regulation and the Repair of the Self.* New York: W.W. Norton.

Schroder, T. (1999). *Old Souls: The Scientific Evidence for Past Lives.* New York: Simon & Schuster.

Segal, Z. V., Williams, J. M. G. & Teasdale, J. D. (2002). *Mindfulness-Based Cognitive Therapy for Depression: A New Approach to Preventing Relapse.* New York: Guilford Press.

Seikkula, J. (2011). Becoming dialogical: Psychotherapy or a way of life? *Australian and New Zealand Journal of Family Therapy,* 32(3), 179–193.

Seikkula, J. & Trimble, D. (2005). Healing elements of therapeutic conversation: Dialogue as an embodiment of love, *Family Process,* 44(4), 461–475.

Shapiro, A. K. & Shapiro, E. (1997). *The Powerful Placebo: From Ancient Priest to Modern Physician.* Baltimore: Johns Hopkins University Press.

Sharrock, W. & Read, R. (2002). *Kuhn: Philosopher of Scientific Revolution*. Cambridge: Polity Press.
Singer, M. T. & Lalich, J. (1996). *'Crazy' Therapies*. San Francisco: Jossey-Bass.
Skinner, B. F. (1953a). *Science and Human Behavior*. New York: Macmillan.
Skinner, B. F. (1971a). *Beyond Freedom and Dignity*. New York: Knopf.
Skinner, B. F. (1971b). Beyond freedom and dignity. *Psychology Today* (August), 37–81.
Skinner, B. F. (1976). *Walden Two*. New York: Macmillan.
Slack, S. (1985). Reflections on a workshop with Carl Rogers. *Journal of Humanistic Psychology*, 25(1), 35–42.
Smith, M. L. & Glass, G.V. (1977). Meta-analysis of psychotherapy outcome studies. *American Psychologist, 2*, 752–760.
Spinelli, E. (2007). *Practicing Existential Psychotherapy: The Relational World*. London: Sage.
Spitzer, R. L., Williams, J. B. W. & Skodol, A. E. (1980). *DSM-III:* The major achievements and an overview. *American Journal of Psychiatry*, 137, 151–164.
Stern, D. N. (2000). *The Interpersonal World of the Infant: A View from Psychoanalysis and Developmental Psychology*. New York: Basic Books.
Stevenson, I. (1973). *Twenty Cases Suggestive of Reincarnation*. Charlottesville: University of Virginia Press.
Swales, M. A. & Heard, H. (2008). *Dialectical Behaviour Therapy: Distinctive Features*. Hove: Routledge.
Szasz, T. S. (1961). *The Myth of Mental Illness*. New York: Hoeber-Harper.
Szasz, T. S. (1974). *The Ethics of Psycho-Analysis: The Theory and Method of Autonomous Psychotherapy*. London: Routledge & Kegan Paul.
Szasz, T. S. (1978). *The Myth of Psychotherapy: Mental Healing as Religion, Rhetoric, and Repression*. New York: Anchor Press.
Taylor, C. (1964). *The Explanation of Behaviour*. London: Routledge & Kegan Paul.
Thorne, B. (1992). *Carl Rogers*. London: Sage.
Thorne, B. (1998). *Person-Centred Counselling and Christian Spirituality*. London: Whurr.
Thorne, B. (2002). *The Mystical Power of Person-Centred Therapy*. London: Whurr.
Tinbergen, N. (1951). *The Study of Instinct*. Oxford: Clarendon Press.
Tolman, E. C. (1932). *Purposive Behaviour in Animals and Men*. New York: Century.
Tolman, E. C. (1947). Cognitive maps in rats and men. *Psychological Review*, 55, 189–208.
Valenstein, E. S. (1998). *Blaming the Brain: The Truth About Drugs and Mental Health*. New York: Free Press.
Van Holthoon, F. L. (1987). Common sense and natural law: From Thomas Aquinas to Thomas Reid. In F. L. Van Holthoon (Ed.), *Common Sense: The Foundations for Social Science* (pp. 99–114). New York: Academic Press of America.
Van Holthoon, F. L. & Olson, D. R. (Eds.). (1987). *Common Sense: The Foundations for Social Science*. Lanham, MD: University Press of America.
Vöhringer, P. A. & Ghaemi, S.N. (2011) Solving the antidepressant efficacy question? Effect sizes in major depressive disorder. *Clinical Therapeutics*, 33(12), B49–61. Retrieved 9 April 2014, from http://dx.doi.org/10.1016/j.clinthera.2011.11.019
Wampold, B. E. (2001). *The Great Psychotherapy Debate*. London: Routledge.
Watson, J. B. (1925). *Behaviorism*. New York: W W Norton.
White, A. (1964). *Attention*. Oxford: Blackwell.

Whitehead, A. N. (1978). *Process and Reality: An Essay in Cosmology.* New York: Free Press.
Whyte, L. L. (1967). *The Unconscious Before Freud.* London: Tavistock Publications.
Wilkins, P. (2003). *Person-Centred Therapy in Focus.* London: Sage.
Wittgenstein, L. (1921/1963). *Tractatus Logico-Philosophicus.* London: Routledge & Kegan Paul.
Wittgenstein, L. (1953/2009). *Philosophical Investigations* (4th ed.) [Including 'Philosophy of Psychology – A Fragment']. Chichester: Wiley-Blackwell.
Wittgenstein, L. (1967). *Zettel.* Oxford: Blackwell.
Wittgenstein, L. (1969). *On Certainty.* Oxford: Blackwell.
Wittgenstein, L. (1982). *Last Writings on the Philosophy of Psychology.* Vol 1: *Preliminary Studies for Part II of Philosophical Investigations.* Oxford: Blackwell.
Wittgenstein, L. (1992). *Last Writings on the Philosophy of Psychology.* Vol 2: *The Inner and the Outer.* Oxford: Blackwell.
Wolff, S. M. (1996). Why do American drug companies spend more than $12 billion a year pushing drugs? *Journal of General Internal Medicine,* 11, 637–639.
Woolger, R. (1988). *Other Lives, Other Selves: A Jungian Psychotherapist Discovers Past Lives*: Bantam Books.

Index

Note: Page numbers with 'n' in the index refer to notes in the text.

abduction by aliens 96
Aboyoun, D. C. 19, 197
acceptance and commitment therapy (ACT) 184
accreditation 3
action and bodily movement 54–6
active listening 188–9
actualizing tendency 78–9
ADHD (attention deficit hyperactivity disorder) 163
aesthetic appreciation 90–1
affect regulation 140–2, 188
aliens, abduction by 96
allegiance, therapist 17, 26–7
Allyon, T. 57
ambivalent pattern (attachment theory) 177
American Psychiatric Association 153
analogies, theoretical 31–3
Angus, L. 75
Anna Karenina (Tolstoy) 74–5, 92
antidepressant medication
  effect size 14–15
antirealist philosophy 112
Aristotelian thought, common sense in 42
Aristotle 42, 115
articulation of responses 102, 171
  see also Type C troubles/procedures
assertiveness training 189
astrology 18, 19, 33–4
attachment patterns 176–7, 198
Augustine, Saint 36
Austin, J. 7, 44, 56
Austrian Health Institute 3
authenticity
  Heidegger 135
  see also congruence
automatic thoughts 104–5, 107
aversion therapy 49

avoidance pattern (attachment theory) 176–7
Azrin, N.H. 57

'balance' in therapy
  actualising tendency and social mediation 182
  Greek medicine 180–1, 183
  id and super-ego 181
  Indian healing systems 182–3
  self-concept and organismic experiencing 181
  traditional views 180–3
  see also view and response; zigzag(s)
Baldwin, M. 59
Barkun, M. 96
Barrett-Lennard, G.T. 63
Bartlett, F.C. 93, 111, 112
Bechara, A. 54
Beck, A. 48–9, 99, 100–1, 104, 107, 172, 184
Beck, J.S. 105
behaviour
  and bodily movements 51, 54–6
  explanation of 55, 156–7
behavioural desensitization 48, 189
behaviourism 32
  development of 53–8
  and inner/outer distinction 69–71
  value of 86
behaviour therapy
  affect regulation in 141
  in ancient times 49–50
  common sense core of 47–50, 167–8
  dangers of 57–8
  historical development of 46–7, 53–8
  neuroscience and 141
  theoretical confusion in 50–6
  theory, rejection of 46–7

Index

belief(s)
  believing vs. 'really believing' 108
  believing vs. thinking 106
  cognition and 103–10
  cognitive schemas and 110–14
  core 104, 107
  feeling and 107
  rational 115
  unreasonable 106–7
  see also thought(s)
Bennett, M. R. 40, 94, 113, 114, 148n
Berne, E. 181
Binswanger, L. 132
bio-energetic therapy 4, 18
bipolar disorder 154, 163, 164
bodily movements
  and behaviour 51, 54–6
Bohart, A.C. 15, 19, 182
Boss, M. 132, 135
Bouveresse, J. 87, 90
Bozarth, J. 66
brain
  dysfunction 142–7
  frontal cortex damage 144–5
  hemispheres 141–2, 146; see also left-brain; right-brain
  holograms and 147
  in infant development 141–2
  left-brain dominance 142
  maps in, see mental maps/representations
  programs in 114; see also cognitive schemas
  surgery 146, 147
brain states/processes
  emotions and 91
  human troubles and 143–7
  memory and 94
Brandon, S. 95
Brandon Report 95
British Association for Counselling and Psychotherapy (BACP) 2
British False Memory Society 98
Buccioni, E. 181, 186n
Buddha 49
Buddhism, behavioural procedures in 49–50
Bull, R. 97

Cartesian picture of person 35–6, 44–5, 98, 166, 185, 194–5, 197
  behaviour therapy and 47, 58
  emotion schemes and 123–4
  emotions in 91–2, 145
  inner/outer distinction and 52–3, 68–71, 75
  introspectionist psychology and 51
  neuroscience and 143–7
  person-centred therapy and 68–71, 79
  process-experiential therapy and 128
  psychodynamic therapy and 86–7
  Wittgensteinian rejection of 36
  see also Descartes; misleading pictures
catharsis 125–6
censor 8
chair work 121–2, 191
child development 188–9
  brain development in infants 141–2
  social referencing and 174–6
Chinese medicine 180
Ch'ing Yuan vi
Chomsky, N. 39
clarification of responses 102, 171
  see also Type C troubles/procedures
classical conditioning 53–4
  as artificial abstraction 54
classification, psychiatric 153–6
  see also DSM
client-centred therapy, see person-centred therapy
client's frame of reference 80
client-therapist relationship, see therapeutic relationship
client vulnerability 122
Clifford, T. 180
cognition 103–10
cognitive behavioural therapy (CBT) 46, 99–117
  ABC account (Ellis) 115
  behavioural and cognitive elements 46, 109
  central notion of 114–15
  cognitive procedures 99–101
  common-sense core of 101–3, 169
  incoherence of 184
  'second wave' 99
  'third wave' 103, 184

cognitive behavioural therapy
      (CBT) – *continued*
   as umbrella term   103
   see also behaviour therapy; cognitive therapy
cognitive psychology   32
cognitive revolution   55, 99, 110, 113
cognitive schemas   118
   and beliefs   110–14
   in child psychology   111
   history of concept   111–12
   and memory   111, 112–13
   see also emotion schemes; mental maps/representations
cognitive science   110–11
   Kantian orientation of   112
cognitive therapy
   affect regulation in   141
   dangers of   114–17
   mindfulness-based   184
   neuroscience and   141
   rational debate in   109
   theoretical confusion in   103–10
   see also cognitive-behavioural therapy
common factors in therapy   15, 17, 21, 193
common sense
   account of therapy practice   166–71
   classification of psychological troubles   156–64, 172–6
   core conditions and   64
   everyday language and   41–5
   explanations of behaviour   156–7
   extension and correction of   28–9, 84
   history of phrase   42
   in oratory   42
   theories and   30–45
   in therapy training   195–8
   truth and   23–6
   variable content of   42–3, 197
common-sense core of theories   29
   behaviour therapy   47–50
   cognitive-behavioural therapy   101–3
   person-centred therapy   59–63
   process-experiential therapy   120–2
   psychodynamic therapy   81–4
compulsive behaviour   89
   see also obsessive-compulsive disorder (OCD)
computers, rationality and   116

conditioning   48, 113, 175
   classical, *see* classical conditioning
   operant   54
conditions of worth   66, 67, 75, 78, 121, 142, 191
confession   71
confusion, theoretical, *see* theoretical confusion
congruence   20, 24, 25, 36, 64–5, 68–9, 98, 172
   misleading picture of   71–6
   origin of term   68
   and Type C troubles/procedures   159
   see also incongruence
contextual model of therapy   16, 19–20
Cooper, D.   23
Cooper, M.   189
   effectiveness of therapy   13, 14, 15, 20, 21–3
   existential therapy   132, 135–6, 137, 170, 186
   pluralism   25, 27, 28
   relational depth   63
   therapist training   193, 195, 196
Cooper, R.   153, 154
Copernicus, N.   31
core beliefs   104, 107
core conditions   59–60
   and common sense   64–7
Costall, A.   97
counselling
   origin of term   9n
   psychotherapy and   8–9
   see also pschotherapy
Cozolino, L.   140–2, 144–6, 147
crystal healing   34

Damasio, A.   40–1, 144
dangers, theoretical, *see* theoretical dangers
Darwin, C.   31, 45
Dasein (Heidegger)   133, 134
Daseinsanalysis   132
Da Silva, P.   49–50
defences, and self-deception   84, 190
depression, major, in *DSM*   154
Derrida, J.   23
De Rubeis, R.J.   111

Index

Descartes, R.   32, 37, 51, 77, 87, 91, 115, 144, 185
  see also Cartesian picture of person
description, and understanding   41–2
desensitization   48, 189
dialectical behaviour therapy (DBT)   184
dialectical constructivism   123, 126–9
  see also emotion schemes
disorder *vs.* distress, *see* distress *vs.* disorder
disorganized attachment   177
displacement   84
distress *vs.* disorder   154, 182, 183, 187
  lack of distinction between, in *DSM*   154
'dodo bird' finding   13–14, 15, 17
Doidge, N.   147
Dreyfus, H. L.   111, 114, 115–16
Dreyfus, S. E.   114, 115–16
drives, in ethology   56
Dryden, W.   64, 99, 103, 104, 184
DSM (*Diagnostic and Statistical Manual of the American Psychiatric Association*)   153–6
  descriptive nature of   154–5
  and disorder *vs.* distress   154
  exclusion clauses   154, 165n
  neurophysiological objections to   154
  psychoanalytic objections to   154
Dwivedi, K.N.   75

'East Pole' example   37–9
eclectic therapy   14
effectiveness of therapy   1–2, 13–29
  relative   13–14
  effect size   14–15
ego   181
Ellingham, I.   68
Elliott, R.   37, 118, 119, 123, 126, 129, 130n
Ellis, A.   99, 107–8, 109, 184
emotion-focused therapy (EFT), *see* process-experiential therapy
emotions
  brain states and   91
  importance of context   92–3
  'inner experience' and   70–1, 87–8, 143, 145

emotion scheme(s)   119, 123–4
  interaction of   129
  see also cognitive schemas; dialectical constructivism
empathic affirmation (PET)   122, 191–2
empirically supported treatments (ESTs)   2, 18
empty-chair procedure   121–2, 125–6
Epictetus   104
ethical issues, and Type B therapy   186n
ethology   56, 181
everyday language, *see* ordinary language
evocative unfolding   120, 122, 124, 190–1
evolution, theory of   24, 31
existential anxiety   133
existential philosophy   131–2
  validity of   137
  see also phenomenology
existential therapy   131–9
  agenda of   138
  Cartesian philosophy and   134
  common-sense understanding of   170–1
  dangers of   136–8
  person-centred therapy and   135–6
  philosophical background   131–2, 137
  practice of   135–6
  principles of   132–5
existential uncertainty   133
expectancy effect   17, 193
experience(ing)   5–6, 128
  Cartesian picture   35
  and incongruence   67–9
  pre-conceptual   111–12, 128–9
  social dimension of   175–6
  as theoretical construct   68
  see also 'inner experience'
explanation
  of behaviour   55, 156–7
  scientific   30–3
explanatory pictures, and regularities   30–3
exposure procedures   20, 47, 48, 102, 109, 136, 141, 179, 188
  see also Type B troubles/procedures

eye movement desensitization and reprocessing (EMDR)   18, 20, 34, 193
Eysenck, H.   1, 13, 85

fabricated thoughts and feelings   52, 115
false memory   95–8
False Memory Syndrome Foundation (USA)   97–8
falsification   33
Fancher, R.E.   47
Farias, V.   139n
Fawcett, Col.   38, 40
feelings
  fabricated   52
  see also emotions
felt sense   78, 120, 125
Fenichel, O.   84
Feyerabend, P.   33
Fingarette, H.   65
focusing-oriented therapy   5–6, 80n
focusing procedure   20, 61–3, 192
  in PET   120, 125, 191
  theory of   37
  zigzag nature of   61–3
Fogelin, R.   92
frames, *see* cognitive schemas
Frank, J.D.   15–16, 17, 20, 21, 28, 182 193
Frankl, V.   132
Freud, S.   25
  Cartesian notion of mind   87, 98
  later work   184
  Project for a Scientific Psychology   143, 145–6
  'structure of the mind'   86
  'the unconscious'   20, 24, 65, 67, 83–93, 169, 172
Frigg, R.   31
Frosh, S.   85, 88–9, 91
Fulford, K.W.M.   132
functional psychology   51
function, concept of   181

Galileo   33
Gardner, H.   46–7, 51, 55, 110–11
Geertz, C.   111
Gellner, E.   85

Gendlin, E.T.
  felt sense   78, 191
  focusing-oriented therapy   5, 6
  focusing procedure   61–3, 73, 120, 188, 191, 192
  Heidegger and   139n
  pre-conceptual reality   23, 128
  process model   138
  schizophrenia   162
Ghaemi, S.N.   14
'givens' in human life   168
Glass, E.   13
Glencavage, L.M.   17
'gossamer threads' view of theory (Rogers)   23–4, 186
Graham, G.   132
Greek medicine   180–1, 183
Greenberg, L.   118–26, 130n, 170, 190–2
Grünbaum, A.   85
Guignon, C.   134, 137
'guru', therapist as   137–8

Hacker, P.   40–1, 94, 106, 113, 114, 144, 148n
Hacking, I.   23, 31, 32
hallucinations   77
Hamlyn, D.W.   53, 54, 114, 175
Hammond, C.   96
Harris, R.   111
Haugh, S.   64
Hayes, S.C.   184
health, as balance   180–3
Heard, H.   103
Hegel, G.W.F.   131
Heidegger, M.   131, 133, 134, 135, 137, 138, 139&n, 179
  and Wittgenstein   132, 138
Hesse, M.   31
Hippocratic medicine   180
Hofmann, S.G.   99, 103, 109, 111, 114, 115, 184
Holdstock, T.L.   79
Hollanders, H.   21, 22, 23, 26
holograms   147
homeopathy   34
Horwitz, A.V.   154, 163
Howe, D.   176–7
Hubble, M.   15
Hull, C.   185

Index

humanist therapy 33
 neo-humanism 119
humours, in Greek and mediaeval thought 180
Husserl, E. 131
hypotheses 30

id 181
illness, as imbalance 180–3
illusions, perceptual 77
images, and representation in neuroscience 40–1
inauthenticity
 Heidegger 134
 see also incongruence; self-deception
incongruence 4, 24, 80, 83, 88, 98, 136
 and 'experience' 67–9
 pervasiveness of 66
 and self-deception 65–7
 Wittgensteinian account of 71–6
 see also congruence; inauthenticity; self-deception
Indian healing systems 182–3
infant development, brain in 141–2
'inner experience' 52, 69–71
 see also inner/outer distinction
inner/outer distinction 52–3, 69–71, 75, 198
integrative therapy 14, 166–86
internal maps, *see* mental maps/representations
interpretation 82, 90, 192
introjection 84
 of conditions of worth 66, 75, 78
introspection 52
introspectionist psychology 50–1

Jacobs, M. 81, 82, 83–4, 85–6, 87
Jacobson, N.N. 46, 109
James, W. 51
Jamison, K.R. 154, 164
Jaspers, K. 132, 135
Jennings, J. 131
judgement, personal 116
Jung, C.J. 85

Kakar, S. 182–3
Kant, I. 36–7, 111–12, 115, 127, 128, 129, 185

Kazdin, A.E. 49
Kirsch, I. 14
Kirschenbaum, H. 68
Klein, M. 85
Koch, S. 67
Kohut, H. 76, 142
Kuhn, T.S. 23, 30

Lacan, J. 85
Laing, R.D. 132
Lalich, J. 18, 34
language
 neuroscientists' use of 40–1, 144
 ordinary, *see* ordinary language
 as representation of reality 36
 therapists' use of 44, 107–8
Laungani, P. 79
left-brain
 dominance 142
 magnetic stimulation of 146
Li Chi 138
Linehan, M.M. 184
Lucca, C.A. 131

Mac...
 see also Mc...
MacIntyre, A. 81, 83
Maciocia, G. 180
Mack, J. 96
Macmillan, M. 85, 91
Malcolm, N. 105
Mandler, G. 51
Mandler, J.M. 51
maps, internal, *see* internal maps/representations
Marbe, K. 51, 52
markers (in PET) 120
Masson, J. 86
May, R. 132
Mc...
 see also Mac...
McDougall, W. 184
McEachrane, M. 105
McLeod, J. 8n, 189
 behaviour therapy 46, 48, 50, 57, 109
 narrative therapy 75
 pluralism 14, 21–3, 25, 27, 28, 186
 therapist training 193, 195, 196

McNally, R.   54, 93–5, 96–7, 147, 154–5, 156, 163, 184
meaning, and use of words   43–4, 92
Mearns, D.   26, 63, 67, 78, 79, 136, 142, 181–2, 184, 195
mechanistic explanations   32
medical model of therapy   16
medication, psychiatric   147, 162–4
  as 'intoxication'   164
Melden, A.I.   54
memory(ies)
  brain states and   94
  false   95–8
  motivated failure of   93
  neuroscience and   94–5
  repression and   93–8
  as retained ability   94
  in Rogers' theory   76–7
  as stored experience   95
  traumatic   95–8
mental disorder/illness
  concept of   153
  as imbalance   180–3
  vs. mental distress, see distress vs. disorder
Mental Health Acts   15
mental maps/representations   51, 113–14
  see also cognitive schemas
mental states
  Cartesian picture of, see Cartesian picture of person
  see also emotions; feelings
Merleau-Ponty, M.   131
Merry, T.   60
meta-analysis   13
metaphors   74
misleading pictures   35–41, 75, 76, 147
  captivation by   68, 91, 92, 128
  'cognitive schemas'   113
  of congruence   71–6
  'emotion schemes'   123, 129
  of memory   95
  of 'the mind'   86–7, 98
  see also Cartesian picture of person; theoretical confusion
models, theoretical   31
Moncrieff, J.   163, 164
Moyal-Sharrock, D.   70
Murdoch, I.   186n

myth, therapy as   17–18, 21, 153
Myth of Mental Illness, The (Szasz)   153

narrative therapy   75
natural selection   31, 45
Neenan, M.   64, 99, 103, 104, 184
neo-humanism   119
neural organization technique (NOT)   34
neural plasticity   142, 147
neuroleptic drugs   163
neuro-linguistic programming (NLP)   18, 34
neuroscience   140–8
  images and representation in   40–1
  memory and   94–5
Nevid, J.S.   111
Newton, I.   31, 32
Newton's laws   32
non-directive reflective therapy   63
Norcross, J.C.   14, 17, 19, 197
'normal science' (Kuhn)   30
noumenon, see 'thing-in-itself' (Kant)
Nuttall, A.D.   80

observation, and theory   33, 35
obsessive-compulsive disorder (OCD)   146, 147
  DSM classification   155
  see also compulsive behaviour
Olson, D.R.   42
operant conditioning   54
ordinary language   36, 167
  and common sense   41–5
  and understanding   41–2
ordinary language philosophy   7, 44
Orlinsky, D.E.   15, 158
Ornstein, R.   91
Ost, J.   97
Ott, H.   139n
outcome research   1

Pascal, B.   115
Pascual-Leone, J.   123
Pasenadi, King   49–50
past, knowledge of   76–7
past-life therapy   96
Pavlov, I.   53
Pavlovian conditioning, see classical conditioning

Index

Penfield, W.   94, 95
perception
   cognition and   103–10
   illusions   77
   in Rogers' theory   76–7
   see also view
Perls, F.   121
personal balance   187
   see also 'balance' in therapy
personal development, in training   195
personal judgement   11
person-centred therapy   59–80
   affect regulation in   140–1
   common-sense core of   59–63, 168–9
   core conditions   59–60
   dangers of   77–80
   development of   184
   existential therapy and   135–6
   as individualistic   79
   memory and   76–7
   neuroscience and   140–1
   perception in   76–7
   reflection in   60–1
   relational depth   63–4
   theoretical confusion in   67–77
   truth and   80–1
   variants of   63–4
Persuasion and Healing (Frank)   15–16
Peters, R.S.   54, 185
Phaedrus (Plato)   181, 186n
pharmaceutical industry, financial links with psychiatry   163–4
pharmacological interventions   146–7
phenomenal world   77
   see also experience; perception
phenomenology   131–2
   see also existential philosophy
philosophical pictures, see misleading pictures
philosophy
   existential, see existential philosophy
   as grounding for therapy   7
   ordinary language   7
   process (Whitehead)   138
   realist and anti-realist   112
   Stoic   99
   Wittgensteinian   7
phobias   20, 66, 106, 108, 133, 161, 172, 189
Piaget, J.   111, 123, 127, 129

pictures
   misleading, see misleading pictures
   theoretical   31–3
pinta (dyschronic spirochaetosis)   154
placebo effect   4, 14, 17, 19, 20, 193
Plato   180, 181, 186n, 188
pluralist therapy   6, 20, 21–6, 28, 172
Polanyi, M.   31
Popper, K.   23, 33, 85
Porter, R.   180
Post, H.   139n
postmodernism   4, 5, 7, 21–6, 28, 126
post-traumatic stress disorder (PTSD)   66
practice, implications for   188–93
pre-conceptual experiencing   111–12 128
pre-conscious, the   86, 88
Pribram, K. H.   147
primal scream therapy   34
problematic reaction points   120, 122, 124, 190–1
process-experiential therapy (PET)   37, 118–30
   common-sense core of   120–2, 170
   as a humanistic therapy   119
   theoretical confusion in   123–6
   treatment tasks   120–1, 124–6, 190–2
process model (Gendlin)   138
process philosophy (Whitehead)   138
Prochaska, J.O.   19, 26
programs in brain, see brain, programs in
Project for a Scientific Psychology (Freud)   143, 145–6
projection   84
Protagoras   25
Prouty, G.   162, 173
psyche, see soul
psychiatric classification   153–6
   see also DSM
psychiatry
   financial links with pharmaceutical industry   163–4
   and medication   162–4
psychoanalysis   81
   incoherence of   184
   as mode of hermeneutics   91
   neuroscience and   143
   objections to *DSM*   154

psychoanalysis – *continued*
  scholarly criticisms of 85
  see also psychodynamic therapy
psychodynamic therapy 81–98
  affect regulation in 140
  aim of 82
  basic techniques 82–4
  common-sense core of 81–4, 169
  interpretation in 82
  neuroscience and 140, 143
  'structure of the mind' 86
  theoretical confusion in 85–93
  theoretical dangers in 93–8
  see also psychoanalysis
psychological troubles
  common-sense classification of 156–64, 172–6
  nature of 151–65
psychosis 162–3
'psychosurgery' 146, 147
psychotherapy
  common factors 15
  counselling and 8–9n
  integration 14, 166–86
  as myth 17–18, 21
  non-standard forms of 18
  see also counselling
Purton, C. 5, 25, 52, 62, 64, 66, 78, 80n, 127–8, 181, 184, 186n

rational debate, in CBT 109
rationality 115–16
Read, R. 7, 23
realist philosophy 112
recovered memories 95–8
recovered memory therapy 95–8
reflection 60–1, 63, 188–9, 192
regularities and explanatory pictures 30–3
reinforcement 47, 55
relatedness (Spinelli) 132–3
relational depth 63–4
relationship
  central to human life 173
  therapeutic, *see* therapeutic relationship
  see also social referencing; Type A troubles
relativity, theory of 24

representation(s) 110
  and images, in neuroscience 40–1
  and language 36
  mental maps, *see* mental maps/representations
  see also cognitive schemas
repression 35, 86, 88, 93–8
  recovered memories and 97
Republic (Plato) 186n
response(s)
  articulation/clarification of 102, 160–1, 171; *see also* Type C troubles/procedures
  irrational 106–7, 160–1
  modification of 47–50, 158–9, 171; *see also* Type B troubles/procedures
  and view, *see* view and response
Rice, L. 118
right-brain
  stimulation of 146
  as substrate of the unconscious 143, 145
ritual abuse, and false memories 96
Rogers, C.R. 33, 140–1, 181
  conditions of worth 66, 75–6, 121, 184
  congruence 20, 24, 25, 36, 64–5, 68–9, 98, 172
  'counselling' 9n
  'experience' 40, 67, 68
  memory 76–7
  perception 77
  reflection 60–1, 62
  theory 23, 59–61, 67
Rosen, R. 147
Rosenzweig, S. 14
Royal College of Psychiatrists (UK) 95

Sanders, P. 5, 184
Sartre, J.-P. 131, 132, 134
satanic abuse, and false memoriers 96
schemas, cognitive, *see* cognitive schemas
  see also emotion schemes
schizophrenia 154, 162–3
'schoolism' 14, 21
Schore, A. 91, 140, 142, 143, 173
Schroder, T. 96
scripts, *see* cognitive schemas
Searle, J. 148n

sedimentation (Spinelli) 133–4, 136, 138
Segal, Z.V. 103, 184
Seikkula, J. 162–3
self-concept 67, 68
self-deception 43, 62, 160
 and classification of troubles 161
 common-sense account of 65–7
 in existential therapy 135, 179
 incongruence and 65–7
 in person-centred therapy 62, 65–7, 75, 80
 pervasiveness of 66
 in psychodynamic therapy 83, 84, 86, 88, 169
 the unconscious and 83, 88–91
 see also inauthenticity; incongruence
self-soothing 142
self-therapy 20
sensus communis (Aristotle) 42
sexual abuse, and false memories 96, 97
 retractions of claims 97
Shannon, B. 111
Sharrock, W. 23
Singer, M.T. 18, 34
skill development, in training 195
Skinner, B.F. 54, 57, 172, 185
Slack, S. 60
Smith, M. 13
social constructionism 23, 25, 112
social control 57
social mediation 78–9
social referencing 173–5, 176
Socrates 115
soul
 balancing of 181–2
 in Greek thought 181–2, 183
Spinelli, E. 132–4, 136, 137–8
spirochaetosis, dyschronic (pinta) 154
'splits' (PET) 120–1, 191
'spontaneous remission' 13
statutary regulation 3
Stern, D. 173–4
Stevenson, I. 96
stimulus, concept of 53, 55, 124
Stoic philosophy 99
super-ego 181
Swales, M.A. 103
Szasz, T.S. 26, 153, 182

Tallman, K. 15, 20, 182
Taylor, C. 54
temperaments, in mediaeval thought 180
theoretical confusion
 behaviour therapy 50–6
 cognitive therapy 103–10
 person-centred therapy 67–77
 process-experiential therapy 123–6
 psychodynamic therapy 85–93
 see also pictures, misleading
theoretical dangers
 behaviour therapy 57–8
 cognitive therapy 114–17
 existential therapy 136–8
 person-centred therapy 77–80
 psychodynamic therapy 93–8
theory(ies)
 belief in 24–5, 26–7, 28
 common sense and 30–45
 common-sense core, *see* common-sense core of theory
 confused, *see* theoretical confusion
 danger from, *see* theoretical dangers
 'gossamer threads' view (Rogers) 23–4
 high-level 31
 incoherent 41, 185; *see also* theoretical confusion
 initiation into 25
 low-level 29, 31–2
 observation and 33, 35
 ordinary language and 44
 pictures in 31–3
 reasons for rejecting 33–5
 scientific, development of 23
 styles of 185–6
 in training 194–5
therapeutic relationship 15, 16–17, 171, 192
 see also Type A troubles/procedures
therapist(s)
 as 'guru' 137–8
 seeking therapeutic help 197
 use of language by 44, 107–8
therapist allegiance 17, 26–7
therapist-client relationship, *see* therapeutic relationship

therapist identity and commitment, 26–7
'they-self' (Heidegger) 134, 179
'thing-in-itself' (Kant) 36–7, 112, 127
thinking, *see* thoughts
Thorne, B. 26, 67, 78, 79, 136, 142, 181–2, 184, 196–7
Thornton, T. 132
thought(s)
 automatic 104–5, 107
 cognition and 103–10
 fabricated 115
 thinking *vs.* believing 106
 'thinking that' *vs.* 'having thoughts' 105–6
 'thinking that' *vs.* 'feeling that' 106–7
 see also belief(s)
Tibetan medicine 180
'time at a place' example 39–40
Tinbergen, N. 56
token economy 57
Tolman, E.C. 55, 113
training 193–8
 common sense in 195–8
 personal development in 195
 skill development 195
 theory in 194–5
transactional analysis 181
transference, and self-deception 84
traumatic memories 95–8
Trimble, D. 162–3
truth
 common sense and 23–6, 92
 in person-centred therapy 79–80
 trust and 24
two-chair procedure 121, 125
Type A troubles/procedures 158, 173, 179, 183, 190
 zigzag in 179
 see also therapeutic relationship
Type B troubles/procedures 158–9, 173, 179, 190
 zigzag in 178
Type C troubles/procedures 159–61, 173, 179, 190
 zigzag in 178

unconscious, the 20, 33, 65, 67, 83, 85, 86–93, 169, 172
 belief in 24, 86
 'discovery' of 87
 right-brain as substrate of 143, 145
 self-deception and 83, 88–91
 substantive status of 83
understanding, and description 41–2
unfinished business 121, 125–6
unidentified flying objects (UFOs) 96

Valenstein, E.S. 163
van Deuzen, E. 132, 137
van Holthoon, F.L. 42
view and response 73–5, 102–3, 106, 108, 187–8
 balancing 177–80
 brain development and 142
 mutual modification of 178–9
 zigzag between, *see* zigzags
 see also 'balance' in therapy
Vöringer, P.A. 14
vulnerability, client 122

Wakefield, J.C. 154, 163
Walden Two (Skinner) 57
Wampold, B. 2, 13, 14, 15, 16–21, 28, 185, 193
Watson, J.B. 50, 52
White, A. 7, 65
Whitehead, A. N. vi, 138
Whyte, L.L. 83
Wilkins, P. 78
Wittgenstein, L. vi, 7, 37, 39, 115
 'don't think, but look!' 72
 'forms of life' 168, 176
 Heidegger and 132, 138
 'inner experience' 52, 69–72, 75
 'knots in our thinking' 8
 meaning as use 43, 92
 rejection of Cartesianism 35–6, 47
Wolff, S.M. 164
Woolger, R. 96
working relationship, *see* therapeutic relationship
'worlding' (Spinelli) 133, 137
Wundt, W. 50–1

Yalom, I. 132

zigzag(s) 62, 177–80
  in behavioural therapy 48
  in chair work 126, 191
  in different types of therapy 178–9
  in evocative unfolding 120, 122, 124, 190–1
  in focusing 61–3, 191
  see also 'balance' in therapy; view and response